# The Resolution of International Tax Disputes

**Series on International Taxation**

VOLUME 87

*Series Editors*

Prof. Ruth Mason, University of Virginia School of Law
Prof. Dr Ekkehart Reimer, University of Heidelberg

*Introduction & Contents*

The Series on International Taxation deals with a wide variety of topics in the global tax arena. The authors include many of the field's leading experts as well as talented newcomers. Their expert views and incisive commentary have proven highly useful to practitioners and academics alike.

*Objective*

The volumes published in this series are aimed at offering high-quality analytical information and practical solutions to international tax practitioners.

*Readership*

Practitioners, academics and policy makers in international tax law.

*Frequency of Publication*

2-3 new volumes published each year.

*The titles published in this series are listed at the end of this volume.*

*To Mimi*

# Table of Contents

# List of Figures and Table

# List of Abbreviations

| | |
|---|---|
| A.C. | Appeal Cases |
| AC | Arbitration Convention |
| ADR | Alternative Dispute Resolution |
| ADRC | Alternative Dispute Resolution Commission |
| APA | Advance Pricing Agreement |
| Arb. Int'l | Arbitration International |
| AT Rev | Australian Tax Review |
| B.T.R. | British Tax Review |
| BB | Betriebsberater |
| BEPS | Base Erosion and Profit Shifting |
| BFH | Bundesfinanzhof |
| BFuP | Betriebswirtschaftliche Forschung und Praxis |
| BIT | Bulletin for International Taxation |
| CA | Competent Authority |
| CDFI | Cahiers de Droit Fiscal International |
| CETA | Comprehensive Economic and Trade Agreement |
| COGS | Costs of Goods Sold |
| CUP | Comparable Uncontrolled Price Method |
| DB | Der Betrieb |
| DFI | Derivatives & Financial Instruments |
| DRD | Dispute Resolution Directive |
| DRJ | Dispute Resolution Journal |
| DStR | Deutsches Steuerrecht |
| EJBMR | European Journal of Business and Management Research |

| | |
|---|---|
| ET | European Taxation |
| FR | Finanzrundschau |
| FTR | Florida Tax Review |
| Geo. Mason L. Rev. | George Mason Law Review |
| ICC | International Chamber of Commerce |
| ICSID | International Centre for Settlement of Investment Disputes |
| IFA | International Fiscal Association |
| ILC | International Law Commission |
| Int'l Tax J. | International Tax Journal |
| ISR | Internationale Steuer-Rundschau |
| IStR | Internationales Steuerrecht |
| ITPJ | International Transfer Pricing Journal |
| IWB | Internationale Wirtschaftsbriefe |
| J. Int'l Arb. | Journal of International Arbitration |
| JIDS | Journal of International Dispute Settlement |
| JISSec | Journal of Information System Security |
| MAP | Mutual Agreement Procedure |
| MC | Model Convention |
| MEMAP | Manual on Effective Mutual Agreement Procedures |
| MLI | Multilateral Convention to Implement Tax Treaty-Related Measures to Prevent BEPS |
| MNE | Multinational Enterprise |
| NJW | Neue Juristische Wochenschrift |
| NZG | Neue Zeitschrift für Gesellschaftsrecht |
| OECD | Organisation for Economic Co-operation and Development |
| OECD-MC | OECD Model Tax Convention on Income and Capital |
| Pace L. Rev. | Pace Law Review |
| PCIJ | Permanent Court of International Justice |
| PE | Permanent Establishment |
| PIStB | Praxis internationale Steuerberatung |
| Q.B. | Law Reports, Queen's Bench Division |
| RdW | Österreichisches Recht der Wirtschaft |
| RIW | Recht der internationalen Wirtschaft |
| R.S.C. | Revised Statutes of Canada |
| SchiedsVZ | Zeitschrift für Schiedsverfahren |
| StuW | Steuer und Wirtschaft |
| SWI | Steuer und Wirtschaft International |

| | |
|---|---|
| TFEU | Treaty on the Functioning of the European Union |
| TNMM | Transactional Net Margin Method |
| U. Pa. L. Rev. | University of Pennsylvania Law Review |
| UN | United Nations |
| UN-MC | United Nations Model Double Taxation Convention Between Developed and Developing Countries |
| UNCITRAL | United Nations Commission on International Trade Law |
| UPE | Ultimate Parent Entity |
| VAT | Value Added Tax |
| VCLT | Vienna Convention on the Law of Treaties |
| VJSchr. | Vierteljahresschrift für Steuer- und Finanzrecht |
| WTJ | World Tax Journal |
| ZSS | Zeitschrift für Steuerstrafrecht und Steuerverfahren |

# Preface

This study has been handed in as a dissertation thesis at the Ludwig Maximilians University in Munich in May 2022. The *rigorosum* took place in June 2023. The manuscript was finished in 2021, and thus the status of the literature considered is mainly 2021.

I wrote the thesis during my time as a research associate at the Max Planck Institute for Tax Law and Public Finance. The views expressed are my own and do not necessarily correspond with the position of the German tax administration that I work for since June 2021.

I would like to express my sincere gratitude, first and foremost, to Prof. Dr Dr h.c. Wolfgang Schön not only for supervising this thesis but mainly for providing the best research environment one could think of. At the Max Planck Institute for Tax Law and Public Finance are wonderful researchers and guests from all over the world, many of whom have become friends. The library is extraordinary and helps researchers to source every article and book they dream of – my special thanks to Petra Golombek. Furthermore, the institute supported many travels – in this regard, special thanks to Gabriele Auer – and allowed me to take part in many conferences. Especially beneficial were the WU Vienna's 2018 Rust Conference on Tax Treaty Arbitration and the subsequent discussions of the Vienna Multi-Stakeholder Group on Improving Cross-Border Dispute Resolution. I am also extremely thankful that I had the chance to meet and discuss with Noemi Strotkemper at the Symposium on Dispute Resolution in International Tax Law in Lausanne and Katerina Perrou at the 2019 GREIT Conference in Lisbon.

Many thanks to Prof. Dr Klaus-Dieter Drüen for providing the second opinion on the thesis and to PD Dr Daniel Dürrschmidt for co-examining me as part of the *rigorosum*.

To Prof. Dr Ana Paula Dourado and Prof. Dr Ekkehart Reimer, I am thankful for including the thesis in the Series on International Taxation.

Both my greatest inspiration and my favourite discussion partner was and is Dr Mira Jahani. To my dear friends Dr David Rügamer, Dr Jonathan Schindler, Dr Philipp Streckenbach, and Savvas Kostikidis, I am deeply grateful for reading the thesis, providing thoughtful comments and discussing them with me. Many thanks also to Antonia Kendrick for the linguistic editing of the thesis.

Berlin, January 2024 *David Rüll*

CHAPTER 1

# Introduction

International tax law is in a state of transformation. While measures to tackle base erosion and profit shifting (BEPS) by multinational enterprises are still being implemented, the global tax system is on the brink of a new evolutionary step to face the challenges that result from the digitalisation of the economy and highly mobile taxpayers, on the one hand, and tax competition between national states, on the other hand.

The BEPS measures lead to a higher regulatory density in the area of international tax law, which in turn leads to a steady increase of international tax disputes. Additionally, procedural law might be called upon in this context as a means to address regulatory deficiencies and vagueness in new provisions.[1] Accordingly, the resolving of tax treaty disputes is facing a changing environment, the latest developments being the introduction of the European Dispute Resolution Directive, the Multilateral Instrument as well as the introduction and evolution of arbitration clauses in Model Conventions.

Moreover, the newest developments to address the challenges posed by the digitalisation of the economy – namely the OECD's Two-Pillar Solution – suggest that the response of states will be truly multilateral, which creates a major challenge for the established dispute resolution mechanisms that mostly stem from bilateral agreements, and thus only provide for the resolution of bilateral disputes.

This gives reason to scrutinise the current framework for the resolution of international tax disputes and to explore whether it is capable of dealing with current and future disputes: in this study, I first survey the matters in dispute (Chapter 2) and assess the interests at stake (Chapter 3). Then (in Chapter 4), I examine the established dispute resolution mechanisms. Thereby, I analyse and compare their procedural rules. Building on this, I develop a proposal for a new mechanism (Chapter 5). Therefore, I consider how procedures might be designed and which institutions may be established to support the resolution of international tax disputes. I conclude the study with a draft

1. *See also W. Schön*, Internationalisierung des Internationalen Steuerrechts, p. 944 (K.-D. Drüen et al. eds, Verlag Dr. Otto Schmidt 2018).

convention for the resolution of international tax disputes (Chapter 6) that would implement my suggestions.

CHAPTER 2

# The Matters in Dispute

On an abstract level, one can differentiate between two sources of disputes: disputes can arise (1) in relation to the facts of a case and (2) regarding the correct way to apply the law to these facts.[2]

## 2.1 ESTABLISHING THE FACTS OF A CASE

The facts of an international dispute include both the situation of taxpayers giving rise to taxation and the application of the states' national laws by their authorities.

Correctly and completely establishing the facts of a case is an - if not the - essential prerequisite for the efficient resolution of a dispute over the application of the law. Furthermore, a divergent understanding of or a disagreement about facts can be the core and source of a dispute.

Resolving international tax disputes is made challenging by the fact that most disputes occur after a tax assessment in at least one of the states involved has already taken place. In the course of a tax assessment, the facts of the case are determined in an elaborate and (especially if multinational enterprises are concerned) extensive way. Consequently, at least one - and often all - of the states involved has or have developed their own understanding of the facts when a dispute arises, and it appears questionable whether they will reconsider them later on.

In order to prevent disputes arising from differences in the determination or understanding of facts, it is advisable that states jointly determine the facts in the

2. This correlates with the definition of a *dispute* in Permanent Court of International Justice, Judgment of 30 Aug. 1924, *The Mavrommatis Palestine Concessions (Greece v. Britain)*, Publications of the Permanent Court of International Justice Series A (1923-1930) No. 2, p. 12: *A dispute is a disagreement on a point of law or fact, a conflict of legal views or of interests between two persons.*

assessment procedure. One (relatively new) instrument to achieve this is a joint audit.[3] The OECD, as of 2019, defines a joint audit as:

> two or more tax administrations joining together to
>
> - examine an issue(s)/transaction(s) of one or more related taxable persons (both legal entities and individuals) with cross-border business activities, perhaps including cross-border transactions involving related affiliated companies organised in the participating jurisdictions, and in which the tax administrations have a common or complementary interest;
> - proceeding in a pre-agreed and co-ordinated manner guaranteeing a high level of integration in the process and including the presence of officials from the other tax administration
> - where the tax administrations jointly engage with the taxpayer, enabling the taxpayer to share information with them jointly
> - and the teams include Competent Authority representatives from each tax administration for the exchange of information.[4]

Joint audits are also a promising tool to narrow down legal questions that can be dealt with under dispute resolution mechanisms, helping to make the resolution of disputes more effective.[5]

Without a joint determination but with separate and extensive audits in several states, however, fact-finding and unification become (or rather remain) an important part of dispute resolution mechanisms: it is very likely that states as well as taxpayers have their own versions of what exactly constitutes the facts of a case. One reason for this might be that the fact-finding procedure during the audit aims to apply legal norms whose scope and characteristics may narrow the focus while determining the facts.[6]

## 2.2 APPLICATION OF THE LAW: TREATY INTERPRETATION

Once the facts are established, the law is to be applied to these facts. The *law* in international tax disputes mainly consists of treaties.[7] There are tax treaties which

---

3. For an overview on joint audits, *see D. Criclivaia*, Joint Audits – Ten Years of Experience: *A Literature Review*, 12 WTJ 3 (2020) DOI: 10.59403/2b17dfr. In detail on the practical implementation, the legal framework and its constraints *T.V. Meickmann*, Die Aufklärung und Bewertung grenzüberschreitender Sachverhalte im Steuerrecht: *Eine Untersuchung unter besonderer Berücksichtigung der rechtlichen und tatsächlichen Rahmenbedingungen gemeinsamer Betriebsprüfungen*, pp. 179-193; 226-335 (Duncker & Humblot 2019); *M. Hendricks*, Joint Audits und Abkommensrecht, pp. 565 ff. (W. Wassermeyer ed., C.H. Beck 2015).
4. OECD, Joint Audit 2019: *Enhancing Tax Co-operation and Improving Tax Certainty*, 22 para. 38 (OECD Publishing 2019), https://doi.org/10.1787/17bfa30d-en (accessed 15 Jan. 2024). They are thereby broadening their definition given in the 2010 report, as already suggested by *N. Čičin-Šain et al.*, Joint Audits: Applicable Law and Taxpayer Rights, 10 WTJ 4, p. 589 (2018).
5. *See also Meickmann, supra* n. 3, at p. 193. Proposing a combination of joint audits and dispute resolution mechanisms *I. Zimmerl*, Joint Tax Audits als Ausgangspunkt zur Effektuierung des Verständigungsverfahrens, p. 156 (C.H.Beck 2022).
6. *See also G. Crezelius*, Steuerrechtliche Verfahrensfragen bei grenzüberschreitenden Sachverhalten, 11 IStR 13, p. 435 (2002); *Meickmann, supra* n. 3, at p. 76.
7. *See also J. Chaisse*, Making Tax Dispute Resolution Mechanisms More Effective – The Base Erosion and Profit Shifting Project and Beyond, 10 Contemporary Asia Arbitration Journal 1, p. 12 (2017).

distribute the exercise[8] of taxation rights among states to avoid both double taxation and non-taxation in almost all areas of taxation. Most prominent, however, are those concerning the taxation of income and capital. On these matters, the Model Conventions by both the United Nations (UN) and the Organisation for Economic Co-operation and Development (OECD) are instrumental and extraordinarily influential.

Against this background, I will focus my research on the established mechanisms for the resolution of disputes that arise from the interpretation and application of treaties regarding the taxation of income and capital.[9] My suggestions (Chapter 5), however, should be applicable to other tax treaty disputes as well.

As a general rule, the terms used in tax treaties are to be interpreted autonomously.[10] The default methodology for the interpretation – that is to be applied as long as there are no treaty-specific interpretation rules – is set out in the Vienna Convention on the Law of Treaties (VCLT)[11].[12] The VCLT is assumed not only to be binding for all its 116 signatories[13] but also to express customary international law.[14] Pursuant to Article 31(1) VCLT, the starting point[15] is a literal interpretation (respecting the *ordinary meaning* of a term).[16] The literal interpretation is complemented by a systematic interpretation (*in its context*) as well as a teleological interpretation (*in the light of its objective and purpose*) as further general rules of interpretation. Furthermore, Article 31(2) VCLT describes the elements, which are considered to be the *context* of the terms of a treaty. According to Article 32 VCLT, the three general rules of interpretation (wording, context as well as objective and purpose) may be supported

8. Stressing that tax treaties do not distribute taxing rights but only the exercise of taxing rights *K. Vogel*, Transnationale Auslegung von Doppelbesteuerungsabkommen, 12 IStR 15, p. 524 (2003).
9. For VAT disputes *see*, for example, *W. Hellerstein*, Dispute Resolution and Dispute Prevention under the EU VAT: A Global Perspective (M. Lang ed., Linde 2017).
10. *Vogel*, *supra* n. 8, 12 IStR 15 (2003), at p. 524; *M. Lehner*, Grundlagen des Abkommensrechts m.no. 96 (K. Vogel/M. Lehner eds, C.H. Beck 2015); BFH, Judgment of 8 Jul. 1998, I R 57/97, m.no. 19; *H. Flick*, Zur Auslegung von Normen des internationalen Steuerrechts, 158 (G. Felix ed., Pöschel 1958); *F.E. Koch*, The Double Taxation Conventions, p. 19 (Stevens 1947); *E. van der Bruggen*, Unless the Vienna Convention Otherwise Requires: *Notes on the Relationship Between Article 3(2) of the OECD Model Tax Convention and Articles 31 and 3 32 of the Vienna Convention on the Law of Treaties*, 43 ET 5, pp. 153 f. (2003); *D. Gosch*, Über die Auslegung von Doppelbesteuerungsabkommen, 2 ISR 3, pp. 88 f. (2013); *M. Lehner*, Die autonome Auslegung von Doppelbesteuerungsabkommen im Kontext des Art. 3 Abs. 2 OECD-MA, pp. 400 f. (J. Lüdicke et al. eds, Haufe-Gruppe 2013); *M. Lang*, Die Bedeutung des originär innerstaatlichen Rechts für die Auslegung von Doppelbesteuerungsabkommen (Art. 3 Abs. 2 OECD-MA), p. 290 (G. Burmester/D. Endres eds, C.H. Beck 1997). Promoting a priority of definitions under national law if terms are not defined in the treaty, however, *F. Wassermeyer et al.*, Art. 3 OECD-MA, 71 (F. Wassermeyer et al. eds, C.H. Beck); *K. Vogel/R.G. Prokisch*, General Report: *Interpretation of Double Taxation Conventions*, 78a CDFI, pp. 81 f. (1993).
11. Concluded in Vienna on 23 May 1969, entry into force on 27 Jan. 1980, UN Treaty Series Vol. 1155, p. 331.
12. *See also M. Lang*, Introduction to the Law of Double Taxation Conventions, section 4.1. (IBFD 2013).
13. As of 15 May 2019.
14. *M. Herdegen*, Interpretation in International Law, 7 (A. Peters/R. Wolfrum eds); *K. Vogel/A. Rust*, Introduction m.no. 81 (E. Reimer/A. Rust eds, Wolters Kluwer Law & Business 2015).
15. *See also Herdegen*, *supra* n. 14, at m.no. 11.
16. *See* in detail *K. Vogel*, Doppelbesteuerungsabkommen und ihre Auslegung: *Teil I*, StuW 2, p. 121 (1982).

by supplementary means of interpretation: (a) to confirm the interpretation, or (b) if the meaning still remains unclear after the general rules have been applied, or (c) the result of the interpretation is *manifestly absurd or unreasonable*. One supplementary method mentioned in Article 32 VCLT is the method of historical interpretation (*including the preparatory work of the treaty and the circumstances of its conclusion*).

A possible source of conflicts appears even on this abstract level: conflicts might not only result from a differing interpretation while the same methodology is employed but already stem from a differing approach to the method of interpretation.[17] For example, disputes might arise as to whether supplementary methods can be made use of. A specific example regarding the interpretation of the OECD Model Convention (OECD-MC) is that it is disputed what kind of role the OECD commentary plays with regard to the interpretation of tax treaties based on it.[18]

For specific questions, treaties may refer[19] to the interpretation of terms under national law. The OECD Model, for example, specifically refers to the meaning under national law on several occasions[20] and, generally, in relation to terms which are not defined in the treaty *unless the context otherwise requires or the competent authorities agree to a different meaning pursuant to the provisions of Article 25*[21] in Article 3(2).[22]

Once the reference to national law is possible, *conflicts of qualification* may arise that stem from the different legal treatment of a situation under the tax laws of the contracting states.[23]

17. Furthermore, *K. van Raad*, International Coordination of Tax Treaty Interpretation and Application, p. 218 (K. van Raad ed., Kluwer Law International 2002) highlights that the likelihood of a divergent interpretation is also increased because national tax authorities are not as familiar with tax treaties and their interpretation as with national provisions.
18. On this question *see E. Reimer*, Interpretation of Tax Treaties, 39 ET 12, pp. 467 ff. (1999); *N. Strotkemper*, Das Spannungsverhältnis zwischen Schiedsverfahren in Steuersachen und einem Internationalen Steuergerichtshof: *Möglichkeiten zur Verbesserung der Streitbeilegung im Internationalen Steuerrecht*, 85 n. 89 (Nomos 2017); *J.M. Mössner*, Zur Auslegung von Doppelbesteuerungsabkommen, p. 411 (K.-H. Böckstiegel et al. eds, Carl Heymanns Verlag KG 1988); *A. Meindl-Ringler*, Beneficial Ownership in International Tax Law, pp. 8 f. (Kluwer Law International 2016).
19. In the case of Art. 3(2) OECD-MC, it is disputed whether it is a *reference* to national law, a renvoi or a rule of interpretation, *see* K.-H. Böckstiegel et al. eds, Law of Nations. Law of International Organizations. World's Economic Law: *Liber Amicorum honouring Ignaz Seidl-Hohenveldern* pp. 420 ff. (Carl Heymanns Verlag KG 1988).
20. In Art. 4(1) to determine whether a person is a resident, for the term *immovable property* in Art. 6(2) as well as partly in Art. 10(3) for the definition of dividends.
21. The addition *or the competent authorities agree to a different meaning pursuant to the provisions of Article 25* was inserted in the 2017 update of the Model.
22. On the question of what amounts to the context, *see Lang, supra* n. 10, at pp. 287 f. On the interpretation of the term *requires* which leads to the question of whether an autonomous interpretation prevails, *see* n. 10 above. For a good overview on Art. 3(2) OECD-MC *see also Meindl-Ringler, supra* n. 18, at pp. 291 ff.
23. *See* in general *A. Ramos Huerta*, Conflicts of Qualification and the Interpretation of Tax Treaty Law, pp. 24 ff. (E. Burgstaller/K. Haslinger eds, Linde 2007); *A. von Poser und Groß-Naedlitz*, Der Qualifikationskonflikt bei Doppelbesteuerungsabkommen, pp. 111 ff. (1972); *S. Widmann*, Zurechnungsänderungen und Umqualifikationen durch das nationale Recht in ihrem Verhältnis zum DBA-Recht, p. 258 (K. Vogel ed., Dr. Otto Schmidt KG 1985); *van Raad, supra* n. 17, at pp. 220 ff.; *M. Lang*, Qualification Conflicts (R. Vann et al. eds, IBFD 2014); *K. Vogel*, Doppelbesteuerungsabkommen und ihre Auslegung: *Teil II*, StuW 3, 292-295 (1982). Fundamentally on

## 2.3 TYPICAL LINES OF CONFLICT IN INTERNATIONAL TAX DISPUTES

To grasp typical scenarios in which international tax disputes occur, I will outline a few matters that often cause or are likely to result in disputes.[24]

### 2.3.1 Transfer Pricing

Transfer pricing issues raise a number of questions, both of a factual and of a legal nature.[25] The aim of transfer pricing rules is to counter the ability of multinational enterprises (MNEs) to shift profits or losses in order to achieve tax benefits.[26] First, for transfer pricing rules to apply there need to be associated enterprises according to Article 9(1) of the OECD/UN Model. This is a legal question which may be answered based on facts regarding the participation of an enterprise or shareholders. After affirming this preliminary question, the way to the heart of transfer pricing issues is clear: the *arm's length principle* is to be applied.[27] In short, the arm's length principle states that the terms of transactions between associated enterprises shall be equivalent to those unrelated enterprises would have agreed on. A thorough analysis of all the facts concerning the parties of the transaction and the transaction itself is vital to allow for a well-reasoned comparison with third-party transactions.[28] In a first step, this analysis usually contains three elements: (1) the functions performed, (2) the risks assumed and (3) the assets used by the parties. The identification of the roles played by the parties is important to determine their exposure to the economic outcome. After this analysis, comparable transactions need to be identified. Depending on the nature of the transaction (and the laws and rules of the states involved), a certain transfer pricing method is to be applied. Five methods are widely accepted: three methods can

---

the term *E. Herzfeld,* Probleme des internationalen Steuerrechts unter besonderer Berücksichtigung des Territorialitätsprinzips und des Qualifikationsproblems, 6 VJSchr., 456-461 (1932). On methods to avoid conflicts of qualification *C. Pleil/S. Schwibinger,* Confronting Conflicts of Qualification in Tax Treaty Law: The Principle of Common Interpretation and the New Approach Revisited, 10 WTJ 3, pp. 427 ff. (2018) DOI: 10.59403/her9d7. On how to solve these conflicts under the 'New Approach', *see A. Rust,* Art. 3 OECD Model m.no. 118 (E. Reimer/A. Rust eds, Wolters Kluwer Law & Business 2015).

24. For an illustration of the practical relevance, *see* the statistics in sections 4.1.3. and 4.5.6. *See also W.W. Park/D.R. Tillinghast,* Income Tax Treaty Arbitration, pp. 46 f. (Sdu Fiscale & Financiele Uitgevers 2004).
25. *See also M.A. Markham,* Arbitration and Tax Treaty Disputes, 35 Arbitr Int 4, pp. 478 f. (2019) DOI: 10.1093/arbint/aiz023.
26. *See* in greater detail *M. Johnson et al.,* Chapter 1: *Overview/Best Practices,* pp. 6 f. (Duff & Phelphs ed., Kluwer Law International 2017); OECD, OECD Transfer Pricing Guidelines for Multinational Enterprises and Tax Administrations: *July 2017,* para. 1.6 (2017).
27. On the theoretical application of the *arm's length principle* in contrast to formulary apportionment, *see J. Monsenego,* Introduction to Transfer Pricing, pp. 11 ff. (Kluwer Law International 2015).
28. In detail on the importance of fact-finding for transactional adjustments, *see A. Navarro,* Transactional Adjustments in Transfer Pricing, Chapter 3 (IBFD 2016) and on difficulties in determining the 'correct' facts *M. van Herksen,* 2003 IRS Report on APAs: A Case for Increased Arbitration Procedures, 10 ITPJ 5, p. 173 (2003).

be described as traditional transaction methods[29] and two methods focus on the transactional profit.[30]

While the facts concerning the tested party can and should be determined without leaving any room for doubt, the legal assessment cannot live up to the claim of the greatest precision and sharpness since, as the OECD puts it, *transfer pricing is not an exact science but does require the exercise of judgment on the part of both the tax administration and taxpayer.*[31] As a consequence, there is not one single correct transfer price but rather a range of acceptable transfer prices.[32] Due to this uncertainty, many disputes revolve around the correct definition of the transfer price range.[33] While determining the method which should be applied in a concrete case is often problematic in itself, the main challenge in relation to all methods except for the profit-split method is something different: finding appropriate comparables.[34] But even the profit-split method comes with its own challenges, mostly in relation to the composition of the allocation formula.[35]

Disputes usually emerge if one state does not accept the transfer prices set out and documented by an enterprise as being in the range of acceptable transfer prices, but makes an adjustment pursuant to Article 9(1) OECD-MC without the other state reacting with a respective counter-adjustment pursuant to Article 9(2) OECD-MC.[36] This counter-adjustment is not as compelling as one might assume from the wording of Article 9(2) OECD-MC (*shall make an appropriate adjustment*): according to the OECD's commentary, *the adjustment is due only if State B considers that the figure of adjusted profits correctly reflects what the profits would have been if the transactions had been at arm's length.*[37]

29. These are (1) the comparable uncontrolled price (CUP) method, which is quite straightforward in that it compares the transaction on hand regarding its prices to transaction prices either between a group member of the MNE and an independent party (internal CUP), or to prices that unrelated parties have agreed on (external CUP); (2) the resale price method, which focuses on the gross margin of a transaction and adjusts the costs of goods sold (COGS) if it is not at arm's length; and (3) the cost plus method, which focuses on the transaction costs and a mark-up which needs to be at arm's length.
30. These are (1) the transactional net margin method (TNMM), for which the net margin is decisive (in contrast to the gross margin, the net margin includes operating expenses); as an object of comparison, the return-on-sales-quota thereby comes into consideration and (2) the profit-split method, which divides the profit of a global value chain according to an allocation key with flexible elements.
31. OECD, *supra* n. 26, at para. 1.13.
32. As described by *Monsenego, supra* n. 27, at pp. 25 ff. *R.S. Avi-Yonah,* The Rise and Fall of Arm's Length: A Study in the Evolution of U.S. International Taxation, 15 Virginia Tax Review 1, p. 149 (1995) calls this, with reference to the economic literature, the *continuum price problem.*
33. In detail on possible scenarios that might cause disputes *Strotkemper, supra* n. 18, at pp. 489 ff.
34. *See also R. Biçer,* The Effectiveness of Mutual Agreement Procedures as a Means for Settling International Transfer Pricing Disputes, 21 ITPJ 2, p. 78 (2014) DOI: 10.59403/x4zpjq.
35. On this *S. Reif,* Die Profit-Split Methode zur Bestimmung von Verrechnungspreisen (Dissertation, Ludwig-Maximilians-Universität München, 2019), pp. 128-133.
36. In detail *Strotkemper, supra* n. 18, at pp. 512 ff. *See also Navarro, supra* n. 28, at p. 201.
37. OECD, Model Tax Convention on Income and on Capital 2017: *Full Version,* Commentary on Art. 9 para. 6 (OECD Publishing 2019), https://doi.org/10.1787/g2g972ee-en. *See also X. Ditz,* Art. 9 OECD-MA m.no. 142 (J. Schönfeld/X. Ditz eds, Verlag Dr. Otto Schmidt 2019).

### 2.3.2 Permanent Establishments and Profit Allocation

The taxation of enterprises follows two conflicting principles that are expressed in Article 7(1) first sentence OECD/UN-MC: generally, enterprises are to be taxed in the state of residence, *unless* they carry out a business in the source state through a permanent establishment. Thus, a permanent establishment is the requirement to allow for the source taxation of business profits. The term *permanent establishment* is defined in Article 5(1) OECD/UN-MC (which vary in detail). This definition is rather complex, which makes it prone to sparking disputes.[38]

Once it is determined that there is a permanent establishment, a very likely source of disputes is the amount of profits that is to be allocated to this permanent establishment and consequently can predominantly be taxed by the source state.[39] Therefore, Article 7(2) OECD/UN-MC states that how profits are attributed should be based on the arm's length principle. Consequently - just as under Article 9 OECD/UN-MC, disputes are likely to arise if one state makes an adjustment and the other state does not react with a counter-adjustment pursuant to Article 7(3) OECD-MC. Again, the term *shall* in Article 7(3) OECD-MC is not as compelling as it might sound because it presupposes the state to consider *that the adjusted profits conform with paragraph 2.*[40] Furthermore, an alternative clause to Article 7(3) OECD-MC is widespread[41] in treaties. This clause states:

> Where, in accordance with paragraph 2, a Contracting State adjusts the profits that are attributable to a permanent establishment of an enterprise of one of the Contracting States and taxes accordingly profits of the enterprise that have been charged to tax in the other State, the other Contracting State shall, to the extent necessary to eliminate double taxation on these profits, make an appropriate adjustment if it agrees with the adjustment made by the first-mentioned State; if the other Contracting State does not so agree, the Contracting States shall eliminate any double taxation resulting therefrom by mutual agreement.[42]

Due to this clause, a counter-adjustment is not obligatory even if the state considers the adjustment to be in line with Article 7(2) OECD-MC. It is, however, compulsory for the states to have a mutual agreement procedure (MAP) - and, if necessary and provided for in the treaty, subsequent arbitration[43] - and to actually agree[44] on a solution that eliminates double taxation in this case.

38. *See*, with a few examples, *van Raad, supra* n. 17, at p. 222.
39. In detail *R. Collier/J. Vella,* Five Core Problems in the Attribution of Profits to Permanent Establishments, 11 WTJ 2, p. 160 (2019) DOI: 10.59403/vd7jxr.
40. OECD, *supra* n. 37, at Commentary on Art. 7 para. 59.
41. As analysed by *J. Sasseville/R. Vann,* Article 7: Business Profits section 6.1.3.6. n. 402 (R. Vann et al. eds, IBFD 2014).
42. This alternative clause is suggested in OECD, *supra* n. 37, at Commentary on Art. 7 para. 68.
43. As clearly stated in OECD, *supra* n. 37, at Commentary on Art. 7 para. 68.
44. Thus, not only to *endeavour* to find a solution - on this later in section 4.1.1.2.3.

### 2.3.3 Residence

Dual residence of companies and other non-individuals is addressed in Article 4(3) OECD/UN-MC. Until 2017, the *place of effective management* was the single decisive criterion to determine the residence. This term, however, has no internationally uniform meaning which means that it is likely to be disputed.[45] In order to counter the opportunity of MNEs to artificially move their treaty residence,[46] since 2017, Article 4(3) OECD/UN-MC has required a mutual agreement between the contracting states to make a choice.[47] As criteria which might be considered, the paragraph mentions not only the *place of effective management* but also *the place where* the enterprise *is incorporated or otherwise constituted and any other relevant factors*. The provision, however, only requires the states to *endeavour* to find an agreement and not to actually agree on a single state of residence.[48] Yet, in lack of a fallback provision on where to allocate the residence, taxpayers are only entitled to reliefs or exemptions under tax treaties concluded according to the 2017 models if there is an effective agreement. Consequently, there will be a MAP in every case of dual residence of non-individuals. With this in mind, it is surprising to see that it does not seem to be self-evident that taxpayers can request an arbitration procedure to be started if the states involved fail to determine a single residence.[49]

For individuals, Article 4(2) OECD/UN-MC still provides a multi-level tie-breaker rule in case of a dual residence. This clause determines a taxpayer's residence by looking at their: (1) permanent home or centre of vital interests, (2) habitual abode or (3) nationality. If none of these criteria qualify for breaking the tie, the contracting states *shall settle* the question of residence by mutual agreement. Interestingly, this wording deviates from Article 4(3) OECD/UN-MC, which only requires states to *endeavour to determine* the question of residence by mutual agreement.

The criteria of the tie-breaker rule are to be interpreted autonomously – Article 3(2) OECD/UN-MC does not apply.[50] The criteria under (1) and (2) demand the establishment of a solid factual basis. Once the facts have been established, a legal

45. *See* in detail *B.R. Obuoforibo,* Article 4: Resident 5.2.2.2. (R. Vann et al. eds, IBFD 2014). Proposing an autonomous treaty definition *G. Maisto et al.,* Dual Residence of Companies under Tax Treaties, 1 Intl. Tax Stud. 1, pp. 32 ff. (2018) DOI: 10.59403/3sb8799.
46. *See* OECD/G20 Base Erosion and Profit Shifting Project, Preventing the Granting of Treaty Benefits in Inappropriate Circumstances: *Action 6: 2015 Final Report,* pp. 72 ff. (OECD 2015).
47. On the corresponding provision in the MLI with the noteworthy interpretation of the term *such person* that mutual agreements can also be ones that state abstract and general criteria that apply to all taxpayers *E. Reimer,* Meilenstein des BEPS-Programms: Das Multilaterale Übereinkommen zur Umsetzung der DBA-relevanten Maßnahmen, 26 IStR 1, p. 3 (2017).
48. According to the OECD's Commentary, the motivation for this amendment was to counter tax-avoidance, *see* OECD, *supra* n. 37, at para. 23 on Art. 4. Criticising the OECD's motivation for the revision of Art. 4(3) *Maisto et al., supra* n. 45, 1 Intl. Tax Stud. 1 (2018), at pp. 42 ff. Paragraph 24.5 of the OECD's Commentary explicitly allows for contracting states to stick to the *place of effective management* concept and thus to agree on the wording of pre-2017 Art. 4(3).
49. *See Maisto et al., supra* n. 45, 1 Intl. Tax Stud. 1 (2018), at p. 54; specifically for the Dispute Resolution Directive *R. Ismer/S. Piotrowski,* Article 25 OECD and UN MC m.no. 172 (E. Reimer/A. Rust eds, Wolters Kluwer Law & Business 2015).
50. *See R.X. Resch,* Home Sweet Home: Tax Treaty Interpretation and the Problem with Language under Consideration of the Permanent Home Tie-Breaker, B.T.R. 2, p. 206 (2019); *J. Sasseville,*

assessment is to be made. As the criteria are couched in rather vague terms, there is broad leeway for interpretation.[51]

### 2.3.4 Anti-abuse Rules

Not least since the implementation of BEPS measures, anti-abuse rules are becoming increasingly frequent in tax treaties.[52] An established provision that is already widely used is the beneficial ownership test in the provisions on the taxation of dividends, interests and royalties.[53] This beneficial ownership test is a likely source of disputes because the concept of beneficial ownership is not a uniform one but varies between jurisdictions and is contentious in scholarly discussions.[54]

Furthermore, Article 29 of the 2017 OECD/UN-MC as well as Article 7 of the MLI provide a toolbox of anti-abuse provisions. This includes limitation on benefits clauses in Article 29(1) through (7) OECD/UN-MC and Article 7(8) through (13) MLI as specific anti-abuse rules as well as a principal purpose test in Article 29(9) OECD/UN-MC and Article 7(1) MLI as a general anti-avoidance rule. More often than not, the application of the principal purpose test will lead to disputes[55] due to its vague wording that leaves broad discretion to the applying authorities[56] and serious consequences looming for taxpayers. Pursuant to the principal purpose test, taxpayers can be denied treaty benefits *if it is reasonable to conclude, having regard to all relevant facts and circumstances, that obtaining that benefit was one of the principal purposes of any arrangement or transaction that resulted directly or indirectly in that benefit, unless it is established that granting that benefit in these circumstances would be in accordance with the object and purpose of the relevant provisions.*[57]

History and Interpretation of the Tiebreaker Rule in Art. 4(2) of the OECD Model Tax Convention: *Chapter 7,* Section 7.3. (G. Maisto ed., IBFD 2010).

51. Critical in this regard *M. Lehner,* Art. 4 m.no. 174 (K. Vogel/M. Lehner eds, C.H. Beck 2015).
52. For the pre-BEPS situation, *see L. de Broe,* International Tax Planning and Prevention of Abuse, Chapter 7 (IBFD 2007); *C. Bergedahl,* Anti-Abuse Measures in Tax Treaties Following the OECD Multilateral Instrument – Part 1, 72 BIT 1, pp. 12 ff. (2018) DOI: 10.59403/3knbtmw.
53. Articles 10(2), 11(2) and 13 OECD/UN-MC. It is disputed, however, whether the beneficial ownership test is an anti-abuse provision as presented by *F. Navisotschnigg,* Chapter 4: The Beneficial Ownership Test, sections 4.2.2. and 4.2.3. (M. Lang et al. eds, IBFD 2019).
54. As thoroughly analysed by *Meindl-Ringler, supra* n. 18. *See also* M. Lang et al. eds, Beneficial Ownership: *Recent Trends* (IBFD 2013); *Navisotschnigg, supra* n. 53.
55. *See also S. Govind/L. Turcan,* Cross-Border Tax Dispute Resolution in the 21st Century: A Comparative Study of Existing Bilateral and Multilateral Remedies, 19 DFI 5, section 2.1.1.2. (2017) DOI: 10.59403/1czqs6m.
56. *See* especially regarding the criterion '*one of the* principal purposes' *Bergedahl, supra* n. 52, 72 BIT 1 (2018), at p. 23. Also assuming differing interpretations due to the vague wording *D. Kleist,* A Multilateral Instrument for Implementing Changes to Double Tax Treaties: Problems and Prospects, 44 Intertax 11, p. 829 (2016) DOI: 10.54648/taxi2016075.
57. In detail on the principal purpose test *S. Buriak,* Chapter 2: The Application of the Principal Purpose Test under Tax Treaties (M. Lang et al. eds, IBFD 2019); *Bergedahl, supra* n. 52, 72 BIT 1 (2018), at pp. 22 ff.; comparing it to the Guiding Principle requirements *A. Báez Moreno,* GAARs and Treaties: From the Guiding Principle to the Principal Purpose Test. What Have We Gained from BEPS Action 6?, 45 Intertax 6/7, pp. 435 ff. (2017) DOI: 10.54648/taxi2017036; *P. Blessing,* Article 29: Entitlement to Benefits (Global Perspective) section 2.2. (R. Vann et al. eds, IBFD July 2020).

Limitation on benefits clauses are also likely to be disputed, especially in the light of their 'mind-numbing complexity':[58] these clauses contain further criteria which have to be met before treaty benefits may be granted, such as the taxpayer being a *qualified person* (Article 29(1) and (2) OECD/UN-MC, Article 7(8) and (9) MLI).[59]

### 2.3.5 Treaty Overrides

Disputes as to the application of tax treaties can also arise if states sign treaties but provide in their national law that particular provisions of these treaties are not to be applied in specific scenarios. From the perspective of public international law, these treaty overrides can be a violation of the *pacta sunt servanda* rule if they go beyond the (permissible and reasonable) interpretation of tax treaty rules that allow for the non-application of their provisions (e.g., in cases of abuse).[60] Whether or not it is justified not to apply a tax treaty is a likely source of disputes.[61]

### 2.3.6 Possible Conflicts to Come in the Light of the OECD's Two-Pillar Solution

The international debate on how to address the tax challenges arising from digitalisation continued after the conclusion of the BEPS project. This issue was debated in BEPS Action 1 but remained unresolved.[62] The Inclusive Framework continued its work and developed a solution based on two pillars: Pillar 1 was initially discussed as a measure to establish a new nexus and profit allocation rule to allow for an allocation of taxing rights with respect to business profits that no longer exclusively refers to physical presence (Amount A)[63] and to provide for a simplification measure for baseline marketing and distribution activities (Amount B). Pillar 2, on the other hand, seeks to

58. *C. J. Fleming, Jr.*, Searching for the Uncertain Rationale Underlying the US Treasury's Anti-treaty Shopping Policy, 40 Intertax 4, p. 249 (2012) DOI: 10.54648/taxi2012028 criticising the limitation on benefits clause in Art. 22 of the 2006 US Model. *See also L. de Broe/J. Luts*, BEPS Action 6: Tax Treaty Abuse, 43 Intertax 2, p. 128 (2015) DOI: 10.54648/taxi2015011; *Bergedahl, supra* n. 52, 72 BIT 1 (2018), at p. 25.
59. In detail *L. Ramharter/R. Szudoczky*, Chapter 3: Limitation on Benefits Clauses: Limiting the Entitlement to Treaty Benefits (M. Lang et al. eds, IBFD 2019); *Blessing, supra* n. 57, in section 2.3.
60. *See R. Ismer/S. Baur*, Verfassungsmäßigkeit von Treaty Overrides, 23 IStR 12, p. 423 (2014), who also point out that the other contracting state might consent to the treaty override. More generally on treaty overrides *C. de Pietro*, Tax Treaty Override and the Need for Coordination between Legal Systems: Safeguarding the Effectiveness of International Law, 7 WTJ 1 (2015).
61. *See S. Sachdeva*, Overriding Tax Treaty Overrides: Proposing a Solution, 53 ET 9, p. 473 (2013) DOI: 10.59403/10ev17w. On an international level, this question is independent from the admissibility of treaty overrides under national constitutional law – *see*, for example, *F. Haase*, Internationales und Europäisches Steuerrecht, 624 (C.F. Müller 2020).
62. OECD/G20 Base Erosion and Profit Shifting Project, Addressing the Tax Challenges of the Digital Economy, Action 1 – 2015 Final Report, p. 149 (OECD Publishing 2015).
63. OECD/G20 Base Erosion and Profit Shifting Project, Tax Challenges Arising from Digitalisation – Report on Pillar One Blueprint: *Inclusive Framework on BEPS* (OECD Publishing 2020).

ensure that MNEs pay a minimum level of tax regardless of where they are headquartered or which jurisdictions they operate in.[64]

As a result of the discussion in the Inclusive Framework, Amount A of Pillar 1 will be based on the establishment of a multilateral convention[65] to redistribute a share of the largest and most profitable MNEs' profits to market jurisdictions. Amount A could lead to many disputes because of the rather complex design of the drafted rules. Matters that may cause disputes range from the scope of eligible MNEs (in scope are MNEs with a global revenue of more than EUR 20 billion and total profits greater than 10% of their global revenue; exclusions apply especially for extractives, regulated financial services and defence) over the tax base (to be reallocated is 25% of the MNEs 'excess profit', i.e., a group profit higher than 10% of the group's revenue) to the exact profit allocation to market jurisdictions and the elimination of double taxation. The Inclusive Framework is aware of this liability for disputes. Consequently, Amount A will be accompanied by the introduction of a Tax Certainty Framework (Part V, section 2 of the MLC): MNEs shall (1) be given the option to file for a *scope certainty review* (Article 22 MLC) if they seek for certainty as to whether they are in scope or (2) for an *advance certainty review* (Article 23(2) MLC) if they seek for certainty whether and how Amount A will be applied in the future, provided a set of critical assumptions is fulfilled, as well as (3) for a *comprehensive certainty review* (Article 23(1) MLC) over all aspects of the application of the MLC in past periods.[66] All tax certainty mechanisms start with an application of the MNE parent entity at its so-called lead tax administration (LTA, usually the tax administration in its state of residency). A review is undertaken by either the LTA or a multilateral review panel consisting of affected tax authorities (Article 24 f. MLC) in the endeavour to find or agree on a solution. If no agreement can be reached, the remaining issues are to be solved by a determination panel (Article 27 MLC).

Another feature of Amount A is a mechanism to resolve so-called Related Issues (Part V, section 3 MLC). Under this mechanism, issues that concern the application or interpretation of provisions of tax treaties that resemble Article 5, 7 or 9 UN/OECD-MC and are related to Amount A in the way described in Article 34(1) MLC can be made subject to a MAP procedure (Article 33 MLC) with subsequent mandatory binding arbitration (Article 35 MLC, with the exception of jurisdictions to which only an *Elective Binding Dispute Resolution Mechanism* pursuant to Article 36 MLC applies).

Under Pillar 2, the Inclusive Framework has drafted a set of model rules that jurisdictions can incorporate in their national law to implement three main components of Pillar 2:[67] (1) the Qualified Domestic Minimum Top Up Tax, (2) the Income Inclusion Rule and (3) the Undertaxed Payments Rule. Consequently, the disputes regarding the application of these rules will first and foremost be ones under the

64. OECD/G20 Base Erosion and Profit Shifting Project, Tax Challenges Arising from Digitalisation – Report on Pillar Two Blueprint: *Inclusive Framework on BEPS* (OECD Publishing 2020).
65. *See* https://www.oecd.org/tax/beps/multilateral-convention-to-implement-amount-a-of-pillar-one.htm (accessed 13 Jan. 2024).
66. OECD/G20 Base Erosion and Profit Shifting Project, *supra* n. 63, at para. 728.
67. On the GloBE rules, *see M. Schwarz*, Report on Pillar Two Blueprint: *Endlich mehr Klarheit zur Income Inclusion Rule und zur Switch-Over-Klausel*, 30 IStR 5, pp. 159 ff. (2021); *M. Schwarz*,

mechanisms provided for in the respective domestic law. In case of mismatches in the application of the rules, there is, as of now, no international binding dispute resolution mechanism. One option to achieve this would be a multilateral convention.[68] Apart from this, a dispute resolution mechanism could also be based on the equivalent of Article 25(3) UN/OECD-MC in tax treaties.[69]

Report on Pillar Two Blueprint: *Neue Details zur Undertaxed Payments Rule und zur Subject-to-tax-Klausel*, 31 IStR 6, pp. 198 ff. (2021). *See also* OECD/G20 Base Erosion and Profit Shifting Project, *supra* n. 64, in sections 6 and 7.

68. As already contemplated by OECD/G20 Base Erosion and Profit Shifting Project, *supra* n. 64, at para. 715.
69. As suggested by *R. Danon et al.*, The OECD/G20 Global Minimum Tax and Dispute Resolution: A Workable Solution Based on Article 25(3) of the OECD Model, the Principle of Reciprocity and the Globe Model Rules, 14 WTJ 3 (2022).

# CHAPTER 3
# The Interests at Stake

## 3.1 THE INTERESTS OF TAXPAYERS

Taxpayers have both material and procedural interests regarding international tax disputes. Materially, they are first and foremost interested in eliminating or avoiding double taxation. Second, there may be varying reasons why taxpayers wish to pay their taxes in one specific country. One motive might be to pay as little tax as possible. To achieve this goal, taxpayers could try to allocate the taxes in the state with the most advantageous regulatory setting.[70] Other taxpayers might, however, seek to pay taxes in the state from whose infrastructure and facilities they benefit or intend to benefit the most. If an enterprise needs highly skilled workers and engineers to run its business, the enterprise may consider its contribution to a state's budget as a necessary investment in the maintenance of the state's research and education landscape.[71]

Another viable taxpayers' interest is certainty.[72] This desire for certainty is not necessarily limited to finding a solution to a singular dispute but may also encompass the aim to have certainty that a specific – and, from the enterprise's point of view, typical – scenario will always be treated the same way by the states involved in the dispute so that they can adjust their actions accordingly.

The procedural interests of taxpayers are aimed at having a mechanism at their disposal which helps them accomplish their material interest of avoiding double taxation in an effective manner. Regarding the mechanism itself, it is in their interest to

70. *See also R. Ismer*, Compulsory Waiver of Domestic Remedies Before Arbitration under a Tax Treaty – A German Perspective, 57 BIT 1, p. 21 (2003); *Strotkemper, supra* n. 18, at p. 402.
71. With similar considerations, *see* the World Bank's webpage https://www.doingbusiness.org/en/data/exploretopics/paying-taxes/why-matters (accessed 15 Jan. 2024).
72. For a very detailed discussion, *see J. Hey*, Steuerplanungssicherheit als Rechtsproblem, pp. 185 ff. (Dr. Otto Schmidt KG 2002). *See also Z.D. Altman*, Dispute Resolution under Tax Treaties, p. 246 (IBFD 2006). On this also OECD/IMF, 2019 Progress Report on Tax Certainty p. 39, https://www.oecd.org/tax/g20-report-on-tax-certainty.htm (accessed 15 Jan. 2024).

have influence and control, to be able to make their point and to know about the procedural progress.[73]

Whether or not taxpayers are able to actively participate in the resolution of the dispute, they have a strong interest in being heard – to be sure both that their legal assessment is considered and that the facts are established correctly.[74] Especially if taxpayers are not actively involved in every step of the procedure, it is in their interest to at least be informed about the negotiations between the states involved.

## 3.2 THE INTERESTS OF STATES

The states involved might typically be in a conflict of interest. Most disputes result from an assessment of the states' tax authorities concluding that they have a right to tax. Consequently, it is in the states' interest to claim the revenue they believe to be rightfully theirs.

In contrast, states seek to avoid double taxation because it hinders international investment in their state. International investment vastly benefits their economies.[75] They know that one state needs to give way in order to avoid double taxation.[76] For the decision of which state gives way not to be arbitrary or – even worse – to be a result of the Law of the Strongest, it is in the states' best interest to have a binding regulatory framework[77] with rules that they can argue with, and which are – in the case that no agreement can be reached – applied by an independent third party.

One might think that handing over the power to decide the question of which of two or more states has the right to tax to an independent third party is against the states' interest since it constitutes an intervention in their sovereignty.[78] This thought, however, is not pertinent. States already give up a piece of sovereignty by signing agreements with other states in which they explicitly agree to waive the exercise of their national tax laws under certain prerequisites. They accept this trade-off for the

73. *See also Park/Tillinghast, supra* n. 24, at p. 43.
74. *See also D. van Hout,* Introduction, p. xxxv (P. Pistone/J.J. de Goede eds, IBFD 2021).
75. On the importance of dispute resolution mechanisms to attract foreign direct investments *Strotkemper, supra* n. 18, at p. 338. Stressing the benefits for the *business climate van Hout, supra* n. 74, at p. xxix.
76. On the challenges in providing reasons for the determination which state should be allowed to exercise its taxing rights *W. Schön,* International Tax Coordination for a Second-Best World (Part I), 1 WTJ 1, pp. 67 ff. (2009) DOI: 10.59403/hzk01m; *W. Schön,* Persons and Territories: *On the International Allocation of Taxing Rights,* B.T.R. 6, pp. 554 ff. (2010).
77. On this *see* convincingly *E. Becker,* Die Selbständigkeit der Begriffsbildung im Steuerrecht und ihr Einfluß auf die Auslegung der internationalen Doppelbesteuerungsverträge vom Standpunkt der deutschen Entwicklung aus betrachtet, II CDFI, 2-3 (1939).
78. This is discussed, for example, regarding the arbitration of tax disputes by *J. Kollmann et al.,* Arbitration in International Tax Matters, 77 Tax Notes Int'l 13, pp. 1190 f. (2015); *G. Groen,* Arbitration in Bilateral Tax Treaties, 30 Intertax 1, p. 3 (2002) DOI: 10.54648/357735; *M. Markham,* Mandatory Binding Tax Arbitration – Is This a Pathway to a More Efficient Mutual Agreement Procedure?, 35 Arbitr Int 2, pp. 154 ff. (2019) DOI: 10.1093/arbint/aiv070; *M.J. Ellis,* Issues in the Implementation of the Arbitration of Disputes Arising under Income Tax Treaties – Response to David Tillinghast, 56 BIT 3, p. 100 (2002); *Park/Tillinghast, supra* n. 24, at pp. 11 f. Raising doubts in this direction already *P. Kerlan,* International Disputes With Respect to Tax Conventions – The French View, p. 258 (V. Di Francesco/N. Liakas eds, Matthew Bender 1978),

greater good of building trust and allowing for international investment in their country and the international involvement of their citizens in and with other countries.[79] Consequently, it is in their best interest not to make this decision a hollow promise but to agree to be bound by it when it matters.[80] Signing tax treaties while at the same time opposing their interpretation and implementation via a dispute resolution mechanism – often wrapped in arguments regarding a state's national constitution[81] – equals the wish to have one's cake and eat it;[82] furthermore, it is not in line with the principle *pacta sunt servanda* as stated in Article 26 VCLT.[83]

## 3.3 THE INTERESTS OF THE PUBLIC

Additionally, the public (i.e., those not involved in a single dispute) has an (at least abstract) interest in how dispute resolution mechanisms should be designed.

One element the public has an interest in is for disputes to foster tax certainty by addressing and resolving interpretative issues that have not been clarified yet.[84] Another element the public has a genuine interest in is the equal enforcement of tax laws because their willingness to adhere to these laws and to contribute their share to the community hinges on the confidence that everyone else is following suit.

In order to meet both objectives, it is necessary that decisions are rule-based (and not made *ex aequo et bono*) and that the procedure is transparent. In particular, the public's interest is at least to know of and to be able to understand decisions to ensure that the law is equally enforced and at best for the procedure to be public and for decisions to be published in full. Furthermore, the publication of reasoned decisions could contribute immensely to tax certainty in that it helps building a body of international tax law.

79. *See also J.M. Mössner,* Internationale Streitbeilegung und internationales Steuerrecht, 29 RIW 5, p. 362 (1983); *Strotkemper, supra* n. 18, at p. 460 and the Report of the Twelfth Session of the UN's Committee of Experts on International Cooperation in Tax Matters (E/C.18/2016/CRP.4) of 7 Oct. 2016, p. 65, available at https://www.un.org/esa/ffd/wp-content/uploads/2016/10/12STM_CRP4_Disputes.pdf (accessed 1 Mar. 2021).
80. *See also Strotkemper, supra* n. 18, at pp. 331 f. and already *G.K. Kwatra,* Arbitration in International Tax Disputes: A New Approach, 5 J. Int'l Arb. 4, p. 161 (1988) DOI: 10.54648/joia1988053.
81. Extensively on the validity of this line of argument *L.E. Schoueri,* Chapter 8: Arbitration and Constitutional Issues (M. Lang et al. eds, IBFD 2015). Especially for India *see S. Govind/S. Rao,* Designing an Inclusive and Equitable Framework for Tax Treaty Dispute Resolution, 46 Intertax 4, pp. 327 ff. (2018) DOI 10.54648/taxi2018032 and for Japan *Y. Masui,* Treaty Arbitration from a Japanese Perspective, 58 BIT 1, pp. 14 ff. (2004).
82. *See also* the considerations of *Park/Tillinghast, supra* n. 24, at p. 29.
83. In the same direction *Mössner, supra* n. 79, 29 RIW 5 (1983), at p. 362 as well as the Report of the Committee of Experts, *supra* n. 79, at p. 63 (section 3.1.2.). *See also M. Markham,* Litigation, Arbitration and Mediation in International Tax Disputes: *An Assessment of Whether This Results in Competitive or Collaborative Relations,* 11 Contemporary Asia Arbitration Journal 2, p. 287 (2018). In detail on the *pacta sunt servanda* rule *A. Aust,* Pacta Sunt Servanda (A. Peters/R. Wolfrum eds).
84. Stressing the importance of tax certainty and predictability – especially in the context of the implementation of BEPS measures – *M. Butani,* Chapter 16: Action 14: Making Dispute Resolution Mechanisms More Effective – An Asian Perspective, section 16.3. (S. Sim/M.-J. Soo eds, IBFD 2017).

CHAPTER 4

# The Mechanisms in Place

On an international level, there are already several established mechanisms for the resolution of international tax disputes. Of international importance are the mechanisms proposed by the UN and the OECD in their Model Conventions as well as the one in Chapters V and VI of the Multilateral Instrument (MLI). Of rather regional importance are the mechanisms established in the European Union (EU): first, the Arbitration Convention and second the Dispute Resolution Directive. Apart from these mechanisms, there are special clauses proposed by and concluded between single states.

This chapter seeks to present the variety of dispute resolution mechanisms and their procedural rules as well as to highlight challenges in their application. First, I will examine the mechanism established under the OECD Model Convention (4.1.) and, against this background, sketch the mechanisms both under the UN Model Convention (4.2.) and under the Multilateral Instrument (4.3.). After a glance at special clauses such as the US arbitration clause and the one between Austria and Germany that refers to the CJEU (4.4.), I present the Arbitration Convention (4.5.). Based on this, I analyse the Dispute Resolution Directive in detail (4.6.). Finally, I briefly consider whether it is a viable alternative to solve tax disputes under investment treaties (4.7.) and take a look at the Tribute initiative (4.8.).

## 4.1 THE OECD MODEL CONVENTION

Ever since its first version was published in 1963, the OECD Model Convention (OECD-MC) has provided a dispute resolution mechanism in the form of a mutual agreement procedure (MAP) in its Article 25. Since the version of 2008, the OECD-MC additionally contains a provision for the mandatory settlement of disputes in Article 25(5).

### 4.1.1 The Mutual Agreement Procedure, Article 25(1) Through (4)

#### *4.1.1.1 Types of MAPs*

In general, one can differentiate between a MAP initiated by taxpayers and a MAP initiated by states.

Taxpayers are, pursuant to Article 25(1) first sentence OECD-MC, allowed to file a case if they *consider that the actions of one or both of the contracting states result or will result for them in taxation not in accordance with the convention.* According to the 1963 Model, the case should be presented in the taxpayers' state of residence. The versions from 1977 to 2014 additionally contained the option to present the case in the state in which a taxpayer is a national if the case was about the non-discrimination clause in Article 24(1) of the Model. Since 2017, there has been no limitation as to where a case can be presented; it may now be presented in *either state.* This also implies the option to present the case in both states at the same time.[85]

Article 25(1) sentence two of the 1977 version of the model introduced a deadline, which is still part of the model today: *the case must be presented within three years from the first notification of the action resulting in taxation not in accordance with the provisions of the convention.*

Once a case is presented to a state, it is, according to Article 25(2) OECD-MC, for the competent authority (CA) of this state to determine whether the case is justified from its point of view.[86] If it is considered justified, the state examines whether the issue at hand can be resolved with a unilateral solution. If no unilateral solution can be achieved, the CA *shall endeavour to resolve the case by mutual agreement with the CA of the other state, with a view to the avoidance of taxation which is not in accordance with the convention* which means that, as a second step, the actual MAP will be started.

For states, the option to initiate a MAP is provided for in Article 25(3) OECD-MC. The wording of this provision has remained unaltered since 1963. A basic negotiation provision that shows similarities to today's Article 25(3) OECD-MC – at least for matters of residence – was already part of one of the first tax treaties, i.e., the treaty between Austria-Hungary and Prussia of 21 June 1899.[87]

Article 25(3) OECD-MC states:

> [1]The competent authorities of the Contracting States shall endeavour to resolve by mutual agreement any difficulties or doubts arising as to the interpretation or application of the Convention.[2] They may also consult together for the elimination of double taxation in cases not provided for in the Convention.

85. OECD, *supra* n. 37, at Art. 25 para. 17.
86. *See also R. Ismer,* Article 25 m.no. 65 (E. Reimer/A. Rust eds, Wolters Kluwer Law & Business 2015).
87. *See* Art. 7 of the treaty that is printed in 18 FinanzArchiv 1, p. 287 (1901), accessible via https://www.jstor.org/stable/40905110 (accessed 15 Jan. 2024). On this *see also W. Haslehner,* Tax Treaty Disputes in Germany, p. 325 (E. Baistrocchi ed., Cambridge University Press 2017). On even earlier examples from treaties on financial matters, *see G. Lippert,* Handbuch des internationalen Finanzrechts, p. 206 (Österreichische Staatsdruckerei 1928).

Thus, there are two main and different application scenarios for Article 25(3): on the one hand, interpretation (or application) issues of existing provisions which do not need to affect a specific case, and, on the other hand, the clarification of issues which are not regulated under the treaty.[88]

Pursuant to Article 3(2) OECD-MC, the states have the power to define terms in the MAP in a way that this definition prevails over those in the national laws of these states.[89]

I will not elaborate on the state-state MAP further but focus on the MAP that can be initiated by taxpayers because this deserves special attention regarding its procedural rules, especially in the light of the taxpayers' participation in the procedure.[90]

For an overview of the MAP procedure, please *see* Figure 4.1.

88. *See also R. Ismer/S. Piotrowski,* Artikel 25. Verständigungsverfahren m.no. 151 (R. Ismer ed., C.H. Beck 2021).
89. Critical regarding the intention the provision was introduced with *Schön, supra* n. 1, at pp. 945 f.
90. For further details on the state-state MAP, *see Ismer/Piotrowski, supra* n. 49, at m.no. 87-97; *Strotkemper, supra* n. 18, at pp. 77 ff.; in great detail *K. Flüchter,* Art. 25 m.no. 214-257 (J. Schönfeld/X. Ditz eds, Verlag Dr. Otto Schmidt 2019).

*Figure 4.1 Overview of the MAP Procedure*

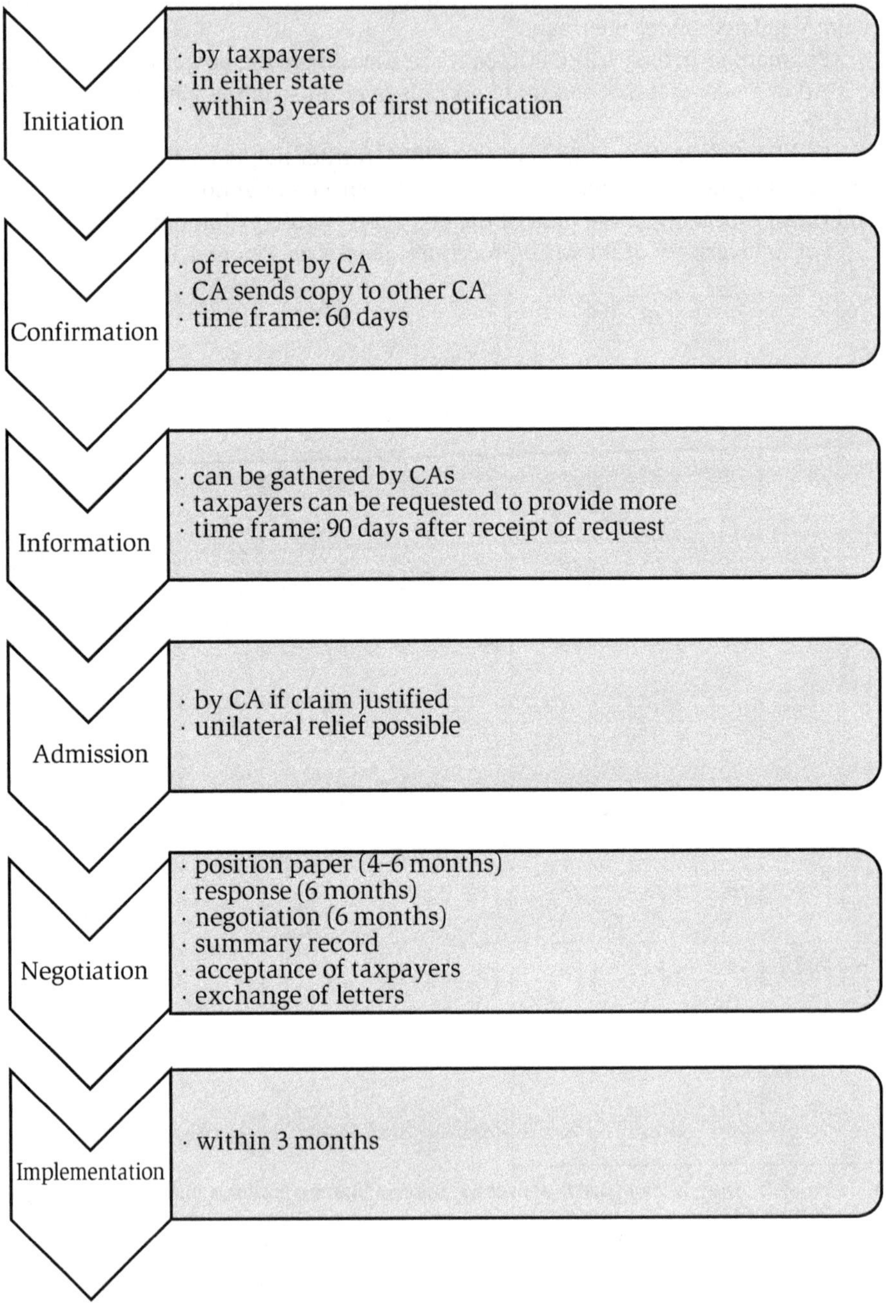

#### 4.1.1.2 *Procedural Rules for MAPs Initiated by Taxpayers*

The procedural rules concerning the initiating taxpayers set out in Article 25 OECD-MC itself are limited to determining which state(s) to address and the deadline to file the case. States then are required to review the justification of a taxpayer's claim, to consider unilateral measures and to contact the other state's CA in the endeavour to reach a mutual agreement. The contact with another state's CA is regulated by Article 25(4) OECD-MC: this paragraph allows for the CAs to communicate with each other directly (also by building a joint commission). Accordingly, communication between states is not restricted to diplomatic channels (e.g., via the states' ministries of foreign affairs[91]).[92]

Consequently, the OECD-MC itself provides only a limited set of procedural rules. The actual requirements for a claim to be filed by taxpayers, for example, are not specified in the convention but can be defined by the states themselves.[93] The OECD makes a few suggestions regarding the typical application requirements in its Manual on Effective Mutual Agreement Procedures (MEMAP).[94] Furthermore, the OECD provides some information and often points to guidance from the states in its MAP profiles.[95]

##### 4.1.1.2.1 *Application Requirements*

###### 4.1.1.2.1.1 Eligible Persons

The claimant needs to be a *person*.[96] According to the definition in Article 3(1)(a) OECD-MC, this term includes an individual, a company and *any other body of persons*. By way of systematic comparison and teleological interpretation, states do not - even though they might be defined as *bodies of persons* - count as persons in this sense because, for them, the inter-state MAP in Article 25(3) OECD-MC applies. PEs themselves cannot file an application.[97]

91. *Ismer/Piotrowski, supra* n. 88, at m.no. 189.
92. *M. Lehner,* Art. 25 m.no. 181 (K. Vogel/M. Lehner eds, C.H. Beck 2015).
93. *See* OECD, *supra* n. 37, at Commentary on Art. 25, para. 16.
94. OECD, Manual on Effective Mutual Agreement Procedures, https://web-archive.oecd.org/2012-06-14/75147-manualoneffectivemutualagreementprocedures-index.htm (accessed 15 Jan. 2024).
95. http://www.oecd.org/tax/dispute/country-map-profiles.htm (accessed 15 Jan. 2024).
96. In detail on the personal scope *S. Govind,* Chapter 10: *Personal Scope of the Mutual Agreement Procedure and Arbitration Provisions, and the Mutual Assistance Provisions,* section 10.2.2.1. (M. Lang et al. eds, IBFD 2019).
97. *Ismer/Piotrowski, supra* n. 49, at m.no. 25; in detail also *Flüchter, supra* n. 90, at p. 45. Criticising this, however, *A. Bödefeld/E. Krüsmann,* Abkommensberechtigung für Betriebsstätten in Verständigungsverfahren nach dem OECD-MA, 27 IStR 2, pp. 46 ff. (2018).

As mentioned before, since the 2017 version of the OECD-MC, the claimant no longer needs to be a resident of either state.[98]

#### 4.1.1.2.1.2 Admissible Claims

The person needs to *consider* that the *actions of one or both states result or will result in taxation not in accordance with* the treaty. Thus, the required degree of certainty is low(ered) in two respects: (1) the person does not need to be convinced that taxation is not in accordance with the treaty but only needs to *consider* it possible and (2) taxation does not need to be final but can also be imminent.[99] Consequently, the wording indicates that the claim is admissible if the person can outline the mere possibility of a taxation contrary to the treaty. In contrast, the OECD demands in its commentary that the taxation contrary to the treaty is *not merely possible but probable.*[100] In the MEMAP, it states that taxpayers do not have to *prove this to a 51% probability* but shall be given *the benefit of the doubt* in borderline cases.[101]

#### 4.1.1.2.1.3 Form and Content of the Application

There are no formal requirements for MAP applications laid out in Article 25 OECD-MC (in contrast to paragraph 5 for arbitration applications, which are to be in written form). Therefore, it is not entirely comprehensible why the OECD sees an option for the CAs to 'prescribe special procedures which they feel to be appropriate'.[102] It is, however, beneficial for taxpayers to file their application in written form and to provide exhaustive documentation to allow for the assessment of their claim.[103]

In paragraph 2.2.1., the OECD MEMAP suggests a comprehensive list of information to be included in the application if there are no requirements specified by the states.[104] This includes information to identify the taxpayer and to understand their situation and economic structure, information regarding the involved authorities, the years involved and the question in dispute regarding both the facts and the treatment under national and treaty law and a statement of the taxpayer.

98. Concerning the questions under the previous versions, *see Ismer, supra* n. 86, at m.no. 39-41; *J.S. Wilkie,* Art. 25 section 2.2. (R. Vann et al. eds, IBFD 2014) who points out that 'the most likely cases [still] concern residents of one or the other of the contracting states'.
99. *S. Eilers/K.-D. Drüen,* Art. 25 OECD-MA m.no. 30 (F. Wassermeyer et al. eds, C.H. Beck 2019) also work out that a final assessment is not necessary and mention an audit report as a sufficient indication for a threatening taxation not in accordance with a treaty. *See also M. Albert,* DBA-Verständigungsverfahren: *Probleme und Verbesserungsvorschläge,* pp. 16 f. (IFSt 2009).
100. OECD, *supra* n. 37, at Art. 25 para. 14 second sentence. *Ismer,* however, assumes that 'it should be sufficient that the taxpayer expresses doubts rather than a conviction' and states that 'the taxpayer's belief has to be reasonable', *Ismer, supra* n. 86, at m.no. 33.
101. OECD, *supra* n. 94, at para. 2.1.1.
102. OECD, *supra* n. 37, at Art. 25 para. 16.
103. *See also Ismer, supra* n. 86, at m.no. 42; *Eilers/Drüen, supra* n. 99, at m.no. 25; *Strotkemper, supra* n. 18, at 70 n. 36.
104. OECD, *supra* n. 94, at pp. 14 f.

#### 4.1.1.2.1.4 Time Limit

Article 25(1) OECD-MC states that *the case must be presented within three years from the first notification of the action resulting in taxation not in accordance with the provisions of the convention*. Thus, it is decisive to define what qualifies as such a *first notification*. The OECD and many scholars advocate for a narrow interpretation of the term to protect taxpayers.[105] They argue that it should not be sufficient to rely on the publication of a law or a general administrative decision,[106] but there needs to be an individual tax assessment or a comparable measure regarding the taxpayers. When determining the exact starting point of the time limit, the point in time at which the measure has been announced (the *notification*) is crucial. For this purpose, the OECD relies on national law and includes fictions or presumptions of announcement after a specific number of days from when the notice was sent.[107] The reference to a measure taken by the tax authorities in respect of a taxpayer causes problems in cases of: (1) self-assessment or (2) withholding taxes if there has not been a notice by the tax authorities. In these cases, the OECD considers as decisive *the time when the taxpayer would, in the normal course of events, be regarded as having been made aware of the taxation* not in accordance with the treaty (which could result from the availability of a record regarding the transfer of funds or, in cases of withholding taxes, from the payment of the [reduced] income).[108] This link shall not require the taxpayer's subjective assessment of a taxation not in accordance with the convention, but the possible assessment of a *reasonably prudent person in the taxpayer's position*.[109] It is interesting to note, however, that the decisive element for the start of the time limit can be a judicial decision in a comparable case as well if it, from this moment on, leads a reasonably prudent person to hold the established taxation not to be in accordance with the treaty.[110]

Another aspect interesting to note is that the start of the time limit is not congruent with the first opportunity to initiate a MAP. This is due to the fact that a MAP can already be initiated if future taxation against the treaty is to be expected. This makes it unnecessary for the taxpayer to wait until the tax authorities notify them before presenting a case.[111] A case might instead already be filed if, for instance,

105. OECD, *supra* n. 37, at Art. 25 para. 21; *Ismer, supra* n. 86, at m.no. 44; *K. Becker*, Art. 25 OECD-MA m.no. 20 (F. Haase ed., C.F. Müller 2016); arguing with an effective use of the procedure *Lehner, supra* n. 92, at m.no. 38.
106. OECD, *supra* n. 37, at Art. 25 para. 21; *Ismer, supra* n. 86, at m.no. 45.
107. OECD, *supra* n. 37, at Art. 25 para. 22 (in the absence of domestic provisions, the OECD proposes to refer either to the time of the actual physical receipt or to the receipt under ordinary circumstances, striving for the most taxpayer-friendly approach).
108. OECD, *supra* n. 37, at Art. 25 paras 23 et seq. Paragraph 24 states that taxpayers can prove that they became aware of the deduction at a later time, in which case this is to be regarded as decisive.
109. OECD, *supra* n. 37, at Art. 25 para. 23.
110. Cf. OECD, *supra* n. 37, at Art. 25 para. 23. For a restrictive approach *Flüchter, supra* n. 90, at m.no. 101.
111. *J. Schwarz*, Schwarz on Tax Treaties, p. 608 (Croner-i; Kluwer Law International 2018) under para. 27-250.

legislative measures are enacted which might lead to a taxation not in accordance with the treaty.[112]

#### *4.1.1.2.2 Procedure for the Handling of the Taxpayer's Request*

For the handling of the taxpayer's request, there are no strict rules or deadlines in the OECD-MC and no suggestions in the OECD MEMAP. There is, however, a suggestion on how and in which time frame the request should be assessed in paragraph 2.2. of the OECD's 2017 Sample Mutual Agreement on Arbitration. This aims to define an exact starting date of the MAP which is relevant for the question of when the arbitration phase might be initiated pursuant to Article 25(5) lit. b OECD-MC. The first timespan for the CA that received the initial request is one of 60 days during which it shall confirm the receipt of the request to the affected person and send a copy to the other CA. After the CAs have received the request or its copy, both have 90 days to ask the affected person for additional information if they deem it necessary *to undertake substantive consideration of the case*. If they do not need further information, they shall confirm within these 90 days that they have received all the information they deem necessary to evaluate the case. The starting date of the MAP is 90 days after the second CA has received the copy of the initial request from the first CA if the CAs do not both confirm that they have received all necessary information at an earlier date.

If one or both CAs have requested further information and the affected person has provided the relevant information, both CAs have 90 days after they have received the information to either confirm that there is sufficient information or point out what is still missing. These requests can continue until the CAs are satisfied with the information received – which provides a possibility of obstruction to delay the official start of the MAP for CAs.[113] For taxpayers, there is no deadline to provide information. This is because taxpayers act to their own detriment if they delay the start of the MAP. This argument is supported by paragraph 7 of the Sample Mutual Agreement, which states that the MAP can be extended for the respective period if taxpayers fail to provide information requested after the start of the MAP in a *timely manner*.

The MAP officially starts if the requesting CA confirms to the affected person and the other CA that it is satisfied with the information provided or 90 days after the reception of the last piece of information – whichever event comes first.

The sample mutual agreement does not provide for the case in which affected persons file their initial request with both CAs at the same time.[114] From my perspective, this approach is advantageous for affected persons because the first 90-day deadline to ask for further information starts at the same time for both CAs.

---

112. *See Flüchter, supra* n. 90, at m.no. 63.
113. Criticising this opportunity in general *M. Diete*, Das obligatorische Schiedsverfahren in der deutschen DBA-Praxis: *Erweiterung des zwischenstaatlichen Rechtsschutzes bei Doppelbesteuerungskonflikten*, p. 106 (Peter Lang 2014); *Strotkemper, supra* n. 18, at p. 342.
114. On this option *see* OECD, *supra* n. 37, at Art. 25 para. 19.

#### 4.1.1.2.3 Access to the MAP

The taxpayers' access can be divided into two categories: (1) the access to the 'internal' procedure whose purpose is to determine whether the claim appears to be *justified* to the CA and (2) the access to the inter-state MAP.

In the timetable in Annex 1 to the MEMAP as well as in the commentary, the OECD mentions the determination of eligibility for a MAP by the CA which received the request as a step in the first stage.[115] One could argue that this understanding of Article 25(2) OECD-MC is not entirely convincing. Article 25(2) OECD-MC does not give the CA full discretion to decide whether to pursue a request but rather to examine whether it *appears to be justified* which mainly leads to the question of whether there actually seems to be taxation contrary to the convention.[116] Regarding this question, the OECD's commentary is rather generous, however: the claim is already justified if the CA can identify any taxation which is not in accordance with the convention - it does not matter whether this taxation is the one criticised by the taxpayer or whether it stems from the state of the CA or the other state.[117]

With regard to the access to the inter-state MAP, the question arises whether the CAs are legally obliged to start a taxpayer-initiated MAP if the material requirements (taxation not in accordance with the convention and no unilateral relief achievable) are met or whether they have discretion. Only if they have discretion would it be possible for the CAs to state further requirements (such as an upfront payment of the taxes in dispute) before granting access to the MAP or to deny access because of allegedly abusive behaviour.[118] The only term which might allow for discretion in the wording of Article 25(2) sentence one OECD-MC is *shall endeavour*. In the French version of the model, there is no equivalent to this term.[119] The term *shall*, however, does not grant much discretionary power to the authorities: it is generally understood as the imposition of a duty or a requirement.[120] Accordingly, the OECD's commentary sees a duty to negotiate entailed in paragraph 2.[121] Many scholars share this view,[122] while others

115. OECD, *supra* n. 94, at p. 45; OECD, *supra* n. 37, at Art. 25 para. 34 (in the context of pending domestic litigation in the CA's state). With a similar interpretation *M. Lombardo*, The Mutual Agreement Procedure (Art. 25 OECD MC) - A tool to overcome interpretation problems?, p. 467 (M. Schilcher/P. Weninger eds, Linde 2008).
116. *See also Strotkemper*, *supra* n. 18, at p. 71.
117. Clearly pointed out by *Flüchter*, *supra* n. 90, at m.no. 130-131; OECD, *supra* n. 37, at Art. 25 para. 31.1.
118. An overview of cases in which access to the MAP is often denied is given by *Albert*, *supra* n. 99, at pp. 20 f.
119. The French wording is *L'autorité compétente s'efforce* [...] *de résoudre le cas* [...].
120. *See* the entry *shall* in *B.A. Garner*, Black's Law Dictionary (West Academic Publishing 2019).
121. OECD, *supra* n. 37, at Art. 25 para. 37.
122. *See*, for example, *D. Mülhausen*, Das Verständigungsverfahren im deutschen internationalen Steuerrecht, pp. 151 ff. (Duncker & Humblot 1976); *Schön*, *supra* n. 1, at p. 944; *K. Flüchter/D. Liebchen*, Art. 25 OECD-MA m.no. 124-128 (J. Schönfeld/X. Ditz eds, Verlag Dr. Otto Schmidt 2013); *M. Keerl*, Internationale Verrechnungspreise in der globalisierten Wirtschaft, p. 215 (Universitätsverlag Göttingen 2008); *H.M. Peters/L.H. Haverkamp*, Verbesserte Möglichkeiten zur Beseitigung von Doppelbesteuerungen: *Vergleich des Schiedsverfahrens nach Art. 25 Abs. 5 OECD-MA und des EU-Schiedsverfahrens*, BB, p. 1306 (2011). Since 2017, German courts also share this view: Tax Court Cologne, Judgment of 14 Apr. 2016, 2 K 1205/15, EFG 2016, p. 1151.

only assume an obligation to exist if the respective convention also entails a mandatory arbitration clause like Article 25(5) OECD-MC.[123] Others deny an obligation, mainly for practical reasons.[124] The last two approaches are not convincing because they lack any foundation in the wording of the provision.

Consequently, Article 25(2) OECD-MC does not confer discretion to the CAs – they are legally obliged to start a MAP if the material requirements are met.[125] As a result, CAs are not allowed to introduce additional requirements aimed at restricting access to a MAP because the provision does not grant them the right to do so – this especially applies to the refusal of access for alleged abuse.[126]

The right to initiate a MAP cannot be waived – especially not during an audit settlement, as has been pointed out in BEPS Action 14.[127]

Taxpayers can, however, only demand that the MAP be initiated – not that an agreement be reached – because the CAs, pursuant to Article 25(2) OECD-MC, only *shall endeavour to resolve* the case *by mutual agreement*.[128] Article 4(2) lit. d OECD-MC contains an exception to this rule: to determine the status of residence of a person who is a national of both or neither of the two contracting states, the CAs *shall settle the question by mutual agreement*. Furthermore, in every MAP, the CAs are obliged to negotiate and to strive for an agreement.[129]

#### *4.1.1.2.4 Procedure of the Negotiations Between CAs*

Apart from Article 25(4) OECD-MC, which addresses the means of communication between the CAs and allows the establishment of a joint commission, there are no procedural rules regarding the negotiation in the Model Convention.

123. *See*, for example, *Lehner, supra* n. 92, at m.no. 90; likewise *Ismer, supra* n. 86, at m.no. 69.
124. *See also U. Bär,* Verständigungen über Verrechnungspreise verbundener Unternehmen im deutschen Steuerrecht, pp. 225 ff. (Duncker & Humblot 2009); *Albert, supra* n. 99, at p. 22 argues that taxpayers had *no original legal status*, while *R. Ismer,* Rechtswidrige Gewährung von Rechtsschutz? – Zugleich eine Besprechung des Urteils FG Hamburg vom 13. 7. 2000 V 2/97 -, 12 IStR 11, p. 394 (2003) assumed it to be *hardly useful* to have both a duty to negotiate and only an endeavour to agree.
125. With the same line of argument as here Tax Court Cologne, Judgment of 14 Apr. 2016, 2 K 1205/15, EFG 2016, p. 1151, m.no. 40-41. *See also Flüchter, supra* n. 90, at m.no. 140; *Ismer/Piotrowski, supra* n. 49, at m.no. 74; OECD, *supra* n. 37, at Commentary on Art. 25, m.no. 37 mentions a *duty to negotiate.*
126. Arguing in the same way *Ismer/Piotrowski, supra* n. 49, at m.no. 37.
127. OECD/G20 Base Erosion and Profit Shifting Project, Making Dispute Resolution Mechanisms More Effective, Action 14-2015 Final Report p. 19, OECD/G20 base erosion and profit shifting project, http://dx.doi.org/10.1787/9789264241633-en.
128. *See also Schön, supra* n. 1, at p. 944; *L. Hintzen/S. Hintzen,* Die Systematik des völkerrechtlichen Verständigungsverfahrens der Doppelbesteuerungsabkommen (I): *Der Weg zu einer internationalen Steuergerichtsbarkeit – Zugleich eine praktische Anleitung zur Durchführung,* 32 DB 40, p. 1909 (1979); *D. Lüthi/T. Menck,* Art. 25 OECD-MA m.no. 26 (D. Gosch et al. eds, NWB 2019).
129. As the OECD, *supra* n. 37, at Commentary on Art. 25, m.no. 37 states, Art. 25(2) OECD-MC *no doubt entails a duty to negotiate.* In further detail and with a reference to the duties emerging from a *pactum de negotiando Flüchter, supra* n. 90, at m.no. 147.

There is a suggestion on how to conduct the procedure in the OECD MEMAP, however: pursuant to paragraph 3.4.1.,[130] the CA of the state that initiated the challenged measure shall provide a position paper that takes into account the following information:

a) Legal name and address and taxpayer identification number of the person requesting assistance, its related persons in the other country, if applicable, and the basis for determining the association;
b) The contact details of the competent authority official in charge of the case;
c) Overview of the issue, transactions, business, and basis for adjustment;
d) Applicable taxation years;
e) Amount of income and tax adjusted for each taxable year, if applicable;
f) Summary of relevant information from the original tax return;
g) Description of the exact nature of the issue or adjustment and the relevant domestic laws and treaty articles;
h) If relevant, calculation with supporting data (may include financial and economic data and reports relied upon and explanatory narratives as well as taxpayer documents and records where relevant and appropriate);

as well as in transfer pricing cases:

i) Outline of comparable transactions and methods for adjusting differences;
j) Description of the methodology employed for the adjustment;
k) An explanation of the appropriateness of the transfer pricing methodology employed for the adjustment (i.e. an explanation why it believes the adjustment achieves an arm's length outcome; identification of tested party, if applicable; industry and functional analysis, if a relevant study is not already included elsewhere in the taxpayer's submission).

This shall be done within four months but no later than six months after the CAs agree to enter into MAP consultations.[131]

Subsequently, the other CA shall review the case and respond within six months of receiving the position paper.[132] The response *could* include the following:[133]

a) Indication of whether a view, proposed solution, or relief proposed in the initial position paper can be accepted;
b) Indication of the areas or issues where the competent authorities are in agreement or disagreement;
c) Requests for additional information and explanations necessary to clarify particular issues;
d) Presentation of other or additional information considered pertinent to the case, but not raised in the initial position paper; and
e) Submission of proposals or views to resolve the issue.

130. OECD, *supra* n. 94, at p. 26.
131. *See* the timetable in Annex 1 of OECD, *supra* n. 94, at p. 45.
132. Second stage of the timetable in Annex 1, OECD, *supra* n. 94, at p. 46.
133. OECD, *supra* n. 94, at p. 27.

If the facts are not yet clear, further investigations are necessary, during which the taxpayer may be involved again.[134]

After that, the negotiation between the CAs is to take place in a way that they deem fit - paragraph 3.5. of the OECD MEMAP mentions *letters, facsimiles, e-mail, telephone, and face-to-face conferences*.[135] In Best Practice N°15, the OECD MEMAP stresses the advantages of face-to-face meetings - these being that they *may allow for a more open discussion and collegial approach and perhaps a more relaxed environment*, help advance the case in that they usually *trigger a milestone event* that CAs prepare for and agree on plans to follow and, finally, that they grant a certain degree of commitment because they cannot be postponed as easily as conference calls.[136] *Flüchter* also mentions the option of videoconferences[137] - something which might not have been on people's minds yet when the OECD MEMAP was drafted back in 2007.

The ideal timeline in Annex 1 of the OECD MEMAP allocates six months to the negotiation between the CAs.[138] It is reported that CAs between which disputes arise frequently meet on a regular basis (e.g., every year or every six months, depending on the caseload) to negotiate pending MAP cases.[139] This raises concerns among some authors that individual cases are no longer sufficiently appreciated at these meetings but that *package deals* are being concluded.[140] Representatives of (at least the German) administration reject this assumption.[141]

If they can agree on a solution, the CAs usually draw up a summary record that they report to the taxpayer.[142] Pursuant to the MEMAP, the CAs formally exchange

134. *Flüchter, supra* n. 90, at m.no. 160.
135. OECD, *supra* n. 94, at p. 27.
136. OECD, *supra* n. 94, at p. 28.
137. *Flüchter, supra* n. 90, at m.no. 161.
138. OECD, *supra* n. 94, at p. 46.
139. *K. Becker*, Seminar J: Verfahren zur Lösung von DBA-Konflikten, 16 IStR 16, p. 593 (2007).
140. *See J. Kollmann/L. Turcan*, Chapter 2: Overview of the Existing Mechanisms to Resolve Disputes and Their Challenges, p. 26 (M. Lang et al. eds, IBFD 2015); *M. Hendricks*, Instrumente zur Beseitigung und Vermeidung von Verrechnungspreiskonflikten, 10.21 (F. Wassermeyer/H. Baumhoff eds, Verlag Dr. Otto Schmidt 2014); *Altman, supra* n. 72, at p. 265; speaking of 'horse trading' *van Raad, supra* n. 17, at p. 219; *L. Nobrega e Silva Loureiro*, Mutual Agreement Procedure: Preventing the Compulsory Jurisdiction of the International Court of Justice?, 37 Intertax 10, p. 539 (2009) DOI: 10.54648/taxi2009054; *H.J. Ault*, Improving the Resolution of International Tax Disputes, 7 Florida Tax Review 3, p. 139 (2005); *J. Becker et al.*, Das Verfahrensrecht der Verrechnungspreise: *Grundlagen, Erfahrungen und Perspektiven*, pp. 73 f. (Springer Gabler 2017); *Meickmann, supra* n. 3, at p. 219; *Park/Tillinghast, supra* n. 24, at p. 20; *D.R. Tillinghast*, Issues in the Implementation of the Arbitration of Disputes Arising under Income Tax Treaties, 56 BIT 3, p. 91 (2002) who states that *there is always a fear of being a sacrificial lamb when two competent authorities have several cases to be resolved at the same time*. *Q. Cai*, A Package Deal Is Not a Bad Deal: Reassessing the Method of Package Negotiation Under the Mutual Agreement Procedure, 46 Intertax 10 (2018) DOI: 10.54648/taxi2018081, however, sees benefits in concluding package deals with respect to transaction costs.
141. *S. Greil/S. Rasch*, Germany, p. 286 (International Fiscal Association ed. 2016); *Flüchter, supra* n. 90, at m.no. 151 states that these assumptions *should be classified as belonging to the realm of legends*.
142. Para. 3.1. of OECD, *supra* n. 94, at p. 17; *Flüchter, supra* n. 90, at m.no. 161.

letters if the taxpayer agrees with the solution.[143] The mutual agreement shall be implemented no later than three months thereafter.[144]

If the CAs cannot agree on a solution or encounter difficulties during the negotiations, they are encouraged by paragraph 3.5.2. of the OECD MEMAP to make use of mediation.[145] The primary responsibilities of a mediator include *the clear identification and reinforcement of the goals of the MAP proceedings*, to clarify the facts and to *objectively* show *opportunities for resolution*.[146] The paragraph remains rather abstract and does not contain any details in relation to the selection of a mediator and the procedure to involve mediation.

#### *4.1.1.2.5 Interaction with Other Remedies*

Article 25 OECD-MC alludes to the interaction of the MAP with national remedies on two occasions: paragraph 1 states that the case may be presented to the CAs *irrespective of the remedies provided by domestic law of the states*, and the second sentence of paragraph 2 demands an agreement reached in the MAP to be implemented *notwithstanding any time limits in the domestic law of the contracting states*.

The first phrase is to be read in the sense that the MAP neither requires nor precludes the use of national remedies. Consequently, if taxpayers want to make use of national remedies, they must make sure they observe the respective time limits in national law to challenge tax measures, which expire even if a MAP has been commenced.[147] This may often lead to scenarios in which national remedies are sought parallel to the MAP. The acting authorities will most likely ask the taxpayers whether they want to pursue or suspend the other remedy.[148] If the MAP is pursued first, taxpayers will usually be asked to waive the national remedies before an agreement is implemented.[149] If national remedies are pursued first, however, this situation might lead to the interesting question of whether the MAP can still be resumed after the national remedy has ended with a decision by tax authorities or courts. This question is answered differently from state to state.[150]

143. *Ibid.*
144. OECD, *supra* n. 94, at p. 46.
145. OECD, *supra* n. 94, at pp. 28 f.
146. OECD, *supra* n. 94, at p. 29.
147. *See also S. Rasch/K. Mank*, Verständigungs- und Schiedsverfahren als Instrumente zur Vermeidung der Doppelbesteuerung, 8 ISR 2, p. 72 (2019).
148. On this also *K.-D. Drüen*, Verständigungs- und Schiedsverfahren, 17 (W. Wassermeyer ed., C.H. Beck 2015); *Strotkemper*, *supra* n. 18, at p. 198; *M. van Herksen/D. Fraser*, Comparative Analysis: Arbitration Procedures for Handling Tax Controversy, ITPJ, p. 159 (2009).
149. *Strotkemper*, *supra* n. 18, at p. 199.
150. The different approaches of states can be traced in the MAP profiles published on the OECD's webpage: http://www.oecd.org/tax/dispute/country-map-profiles.htm (for this overview accessed 21 Aug. 2019). Thus, only Bahrain, Brunei, Cameroon, Curaçao, Denmark, Finland, France, Gabon, Greenland, India, the Isle of Man, Liechtenstein, Luxembourg, the Maldives, Monaco, the Netherlands, Pakistan, Saint Kitts and Nevis, Saudi Arabia, Senegal, Serbia, the Seychelles, Sweden, Switzerland and the United Kingdom allow for a deviation from both administrative and court decisions.

#### 4.1.1.2.6 *Taxpayer Participation*

The most relevant, and often the only, opportunity for taxpayers to be heard in the course of the MAP is the application.[151] In their application, taxpayers can and should explain why they see or fear taxation not in accordance with the convention. They can present the facts and detail their legal assessment.[152]

Later in the procedure, there is no institutionalised right for taxpayers to be heard during the MAP.[153] This is being justified by the government-to-government character[154] of the MAP.[155]

While the OECD points out that a disclosure of the files to taxpayers *does not seem to be warranted, in view of the special nature of the procedure*,[156] it advises – at least for transfer pricing cases – that taxpayers *should be given every reasonable opportunity to present the relevant facts and arguments to the competent authorities both in writing and orally*.[157] In the context of Article 25(4) OECD-MC, they even see a *duty* of CAs:

Meanwhile, Argentina, Australia, Austria, Belgium, Benin, Bulgaria, Canada, Chile, Colombia, Costa Rica, Croatia, the Czech Republic, Estonia, Greece, Hungary, Indonesia, Israel, Kazakhstan, Kenya, Korea, Malaysia, New Zealand, Norway, Peru, Poland, Portugal, Romania, Singapore, the Slovak Republic, Slovenia, South Africa, Spain, Turkey and the United States only allow a deviation from administrative decisions but not from court decisions.

Brazil, Côte d'Ivoire, the Democratic Republic of Congo, Egypt, Guernsey, Hong Kong, Iceland (only with new documents), Ireland (if a decision stems from the *Appeal Commissioner*), Italy, Japan, Jersey, Latvia, Lithuania, Macau, Mauritius, Mexico, Nigeria, Qatar, San Marino, Thailand, Tunisia, Uruguay and Vietnam do not allow a deviation from either administrative or judicial decisions. Germany states in its profile that deviations from both administrative and court decisions are possible; supporting this position *Ismer/Piotrowski, supra* n. 88, at m.no. 121; *D. Rüll,* Chapter 14: Germany, section 14.7.2. (M. Lang et al. eds, IBFD 2020). According to *Strotkemper, supra* n. 18, at p. 201, however, this classification is based on an outdated statement by the administration and no longer valid; differentiated *Flüchter, supra* n. 90, at m.no. 119.

151. *See also* IBFD Observatory on the Protection of Taxpayers' Rights, 2018 General Report on the Protection of Taxpayers' Rights, p. 174.
152. Stressing the importance of a detailed presentation of facts H. Schaumburg/M. Hendricks eds, Steuerrechtsschutz 8.41 (Verlag Dr. Otto Schmidt 2018).
153. *See M.P. Bricker,* Arbitration Procedures in Tax Treaties, 26 Intertax 3, p. 101 (1998) DOI: 10.54648/taxi1998017; critical also *S. Nowland,* Three's (Not) a Crowd in International Tax Arbitration: International Tax Arbitration as a Development of International Commercial Arbitration Rather than a MAP Fix, 37 Hastings Int'l & Comp. L. Rev. 1, p. 189 (2014).
154. On this *Ismer/Piotrowski, supra* n. 49, at m.no. 6.
155. *M. Reich,* Das Verständigungsverfahren nach den internationalen Doppelbesteuerungsabkommen der Schweiz, p. 79 (Schulthess Polygraphischer Verlag 1976). Critical, for example, *Eilers/Drüen, supra* n. 99, at m.no. 10; *E. Snodgrass,* Tax Controversies and Dispute Resolution under Tax Treaties: Insights from the Arbitration Sphere, 19 DFI 5, section 4.2. (2017) DOI: 10.59403/1nwv1jp. *See* with very detailed considerations also *L. Riza,* Taxpayers' Lack of Standing in International Tax Dispute Resolutions: An Analysis Based on The Hybrid Norms of International Taxation, 34 Pace L. Rev. 3, 1082-1090 (2014) DOI: 10.58948/2331-3528.1867.
156. OECD, *supra* n. 37, at Commentary on Art. 25, m.no. 61.
157. OECD, *supra* n. 37, at Commentary on Art. 25, m.no. 40 lit. d.

> to give taxpayers whose cases are brought before the joint commission under paragraph 2 certain essential guarantees, namely:
>
> - the right to make representations in writing or orally, either in person or through a representative;
> - the right to be assisted by counsel.[158]

These procedural guarantees, however, do not have a corresponding provision in Article 25 OECD-MC.[159] Furthermore, it is - as *Flüchter* points out correctly - very difficult for taxpayers to comment on a position of CAs they are not familiar with and have no right to obtain.[160]

Consequently, the actual amount of taxpayer participation depends on the goodwill of the CAs conducting the proceedings. This is also outlined in Best Practice N°14 paragraph 3 sentence 2 of the OECD's MEMAP:

> Whilst giving due respect to the confidentiality of government-to-government communications and without allowing taxpayers to become involved in the actual MAP negotiations, competent authorities are encouraged to consider obtaining input from the taxpayer on factual and legal issues that may arise in the course of the MAP.[161]

Usually, taxpayers are involved again before an agreement is implemented, and the implementation depends on their consent.[162] For the MAP, this is not stated as a requirement in Article 25(2) OECD-MC - other than for the implementation of an arbitration decision in Article 25(5) third sentence OECD-MC.[163] It is not clear whether it is possible for taxpayers to deny their consent to the implementation of a MAP agreement and to start a new procedure under a different dispute resolution mechanism.[164]

#### *4.1.1.2.7 Publication of Agreements*

MAP agreements are not published. This is criticised by some scholars who suggest at least an anonymised publication of agreements should take place.[165] I support this

158. OECD, *supra* n. 37, at Commentary on Art. 25, m.no. 60.
159. *See also Albert, supra* n. 99, at p. 43.
160. *Flüchter, supra* n. 90, at m.no. 165.
161. OECD, *supra* n. 94, at p. 25.
162. As described in the MEMAP under section 3.1., OECD, *supra* n. 94, at p. 17.
163. On this and on further possible conditions before implementation *Ismer/Piotrowski, supra* n. 49, at m.no. 81.
164. Denying this option assuming a lack of need for legal protection Tax Court Cologne, Judgment of 4 Jul. 2018, 2 K 2679/17, ECLI:DE:FGK:2018:0704.2K2679.17.00, EFG 2018, p. 1745, m.no. 28-34. Supporting this argument and proposing a rule comparable to the one under the Dispute Resolution Directive *Ismer/Piotrowski, supra* n. 49, at m.no. 81
165. *Lehner, supra* n. 92, at m.no. 119; *Ismer/Piotrowski, supra* n. 49, at m.no. 79; *B.R. Runge*, The German View of the Prevention and Settlement of International Disputes on Tax Law, 25 Intertax 1, pp. 4 f. (1997) DOI: 10.54648/taxi1997002; *L. Hintzen/S. Hintzen*, Die Systematik des völkerrechtlichen Verständigungsverfahrens der Doppelbesteuerungsabkommen (II): *Der Weg zu einer internationalen Steuergerichtsbarkeit – Zugleich eine praktische Anleitung zur*

suggestion for two main reasons. First, the publication of agreements regarding the interpretation of tax treaties could – even if they are not accorded precedential value – help to develop a differentiated body of international tax law.[166] Second, showing that MAP agreements really are based on an interpretation of law and the assessment of the individual case would help to refute the suspicion that, currently, some MAP agreements are based on package deals that do not take account of the individual case.[167]

As of now, however, even the decisions that are communicated to taxpayers mostly do not contain reasons[168] – even though the OECD advises to communicate these reasons.[169] *Flüchter* argues in favour of this practice, given that most agreements are based on a compromise and so agreeing on reasons would further complicate the procedure.[170] This argument is not compelling, however: in the case of an agreement because of a common interpretation of a treaty, this interpretation should be explained to the taxpayers. But even if the CAs do not agree on a common interpretation but on a compromise solution, it could still be communicated that the solution is based on a compromise.

#### 4.1.2 The Arbitration Procedure, Article 25(5) OECD-MC

Since 2008, the OECD-MC contains an arbitration clause in Article 25(5). This clause remained unchanged until the 2014 model. Since the 2017 model, the clause has undergone slight amendments: (1) The two-year period for the conclusion of the MAP no longer begins to run with the initial presentation of the case to one CA, but rather when all of the necessary information has been provided to both CAs and (2) there is now a formal requirement for the request to initiate the arbitration procedure: it has to be made in writing.

Another aspect interesting to note is that the OECD-MC no longer contains a footnote to Article 25(5) stating that *national law, policy or administrative considerations* might hinder states from implementing the arbitration provision. As can be seen from the final report on BEPS Action 14, this change intends to create transparency regarding the states' position towards mandatory binding arbitration because they could simply refer to the footnote without any further explanation or reservation under the 2008-2014 models.[171]

*Durchführung*, 32 DB 41, p. 1957 (1979); *A. Ribes Ribes*, Compulsory Arbitration as a Last Resort in Resolving Tax Treaty Interpretation Problems, 42 ET 9, p. 401 (2002).

166. *See also Schön*, *supra* n. 1, at p. 945.
167. On this suspicion *see* n. 140.
168. As reported by *Flüchter*, *supra* n. 90, at m.no. 171.
169. *See* Best Practice N°17 in OECD, *supra* n. 94, at p. 30.
170. *Flüchter*, *supra* n. 90, at m.no. 171.
171. *See* OECD/G20 Base Erosion and Profit Shifting Project, *supra* n. 127, at paras 22 f.

Apart from these minor changes, the provision remains straightforward: it states that an arbitration procedure can be initiated if the MAP has not ended with an agreement regarding all questions in dispute within two years. The new definition of the beginning of this two-year time period, however, can be seen critically: it is harder to determine the date at which all the necessary information has been provided to both CAs than to focus on the date the request has been submitted.

Furthermore, it is - in contrast to the requirements to start a MAP pursuant to paragraph 1 - necessary that there actually is taxation which is not in accordance with the convention. It is worth mentioning that arbitration is only possible regarding *unresolved issues* (Article 25(5) first sentence). As a consequence, the arbitration phase is not an appeal stage to express disapproval of agreements reached in the MAP. It is much more an extension of the MAP with other means.[172]

Article 25(5) second sentence OECD-MC states that issues on which a decision has already been rendered by a court or administrative tribunal of either state shall not be submitted to arbitration. This sentence can be struck out if both contracting states allow for deviations from court decisions.[173] This question has already been addressed under section 4.1.1.2.5.[174]

If an arbitration decision is achieved, this decision is to be implemented by mutual agreement. It is up to the affected person, however, to decide whether to accept the solution or whether to decline it - an implementation is only possible with their consent (Article 25(5) third sentence OECD-MC).

As to the procedural rules for arbitration, the OECD-MC remains silent. The *mode of application* of Article 25(5) OECD-MC shall, pursuant to its fourth sentence, be settled by mutual agreement between the CAs.[175] The OECD's commentary contains a *Sample Mutual Agreement on Arbitration* as an annex to the commentary on Article 25 to assist the states in agreeing on procedural rules. This sample mutual agreement remained unchanged from 2008 to 2014 and was changed profoundly in 2017. In Figure 4.2 and the following, I will describe the procedure set out in the sample agreement.

172. *See also Ismer, supra* n. 86, at m.no. 105; *M. Desax/M. Veit*, Arbitration of Tax Treaty Disputes: The OECD Proposal, 23 Arb. Int'l 3, pp. 413 f. (2007) DOI: 10.1093/arbitration/23.3.405; *Flüchter, supra* n. 90, at m.no. 288.
173. OECD, *supra* n. 37, at Art. 25 para. 74.
174. Cf. n. 150.
175. Pointing out that many states have not yet agreed to procedural rules and contemplating whether the procedural rules of the Hague Conventions of 1899 and 1907 can be applied in the absence of an agreement *F.A. Koppensteiner*, Das 'Welthandelsgericht' als Forum zur Beilegung von Streitigkeiten im Bereich der direkten Besteuerung im Vergleich zu anderen Direktsteuerverfahren (Wirtschaftsuniversität Wien, 9.10.2009), pp. 240-242.

*Figure 4.2 Arbitration Procedure*

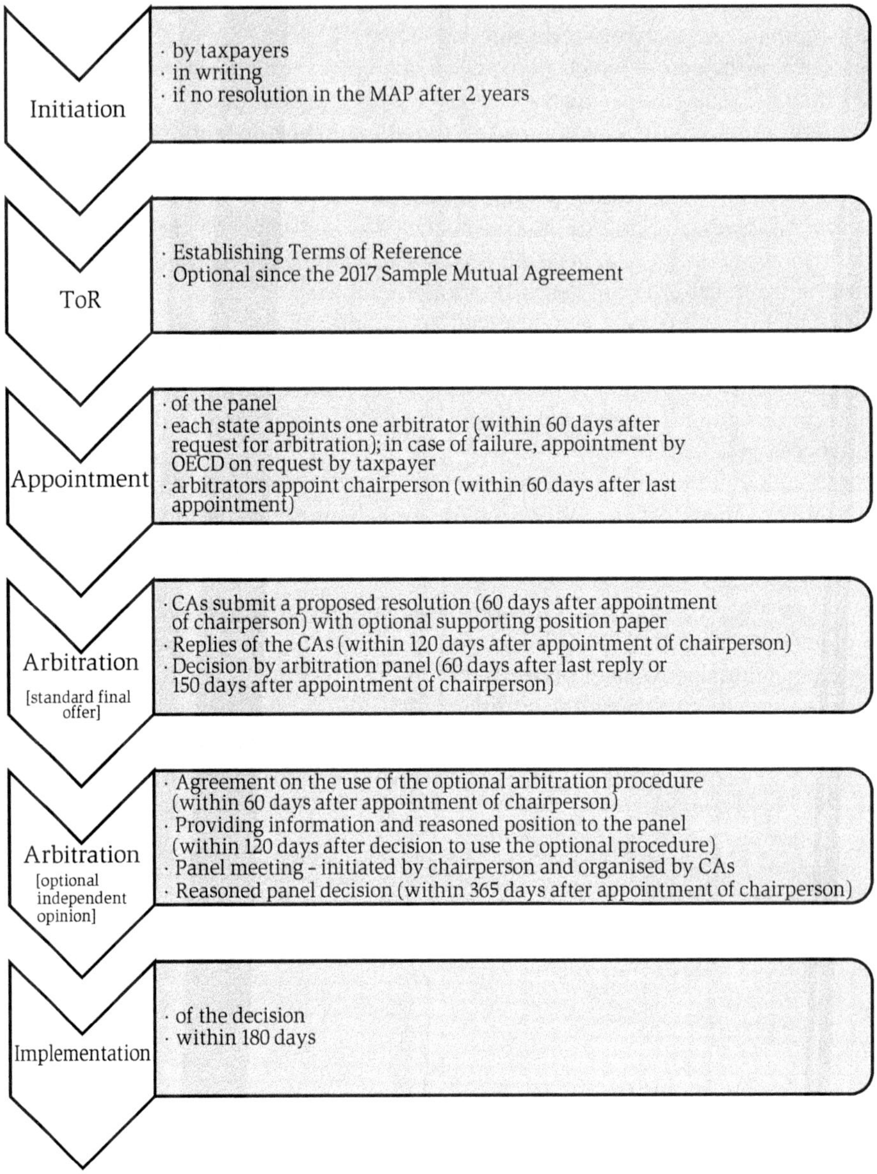


#### *4.1.2.1 The Request for Arbitration*

The affected person has to request arbitration, but the CAs are unable to do so. This request is a precondition for the start of the procedure, as the arbitration process does not start automatically after an unsuccessful MAP.[176] The arbitration procedure provided for in Article 25(5) OECD-MC is mandatory - an approval of the CA is not necessary to initiate the procedure.[177]

The requirement of written form has already been part of the sample mutual agreement since 2008 and is further set out in Article 25(5) OECD-MC since 2017.

The request shall be sent to one and can be sent to both CAs. If it is only sent to one CA, this CA shall send a copy to the other CA within 10 days after the first CA has received the request.

The sample mutual agreement does not go into further detail as to the required content of the request. It only states that the request shall contain sufficient information to identify the case. It is, however, advisable for the affected person not only to point out the existence of the taxation which they deem not in accordance with the convention and to stress the unresolved issues but also to provide a thorough statement regarding the - from their perspective - correct legal assessment to make use of this opportunity to be heard; it might be their only chance to take a stand in the arbitration procedure.

Additionally, the request shall be accompanied by a written statement as to whether a decision has already been rendered by a court or administrative tribunal of one of the states on the same issue in case the treaty does contain a provision which is equivalent to Article 25(5) second sentence OECD-MC.[178]

#### *4.1.2.2 Definition of the First Possible Application Date*

As already mentioned, an arbitration request may only be handed in if the MAP remains - at least partially - unsuccessful after two years. Until 2014, the sample mutual agreement focused on the presentation of the case to both CAs for the definition of the start date of this two-year period. It already provided for the option of a further determination of which information should be regarded as a necessary minimum for the presentation of a case. Since 2017, the definition of the start date is far more elaborate. To allow for an exact determination of the start date, paragraph 2 of the sample mutual agreement in its subparagraph 2 sets out detailed procedural rules on how to handle the initial request for the MAP and how to ask for further information. I have addressed this in detail above (section 4.1.1.2.2).

#### *4.1.2.3 Terms of Reference*

From 2008 to 2014, the sample mutual agreement contained a paragraph on the establishment of *Terms of Reference*: The provision required the CAs to agree on the questions to be resolved by the arbitration panel and send them to the affected person within three months of receiving the arbitration request. In these *Terms of Reference,*

176. *See also* OECD, *supra* n. 37, at Art. 25 para. 70.
177. On the distinction from the concept of *voluntary* arbitration, *see Ismer, supra* n. 86, at m.no. 103.
178. So too *Flüchter, supra* n. 90, at m.no. 351.

the CAs also were free to agree on additional or alternative ad hoc procedural rules for the arbitration. The sample mutual agreement also provided for a multi-level procedure to establish Terms of Reference if the CAs failed to agree on common terms.[179]

Since 2017, the establishment of *Terms of Reference* is not mentioned in the sample mutual agreement anymore, but it is indicated as an option in paragraphs 15.1 and 15.2 in the commentary on the sample mutual agreement.

#### *4.1.2.4 Selection of Arbitrators*

The sample mutual agreement in paragraph 3 provides for an arbitration panel that shall sit in a composition of three arbitrators. The requirements regarding both the skills and the independence of the arbitrators are defined rather vaguely: the arbitrators are to have *expertise or experience in international tax matters*. They must be *impartial and independent* of the contracting states' authorities and of *all persons directly affected by the case (as well as their advisors)* when accepting the appointment, maintain impartiality and independence during the proceedings and *avoid any conduct for a reasonable period of time thereafter which may damage the appearance of impartiality and independence.*

Each state shall appoint one arbitrator *within 60 days after the request for arbitration (or a copy thereof) has been received* by both CAs. If no arbitrator has been appointed within 60 days, the affected person may enquire the *highest-ranking official* of the OECD's Centre for Tax Policy and Administration *who is not a national of either contracting state* to appoint an arbitrator within 10 days after receiving the request.

The chairperson of the panel is to be appointed by the two arbitrators appointed by the states. The chairperson shall be neither a national nor a resident of either state. The appointment has to take place within 60 days of the last appointment by the states. If the arbitrators fail to agree on a chairperson, the affected person may as well request the highest-ranking official of the OECD's Tax Policy Centre to appoint a chairperson within 10 days after receiving the request.

#### *4.1.2.5 Arbitration Procedure*

The sample mutual agreement supports two different types of arbitration procedures being: (1) *independent opinion arbitration* and (2) final-offer arbitration (also called *baseball arbitration*[180]). The term *independent opinion arbitration* describes a procedure in which every CA provides the panel with the necessary facts, and the panel decides by applying the law to these facts independently, giving a reasoned decision. In a final-offer arbitration procedure, however, each party proposes a reasoned solution. The arbitration panel only chooses one proposal over another, usually without giving reasons.

179. In detail *Strotkemper, supra* n. 18, at pp. 243 f.
180. On the history of this term, *see* section 5.3.3.1.

From 2008 to 2014, the sample mutual agreement provided for independent opinion arbitration as standard method and suggested the use of final-offer arbitration in the context of a *streamlined arbitration process* (paragraph 6). Since 2017, however, the sample mutual agreement sees final-offer arbitration as the standard method (paragraph 4) and mentions independent opinion arbitration as an *optional arbitration process* (paragraph 5).

#### *4.1.2.5.1 The Standard Arbitration Procedure (since 2017)*

If the CAs do not agree on another term, they shall, within 60 days of the chairperson's appointment, submit a proposition to resolve all questions that remain open after the MAP to each arbitrator and the other CA. This resolution proposal shall be limited to a *disposition of specific monetary amounts* or, if applicable, to the *maximum amount of tax that may be charged* according to the relevant provisions of the treaty *for each adjustment or similar issue in the case*. The specification of a monetary amount can be difficult if it depends on preliminary questions (described as *threshold questions* by the sample mutual agreement), such as the questions of residence or the existence of a permanent establishment. In such a case, the CAs are to submit alternative proposals for different scenarios.

The reasoning is subject to a *supporting position paper* which *may* be handed to the arbitrators and the other CA, but is not a necessity. Each CA is allowed to reply to the proposed resolution and position paper of the other CA within 120 days of the appointment of the chairperson. The sample mutual agreement does not provide any guidance on how to proceed if only one or no CA submits a proposal. Given the limited mandate of the panel, the consequence most likely is that there is no decision possible if no CA submits a proposal and that the panel has to accept the respective proposal as a decision if there is only one provided.[181] This gives the CAs the chance to obstruct the procedure.

In the course of coming to a decision, the arbitration panel shall select one of the proposed resolutions regarding every single issue and *threshold question*. A simple majority (two out of three arbitrators) is necessary. The panel is not to explain or justify its decision. The sample mutual agreement proposes a term of either 60 days after the reception of the last reply submission or, if there was no reply submission, 150 days after the appointment of the chairperson if the CAs do not agree on another term.

The sample mutual agreement (paragraph 4 subparagraph 4) seeks to avoid an in-person meeting and to promote the use of teleconferencing and videoconferencing technologies for the communication between the arbitrators themselves as well as between arbitrators and CAs for the sake of reducing costs. Face-to-face meetings have to be decided upon by the CAs regarding the questions of when and where (but apparently not regarding the question of whether to have such a meeting at all).

181. Similar *Flüchter, supra* n. 90, at m.no. 374 who additionally points out that the panel has the alternative option not to decide the case at all.

The last sentence of paragraph 4 subparagraph 5 states that the arbitration decision *shall have no precedential value.*

#### 4.1.2.5.2 *The Optional Arbitration Procedure (since 2017)*

The CAs may, within 60 days after the appointment of the chairperson, agree to apply the *independent opinion arbitration method* via the *optional arbitration procedure* pursuant to paragraph 5 of the sample mutual agreement.

In this case, both CAs have 120 days to provide each other as well as the arbitration panel with all the information they deem necessary for the panel to reach an independent decision. This information should include not only a description of the facts and the unresolved issues but also a reasoned position of each CA. Unless otherwise agreed, information coming to light after the beginning of the proceedings will not be taken into account.

The organisation of a meeting of the arbitration panel is in the hands of the CAs: according to paragraph 5 subparagraph 3 of the sample mutual agreement, the chairperson informs the CAs that a meeting should be held, and they decide within 30 days thereafter when and where this meeting is to be held and communicate their decision to the arbitrators.

The decision of the arbitration panel is to be based on the applicable provisions of the convention and, subject to those provisions, on the domestic law of the states in conflict (paragraph 5 subparagraph 4 of the sample mutual agreement). Other legal sources which the CAs identify by mutual agreement shall also be considered.

The arbitrators are to adopt the procedural and evidentiary rules they deem necessary – subject to the provisions of the relevant convention and the (sample) mutual agreement on arbitration (paragraph 5 subparagraph 5).

The panel's decision is to be delivered, unless the CAs agree otherwise, within 365 days of the chairperson's appointment. The decision is to be reasoned and shall indicate the sources of law it relies upon. Paragraph 5 subparagraph 6 explicitly states that the decision formed via the independent opinion arbitration method, like the decision reached through the standard procedure, *shall have no precedential value.*

#### 4.1.2.5.3 *Result of an Arbitration Panel Not Delivering a Decision in Time*

If the arbitration panel – in either procedure – does not deliver a decision in the timespan agreed upon or provided for, the CAs may, pursuant to paragraph 9 of the sample mutual agreement, appoint a new arbitration panel.

#### 4.1.2.5.4 *Withdrawal by the Affected Person or Agreement Between CAs*

Until the arbitrators have delivered their decision, the CAs can continue to try to find an agreement regarding the unresolved issues themselves (paragraph 10 of the sample mutual agreement). If they do so, they shall notify the arbitrators who will not provide a decision. The same applies if the affected persons withdraw their request for arbitration or MAP. In all these cases, the MAP will be considered to have been completed.

#### *4.1.2.6 Participation of Taxpayers*

With regard to the standard procedure, there is no provision that allows affected persons to participate during arbitration. As a consequence, they only have a say at the beginning as well as at the end of the procedure: They can state their position in the application for arbitration, and they can decide whether to accept the result.

Pursuant to paragraph 5 subparagraph 2 of the sample mutual agreement, the affected person is allowed to participate in the optional arbitration procedure to the same extent as in the MAP in writing. There is, however, no unconditional right to present their opinion orally. Such an appearance depends on the consent of the CAs and the arbitrators.

#### *4.1.2.7 Publication of Decisions*

The standard final-offer arbitration procedure (paragraph 4 of the sample mutual agreement) does not provide for a publication of a decision. This can be explained well by the fact that the decision consists only of a position paper of one of the CAs, and the arbitration panel does not give any reasons as to why it has chosen one position paper over another.[182]

A decision rendered in the optional arbitration procedure via the independent opinion arbitration method may be published pursuant to paragraph 5 subparagraph 6 of the sample mutual agreement with the permission of the affected person and the CAs. It shall be redacted to avoid the identification of the affected person and has to mention that it has *no formal precedential value.*

#### *4.1.2.8 Costs of the Procedure*

Paragraph 8 of the sample mutual agreement states the principle that, first, each participant in the arbitration bears their own costs. Each arbitrator is paid for by the CA which appointed or had to appoint them, while the remuneration of the chairperson and their costs are shared between the CAs equally. For meetings of the arbitration panel, the hosting CA has to cover the costs. This provision can be seen critically because it might impair the states' willingness to host meetings and thus delay the procedure.

182. Criticising this correlation for the MLI *J.F. Avery Jones,* Guest Editorial: *Types of Arbitration Procedure,* 47 Intertax 8/9, p. 675 (2019) DOI: 10.54648/taxi2019067.

#### 4.1.2.9 *Implementation of the Decision*

Unless the arbitration decision is found to be unenforceable by the courts of one of the states involved (as provided for under paragraph 11 of the sample mutual agreement), the decision has to be implemented within 180 days after it has been communicated to the CAs. Therefore, the CAs shall adopt the arbitration decision via a mutual agreement (as can also be read from Article 25(5) third sentence OECD-MC). Subsequently, this agreement can be implemented under the national law of the states pursuant to Article 25(2) second sentence OECD-MC.

### 4.1.3 The OECD Model's Mechanism in Practice

*Figure 4.3 OECD MAP Statistics*

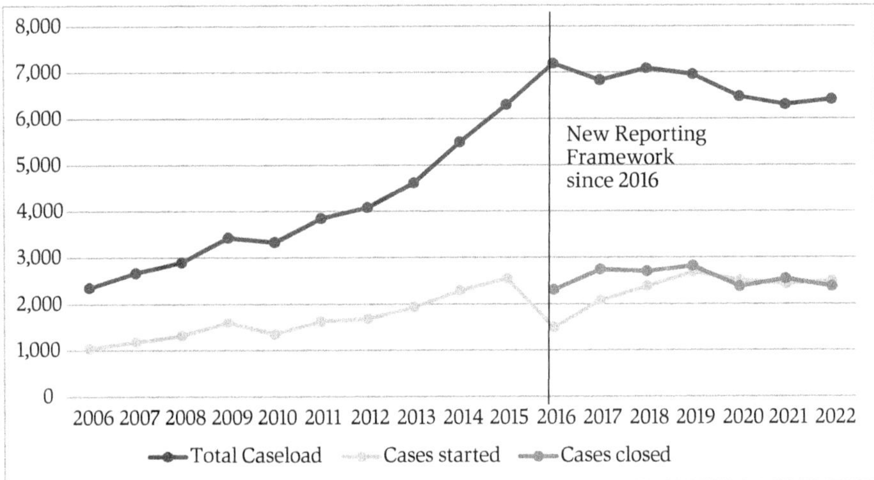


The OECD publishes MAP statistics annually on their webpage.[183] In Figure 4.3, the overall values of all reporting jurisdictions are collected. From 2006 through 2015, they include OECD member countries and the OECD partner economies Argentina, China, Costa Rica, Lithuania and South Africa. Since 2016, the reports have been compiled in accordance with a new Reporting Framework that is a result of BEPS Action 14.[184] This includes reports from members of the Inclusive Framework. The statistics can also be accessed for each jurisdiction separately. By the end of 2022, the jurisdictions that were involved in the most cases were Germany (1,431 cases), France

183. *See* http://www.oecd.org/tax/dispute/mutual-agreement-procedure-statistics.htm (accessed 15 Jan. 2024).
184. For details, *see* http://www.oecd.org/tax/dispute/mutual-agreement-procedure-statistics-reporting-framework.pdf (accessed 15 Jan. 2024).

(1,074 cases), Italy (942 cases), Spain (889 cases), Belgium (851 cases), India (697 cases), the United States (658 cases), the United Kingdom (650 cases), and the Netherlands (528 cases). The OECD MAP statistics do not show arbitration cases separately.[185]

Despite the varying reporting members and the change in the Reporting Framework, the statistics allow for the assessment that the cases piled up steadily from 2006 through 2016 and have stabilised at a level of about 6,000 to 7,000 cases since then. This shows that in the last years, CAs were able to resolve a case number per year that is about as high and sometimes higher than the number of new cases started.

Furthermore, the OECD statistics since the application of the new Reporting Framework contain more details regarding the matters in dispute, the length of procedures and the outcomes. Regarding the matters in dispute, the OECD differentiates between transfer pricing disputes (which include both conflicts regarding the attribution of profits to a permanent establishment and conflicts in relation to the determination of profits between associated enterprises) and *other cases*.

*Figure 4.4 Relation Between Transfer Pricing and Other Cases*

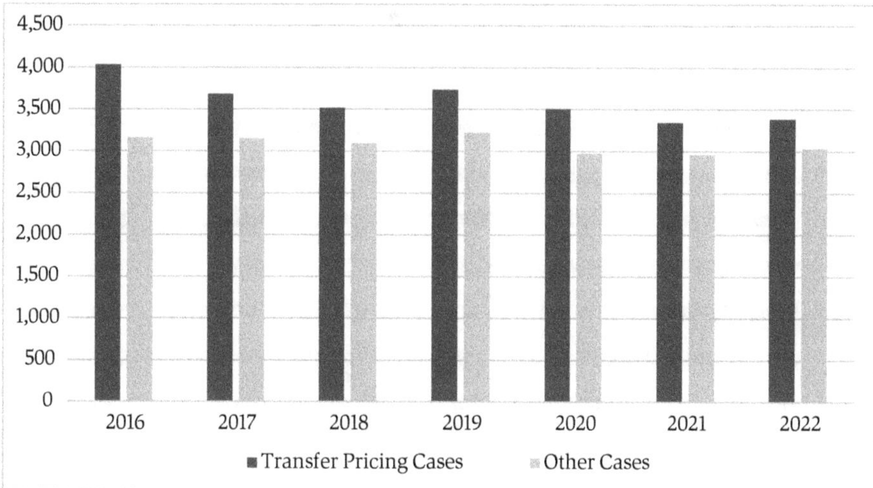


Figure 4.4 shows that transfer pricing cases in all reporting years amount to more than half of all MAP cases. On average, transfer pricing cases take longer to be resolved, which means that the goal set out in BEPS Action 14 to complete a case within 24 months is frequently missed (Figure 4.5).[186]

185. Instead, they are displayed as MAP cases, and their results are reported accordingly as detailed in Annex C to the Reporting Framework at 1(e)(vi)-(viii) and Annex D at 2(a)(vi)-(viii), accessible at http://www.oecd.org/tax/dispute/mutual-agreement-procedure-statistics-reporting-framework.pdf (accessed 15 Jan. 2024).

186. *See* minimum standard 1.3 at OECD/G20 Base Erosion and Profit Shifting Project, *supra* n. 127, at p. 15.

*Figure 4.5 Average Duration of Procedures in Months*

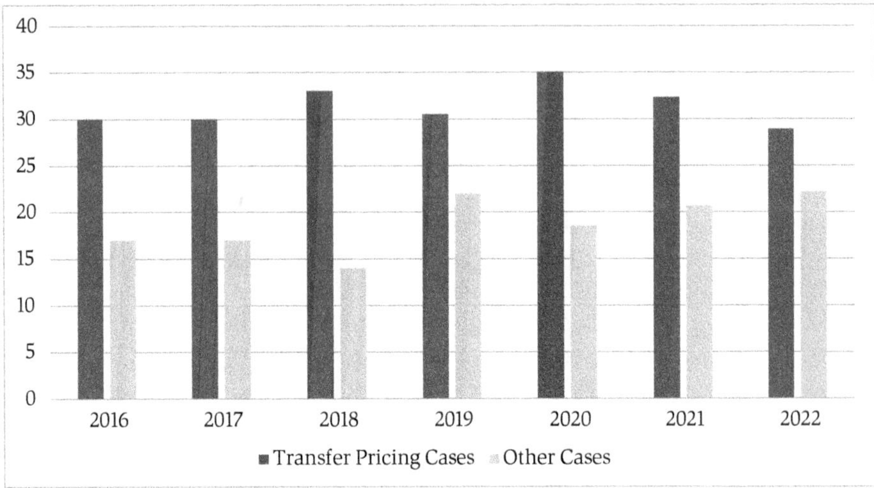


*Figure 4.6 Outcomes in Per Cent*

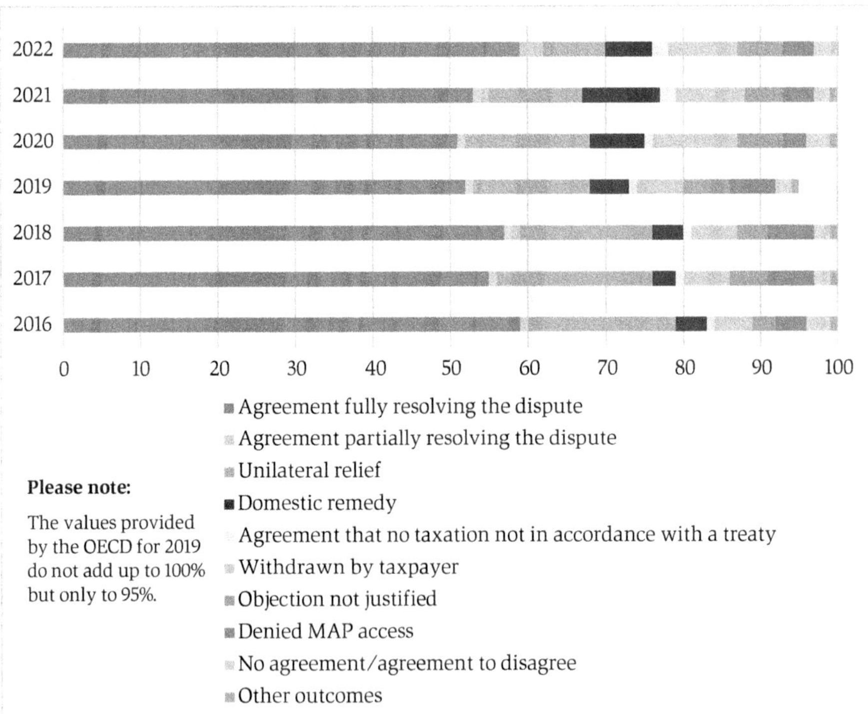


**Please note:**

The values provided by the OECD for 2019 do not add up to 100% but only to 95%.

Overall, more than half of the concluded procedures end with an agreement that fully resolves the dispute (Figure 4.6). Between 70% and 80% of procedures end with a result that benefits the taxpayer at least partially (which also includes mutual agreements partially resolving disputes, unilateral relief by one CA or a successful domestic remedy).

The OECD's dispute resolution mechanism thus has proven to be fairly successful with respect to the concluded cases. Still a bit worrying, however, is the huge number of cases not concluded that date back to years before 2016. At the end of 2022, these cases still amounted to 1,081 which equals a share of 17% of the total caseload of all reporting jurisdictions. *Kaeser* sees the main reason for this as a lack of staffing at the CAs.[187]

## 4.2 THE UN MODEL

Since its first version in 1980, the United Nations Model Double Taxation Convention (UN-MC) has always contained a provision for a MAP in Article 25. This provision was almost identical in wording with the OECD-MC. It only deviated in Article 25(4) from the second sentence on. There, it stated:

> The competent authorities, through consultations, shall develop appropriate bilateral procedures, conditions, methods and techniques for the implementation of the mutual agreement procedure provided for in this article. In addition, a competent authority may devise appropriate unilateral procedures, conditions, methods and techniques to facilitate the above-mentioned bilateral actions and the implementation of the mutual agreement procedure.

The first of these two sentences was changed in the course of the 2011 update by replacing the word *shall* with the word *may* – most likely to acknowledge the fact that only very few states actually agreed upon further procedural rules for the MAP.[188]

Furthermore, the 2011 update introduced an arbitration clause into the UN-MC. A bit more cautious than the OECD-MC, however, the UN-MC includes two alternative versions of Article 25, from which only alternative B contains an arbitration provision in its paragraph 5. Article 25 alternative B (5) UN-MC 2017 mostly resembles Article 25(5) OECD-MC 2008-2014, but deviates in a few points:

(1) Article 25(5) first sentence lit. b allows for three instead of two years for the CAs to settle the case in the MAP.
(2) Most strikingly, it is not the taxpayer who is entitled to apply for arbitration; instead, this right lies with the CAs (end of the second sentence).[189]

187. As reported by *A. Jehlin/S. Löcherbach,* Tagungsbericht zum 18. Münchner Unternehmenssteuerforum: *Verständigungsverfahren im Steuerrecht,* DStR-Beihefter, p. 4 (2016).
188. On this, *see L. Turcan,* Chapter 10: Dispute Resolution, pp. 267 f. (M. Lang et al. eds 2017).
189. In the UN's commentary on Art. 25 alternative B (5), it is furthermore pointed out that the states might also agree on a voluntary arbitration provision if they do not want to grant one CA the right to start the arbitration procedure, *see* United Nations, Model Double Taxation Convention: *Between Developed and Developing Countries – 2017 Update,* p. 594 (United Nations 2018)

(3) The CAs are allowed to deviate from the decision of the arbitral panel within six months after it has been communicated to them (fourth sentence) by agreeing on another solution.

The UN-MC's commentary also includes a sample mutual agreement on arbitration,[190] which is based on the sample which could be found in the OECD-MC's commentary from 2008 to 2014. Interestingly, however, it suggests the use of the final-offer arbitration method as a standard already since its introduction in 2011. For that purpose, the *streamlined arbitration process*, provided for in paragraph 6 of the OECD-MC's sample mutual agreement 2008-2014, is regarded as a standard procedure. Meanwhile, the independent opinion approach can be made use of *if the CAs so indicate in the Terms of Reference* as an alternative pursuant to paragraph 11 of the UN's sample mutual agreement. The streamlined procedure from the OECD's sample mutual agreement was modified, however: the arbitration panel does not – as provided for by paragraph 6 of the OECD's sample mutual agreement – consist of one single arbitrator but of the standard composition pursuant to paragraph 5 of the sample mutual agreement (one arbitrator per state and a chairperson; determination by the Chair of the UN Committee of Experts on International Cooperation in Tax Matters [or the longest serving member of this committee if the chair is a national of one of the states involved] if a state fails to appoint an arbitrator or the two appointed arbitrators are not able to agree on the appointment of a chairperson). In contrast to the standard procedure in the latest OECD sample mutual agreement from 2017, the arbitration panel is obliged to give short reasons explaining why it has chosen one proposal over another.

There are more ways in which the streamlined process deviates from the OECD's sample mutual agreement: it suggests a value threshold before an arbitration procedure may be accepted (paragraph 1 subparagraph 2 of the sample mutual agreement, which does not contain the suggestion of a value) and requires the arbitrators to declare their neutrality regarding the procedure (paragraph 7 second sentence of the sample mutual agreement). Additionally, paragraph 5 of the mutual agreement suggests defining the remuneration of arbitrators. Thereby, the UN's sample mutual agreement goes into more detail than the OECD's. While the OECD's sample (2008-2014) highlights the option of taking the method used in the Code of Conduct on the EC Arbitration Convention as an example, the UN's sample suggests setting a fixed amount per day for the arbitrators, and generally limiting these days to five days (three days for preparation and two for meetings) plus under certain circumstances necessary days for travel.

Finally, a notable difference between the OECD-MC and the UN-MC concerns the finality of the arbitration panel's final decision: paragraph 17 of the UN's sample mutual agreement not only reflects paragraph 18 of the OECD's sample mutual

para. 14. However, it is also mentioned that the states might agree to allow (as it is provided for under Art. 25(5) of the OECD-MC) for the affected person to start the arbitration phase, *see* United Nations, *supra* n. 189, at p. 595 para. 17.

190. United Nations, *supra* n. 189, at p. 618.

agreement (2008-2014) but also adds the option for the CAs to agree on a different solution within six months of the decision being communicated to them.

### 4.3 THE MULTILATERAL INSTRUMENT

The Multilateral Convention to Implement Tax Treaty-Related Measures to Prevent Base Erosion and Profit Shifting (Multilateral Instrument, MLI) includes two parts that address the resolution of disputes: Part V aims at the MAP and Part VI contains arbitration provisions. These two parts differ in their legal nature. While Part V is an inherent part of the MLI, Part VI is a mere option. Thus, the provisions of Part V affect all signatories to the MLI, whereas the signatories can pick single elements of Part VI or ignore the entire Part altogether.[191]

Article 16(1) through (3) of the MLI resemble Article 25(1) through (3) of the OECD-MC 2017. Thus, the MLI seeks to update the MAP provisions in existing treaties to a uniform standard that includes, in particular, the right of affected persons to file the MAP case with either CA[192] and a deadline to file an application of at least three years from the first notification onwards.

In Part VI, the MLI contains comparably detailed[193] provisions for an arbitration mechanism.[194] This mechanism is rather complex because it allows for a range of options that states can choose from.[195] In general, the mechanism applies if two states have a 'match' in that they both chose to apply Part VI (Article 18 second sentence MLI).

191. In general on this conceptual aspect of the MLI *W. Schön*, Seminar E (IFA/OECD): Das Multilaterale Instrument, 26 IStR 16, p. 688 (2017).

192. Article 16(4) lit. a MLI, however, allows for a reservation regarding this right to file the case with either CA: A state might as well stick to the pre-2017 wording that generally provided for an application in the state of residence (or in cases of discrimination on the grounds of nationality in the state of nationality) but add the phrase *and the competent authority of that Contracting Jurisdiction will implement a bilateral notification or consultation process with the competent authority of the other Contracting Jurisdiction for cases in which the competent authority to which the mutual agreement procedure case was presented does not consider the taxpayer's objection to be justified.*

193. *See also Govind/Turcan, supra* n. 55, 19 DFI 5 (2017), in section 2.1.2.2.

194. On this mechanism in general *S. Piotrowski*, Schiedsverfahren in deutschen DBA nach dem MLI, 27 IStR 7, pp. 257 ff. (2018); *P. Nürnberg*, Das Schiedsverfahren nach dem Multilateralen Instrument, IWB 18, pp. 688 ff. (2018); *H.M. Pit*, Arbitration under the OECD Multilateral Instrument: Reservations, Options and Choices, 71 BIT 10, pp. 568 ff. (2017) DOI: 10.59403/gz63b4; *N. Bravo*, Mandatory Binding Arbitration in the BEPS Multilateral Instrument, 47 Intertax 8/9, pp. 693 ff. (2019) DOI: 10.54648/taxi2019069; *O. Rosenberg*, Verständigungs- und Schiedsverfahren nach dem Multilateralen Instrument und der EU-Streitbeilegungsrichtlinie, pp. 165 ff. (W.W. Kraft/A. Striegel eds, Springer Gabler 2019); *S. Govind/L. Turcan*, The Changing Contours of Dispute Resolution in the International Tax World: Comparing the OECD Multilateral Instrument and the Proposed EU Arbitration Directive, 71 BIT 3/4, section 2.3. (2017) DOI: 10.59403/1x9g90e.

195. Seeing possible inefficiencies resulting from the wide range of options *G.M. Luchena Mozo*, A Collaborative Relationship in the Resolution of International Tax Disputes and Alternative Measures for Dispute Resolution in a Post-BEPS Era, 58 ET 1, section 1 (2018) DOI: 10.59403/2mk4aac. On reasons for the optional design *Bravo, supra* n. 194, 47 Intertax 8/9 (2019), at pp. 695 f.

Article 19(1) MLI is based on Article 25(5) OECD-MC 2017. However, the MLI does not entirely defer the setting of procedural rules to the conclusion of a separate mutual agreement (as Article 25(5) last sentence OECD-MC 2017) but spells out a set of procedural rules in the instrument itself. Thus, the start date (and as part of its determination, the procedure at the beginning) of the MAP is determined in Article 19(5) through (9) MLI. The provisions regarding the start date have the same material content as those in paragraph 2 of the OECD's sample mutual agreement 2017 (*see* section 4.1.1.2.2) – the only deviation is that the MLI does not count in days but in calendar months (two/three calendar months instead of 60/90 days).

Article 19(11) MLI allows for the signatories to reserve the right to replace the two-year period for the MAP (as provided for in Article 19(1) lit. b MLI/Article 25(5) first sentence lit. b OECD-MC) with a three-year period (as provided for in the UN-MC). Furthermore, Article 19(1) lit. b MLI enables the CAs to extend the relevant MAP period on a case-by-case basis by an agreement before the period has expired.[196]

The MLI's approach to Article 25(5) second sentence OECD-MC is to be welcomed with regard to the relationship of rule and exception: Article 19(12) lit. a MLI only allows for a reservation for cases not to be submitted to arbitration if states are not able to deviate from a previous national court decision, while the OECD-MC contains this provision as a standard that might be deleted. Consequently, states rather need to justify the application of the rule under the MLI approach.

However, the scope of application can be limited quite freely by formulating abstract criteria in the course of a reservation pursuant to Article 28(2) lit. a MLI.[197] Such reservations can be objected to by other states under the provisions of Article 28(2) lit. b MLI. The result of such an objection is, however, that the entire arbitration procedure does not apply between the state making the reservation and the state objecting to it.[198]

Article 20 MLI provides rules for the appointment of arbitrators which are identical to those in paragraph 3 of the 2017 OECD sample mutual agreement. Article 21 MLI mainly resembles paragraph 6 of the 2017 sample mutual agreement with two minor differences: (1) it is not spelled out that arbitrators shall be designated as authorised representatives of one or both CAs, but rather vaguely that arbitrators (and a maximum of three staff) *shall be considered to be persons or authorities to whom information may be disclosed* and (2) Article 21(1) second sentence MLI provides that information received by arbitrators and passed on to CAs shall be considered to be exchanged under the provision on the exchange of information of the relevant treaty (Article 26 OECD-MC).

Article 22 MLI corresponds with paragraph 10 of the 2017 sample mutual agreement. More interesting is the provision in Article 24 MLI: this provision presents

196. Criticising this option to extend the MAP indefinitely *Govind/Rao, supra* n. 81, 46 Intertax 4 (2018), at p. 324.
197. Arguing in favour of this option *Pit, supra* n. 194, 71 BIT 10 (2017), at p. 573.
198. An overview of the reservations is provided by *Pit, supra* n. 194, 71 BIT 10 (2017), at p. 574 as well as by *Bravo, supra* n. 194, 47 Intertax 8/9 (2019), at p. 710. Especially Germany has made extensive reservations – on this *see Rüll, supra* n. 150, at pp. 351 f.

the option for states to allow their CA to agree on a different solution with the other CA even after (i.e., within three months) the arbitrators have rendered their decision. This is reminiscent of the provision in paragraph 17 of the UN's sample mutual agreement (even though the UN Model provides for a term of six months during which the CAs can agree on a different solution). Pursuant to Article 24(3) MLI, states can limit the possibility to agree on a different solution to cases which have been decided via an independent opinion arbitration.

The procedural rules for the arbitration itself are provided for in Article 23 MLI.[199] The standard procedure is laid out in Article 23(1) MLI. It mostly corresponds to the standard final-offer procedure in paragraph 4 of the 2017 OECD sample mutual agreement. Deviations are that:

(1) there are no deadlines specified – this remains subject to a further agreement (Article 23(1) lit. a first sentence and lit. b third sentence MLI).
(2) it is pointed out in Article 23(1) lit. b second and fourth sentence MLI that all papers (the proposed resolution as well as supporting papers and reply submissions) shall be sent to the other CA *by the date* on which they were *due*. This implies that the papers do not need to be sent to the arbitration panel and the other CA at the same time, but can be held back towards the other CA even if the paper has been sent to the arbitration panel earlier.
(3) there is no equivalent to paragraph 4 subparagraph 4 of the OECD's sample mutual agreement.

States can also make a reservation to apply an independent opinion procedure as standard pursuant to Article 23(2) MLI. The rules, however, are rather tenuous – also in comparison to paragraph 5 of the 2017 OECD sample mutual agreement. There are no deadlines provided for – not even in the way (as for the final-offer procedure) that they shall be agreed upon later on. It is only mentioned for the provision of information to the panel by the CAs that this has to be done *without undue delay*. Furthermore, the affected persons and their right to be heard (as provided for under paragraph 5 subparagraph 2 of the 2017 OECD sample mutual agreement) are not even mentioned.

Article 23(3) MLI stipulates a rule of conflict if two states chose different arbitration procedures. Thus, a state which did not opt for independent opinion arbitration can reserve for the arbitration procedure not to apply until the states have agreed on the type of arbitration.[200]

The signatories can furthermore choose to impose a confidentiality rule on affected persons and their advisors by applying Article 23(5) MLI. Pursuant to Article 23(4) MLI, this rule already applies if one of the involved states made such a choice. Thus, the non-application of the rule requires a reservation pursuant to Article 23(6) MLI. This reservation, however, can be countered by a reservation pursuant to Article 23(7) MLI: then there will be no arbitration phase between a state which has

199. In detail on the procedure also *Bravo, supra* n. 194, 47 Intertax 8/9 (2019), at pp. 703 ff.
200. Critical *Avery Jones, supra* n. 182, 47 Intertax 8/9 (2019), at p. 675.

chosen to apply Article 23(5) MLI and one which has made a reservation for the provision not to apply. The confidentiality rule in Article 23(5) MLI requires affected persons and their advisors to sign an agreement *not to disclose to any other person any information received during the course of the arbitration proceedings* from either CA or the arbitration panel. If either an affected person or an advisor breaches the agreement, the MAP as well as the arbitration procedure will be terminated.

The rule regarding costs in Article 25 MLI reminds one of paragraph 8 of the 2017 OECD sample mutual agreement but is less detailed: as long as there is no other mutual agreement regarding costs, each state bears its own costs and those of its appointed panel member. Other costs and those of the chairperson shall be borne in equal shares.[201]

Article 26 MLI contains rules of conflict with regard to other dispute resolution mechanisms: if an arbitration panel *or similar body* has already been established under another treaty, this case shall not be submitted to arbitration under the MLI pursuant to Article 26(2) MLI. Furthermore, the MLI steps back behind arbitration mechanisms from other conventions that contain *wider obligations* (Article 26(3) MLI).

On its webpage, the OECD provides a tool that allows for an assessment of the relation between two signatories and their choices regarding the application of Chapter VI.[202]

## 4.4 SPECIAL CLAUSES

### 4.4.1 The US Arbitration Clause

The US already concluded tax treaties with arbitration clauses as early as 1989.[203] The clause in Article 25(5) of the 1989 treaty with Germany, however, was only a facultative arbitration clause, stating:

> If a disagreement cannot be resolved by the competent authorities it may, if both competent authorities agree, be submitted for arbitration. The procedures shall be agreed upon and shall be established between the Contracting States by notes to be exchanged through diplomatic channels.[204]

This clause was amended via a protocol in 2006 and thereafter resembled the first (semi-)mandatory arbitration clause the US concluded. It is interesting to note that a comparable clause was also included in Article 26 of the tax treaty between Switzerland

201. Para. 254 of the Explanatory Statement points out that this shall not include *internal costs associated with the logistical arrangements for the meetings of the arbitration panel, such as the use of meeting facilities owned by a Contracting Jurisdiction, related resources, financial management, other logistical support provided by the competent authority of a Contracting Jurisdiction, and general administrative coordination of the proceedings, which would generally be borne by the Contracting Jurisdiction that hosts the meeting.* Thus, the rule effectively is the same as the one in the OECD's sample mutual agreement.
202. *See* http://www.oecd.org/tax/treaties/mli-matching-database.htm (accessed 15 Jan. 2024).
203. For details of the history of US arbitration clauses with other states *see Altman, supra* n. 72, at pp. 21 f.
204. Clearly pointing out the disadvantages of this provision *Park/Tillinghast, supra* n. 24, at p. 22.

and Germany via a protocol on 27 October 2010 (as well as an accompanying mutual agreement).

Since 2016, the United States Model Income Tax Convention (US-MC) also contains an arbitration provision. This provision does not resemble the one introduced in the OECD-MC but rather those previously agreed upon in US tax treaties.[205] The treaty provision already contains general elements of the arbitration procedure in Article 25(7) through (9), while more detailed procedural rules are to be agreed upon in a protocol (or, in the case of Canada, a memorandum) accompanying the respective treaty.

The US arbitration mechanism has several characteristic features that differ from other mechanisms and especially from the mechanism under the OECD-MC: first, the arbitration procedure only starts if *all concerned persons and their authorised representatives or agents* have submitted non-disclosure agreements regarding all information they receive in the procedure, apart from the panel's determination (Article 25(7) lit. d US-MC). Second, the CAs enjoy a high degree of flexibility, in that they can, on the one hand, extend the time limit for the MAP phase by agreeing with each other (Article 25(7) lit. b US-MC), and, on the other hand, exclude cases from arbitration by agreeing with each other in the MAP stage *that the particular case is not suitable for resolution through arbitration* (Article 25(7) second sentence second alternative US-MC). These options make the arbitration provision only semi-mandatory.[206]

The procedural rules provide for arbitration under the final-offer approach. A distinctive feature of the rules for the composition of a panel is that if one CA fails to appoint an arbitrator, the other CA may appoint the second arbitrator (Article 25(9) lit. a US-MC). The two arbitrators appointed by the states (or one state) are to appoint a chairperson who *shall not be a national or lawful permanent resident* of either state. If they fail to do so, they are dismissed, and new arbitrators shall be appointed by the CAs.

The taxpayer who initiated the procedure (defined as the *presenter* in Article 25(8) lit. a US-MC) is allowed to provide the panel with *a paper setting forth the presenter's analysis and views of the case for consideration* through the CAs before their deadline to submit position papers ends (Article 25(9) lit. e US-MC). Their paper only has the purpose of informing the panel and cannot be chosen as a solution, as can be concluded from Article 25(9) lit. j US-MC. The CA's position paper shall provide a proposed resolution that *shall be limited to a disposition of specific monetary amounts (e.g., of income, profit, gain or expense) or, where specified, the maximum rate of tax charged pursuant to the Convention for each adjustment or similar issue in the case* (Article 25(9) lit. f third sentence US-MC) – if there is more than one issue involved, separate dispositions may be provided (Article 25(9) lit. h US-MC). Additionally, the CAs are allowed to include positions regarding so-called *threshold questions* like the

205. These are – in addition to the one with Germany after 1 Jun. 2006 – the ones concluded with Belgium on 28 Nov. 2006 and with Canada on 21 Sep. 2007. *See also K. Burmester*, Chapter 37: United States, p. 827 (M. Lang et al. eds, IBFD 2020).

206. Critical also *Strotkemper, supra* n. 18, at p. 351.

taxpayer's state of residence or the question of whether there is a permanent establishment in the position paper (Article 25(9) lit. g US-MC). Furthermore, the CAs may provide the panel with *additional supporting papers* (Article 25(9) lit. f fourth sentence US-MC). Finally, each CA is allowed to submit a reply to the position paper of the other CA (Article 25(9) lit. I US-MC).

The panel's written determination shall include no more than the indication of which of the proposed CA resolutions they choose to be the solution, without any rationale or other explanation (Article 25(9) lit. j US-MC). For each issue in dispute, they can choose another CA's proposal. The provision also clarifies that *the determination of the arbitration panel shall have no precedential value with respect to the application of this Convention in any other case* (Article 25(9) lit. j third sentence US-MC).

Most deadlines are not yet provided for in the US-MC but shall be mutually agreed upon pursuant to Article 25(10) US-MC. The agreements concluded on further procedural rules so far include detailed deadlines as well as strict limitations as to the maximum page numbers of position papers and additional supporting papers.[207]

Reportedly, the US entered into an agreement with the International Centre for Dispute Resolution (ICDR), the international division of the American Arbitration Association – a private, not-for-profit organisation – to administer its procedures.[208] Apparently, the ICDR also manages (or at least managed) an *international tax treaty roster* and conducts training for potential arbitrators.[209]

### 4.4.2 The Swedish-German Clause: Jurisdiction of the ICJ

A very special clause that makes use of an institutionalised dispute resolution mechanism can be found in the tax treaty between Sweden and Germany from 14 July 1992: Article 41(5) of the treaty refers *for the settlement of disputes regarding international law* to Chapters I, II and IV of the European Convention for the Peaceful

207. The agreements are accessible at https://www.irs.gov/businesses/international-businesses/mandatory-arbitration (accessed 15 Jan. 2024). The Arbitration Board Operation Guidelines for the treaty with Germany, for example, in para. 6.a. state that the position papers shall not exceed 5 and the supporting papers shall not exceed 30 pages, plus annexes. *See also Burmester, supra* n. 205, at pp. 833 f.

208. Reported and criticised by *M. Lennard,* Some Aspects of the Architecture of International Tax Reform (and Their Human Rights-Related Consequences), p. 220 (P. Alston/N. Reisch eds, Oxford University Press 2019). *H. Mooij,* Arbitration Institutes: *An Issue Overlooked,* 47 Intertax 8/9, p. 739 (2019) DOI: 10.54648/taxi2019072 reports this regarding the US and Canada. *See also G. Almeida,* Should Taxpayers Have Access to the International Tax Arbitration Procedure?, SSRN Journal, p. 2 (2018), https://papers.ssrn.com/sol3/papers.cfm?abstract_id=3266492 (accessed 15 Jan. 2024).

209. This can be concluded from an announcement in the ICDR's International Arbitration Reporter, Issue 2, p. 7 from 2011 (accessible at https://www.icdr.org/sites/default/files/document_repository/ICDR_International_Arbitration_Reporter-Vol.2.pdf, last access 7 Jan. 2023). *See also Strotkemper, supra* n. 18, at p. 215.

Settlement of Disputes.[210] Article 1 lit. a of the European Convention for the Peaceful Settlement of Disputes allows for disputes concerning the interpretation of a treaty to be submitted *to the judgment of the International Court of Justice* (ICJ).[211] This should cover most disputes arising from the interpretation of the German-Swedish tax treaty.[212] The procedure before the ICJ is governed by its Statute. Consequently, the procedure is between the states only (Article 34(1) of the Statute), whereas taxpayers are not party to the procedure. Remarkable characteristics of the procedure – compared to other dispute resolution mechanisms – are, however, that hearings are generally public, unless the court decides otherwise or the parties demand for them not to be public (Article 46 of the Statute), minutes are made (Article 47 of the Statute) and – in case of public hearings – published (Article 71(6) of the Rules of the ICJ[213]). Decisions are binding and final (Articles 59 and 60 of the Statute).[214]

As an alternative to a procedure before the ICJ, the states may also agree, pursuant to Article 41(5) sentences 1 to 5 of the German-Swedish tax treaty, to call an arbitration panel that shall consist of professional judges from the contracting or third jurisdictions or international organisations. The procedural rules shall comply with *internationally recognised principles*. It is remarkable that in these cases, taxpayers shall be granted a *full right to be heard* as well as the right to submit their own applications during the procedure. The decision shall not be one *ex aequo et bono* but shall be based on the treaties between the states as well as on international law.

There are no known cases of either dispute resolution clause alternatives, however.

In 2023, Sweden and Germany agreed on a protocol to amend the tax treaty from 1992. Accordingly, the dispute resolution mechanism in Articles 39 ff. will be replaced with the MAP provision from Article 25(1) through (4) OECD-MC.[215] The arbitration mechanism will be deleted, presumably in the light of the Dispute Resolution Directive.

210. Concluded in Strasbourg on 29 Apr. 1957, accessible at https://www.coe.int/en/web/conventions/full-list/-/conventions/treaty/023 (accessed 15 Jan. 2024).
211. An abstract consideration of whether it is advisable to dispute international tax matters in front of the ICJ is made by *Strotkemper, supra* n. 18, at pp. 640 f.
212. *L. Hummel*, Art. 41 DBA Schweden m.no. 14 (F. Wassermeyer et al. eds, C.H. Beck 2019).
213. Accessible at https://www.icj-cij.org/en/rules (accessed 15 Jan. 2024).
214. Contemplating whether and how to mandate the ICJ with international tax disputes in general *M. Züger*, Arbitration under Tax Treaties: *Improving Legal Protection in International Tax Law*, pp. 120 ff. (IBFD 2002); *Strotkemper, supra* n. 18, at pp. 433 ff.
215. Article 16 of the Protocol from 18 Jan. 2023, accessible (in German) at https://www.bundesfinanzministerium.de/Content/DE/Standardartikel/Themen/Steuern/Internationales_Steuerrecht/Staatenbezogene_Informationen/Laender_A_Z/Schweden/2023-01-18-Schweden-Abkommen-DBA-Aenderungsprotokoll-deutsche-Fassung.pdf?__blob=publicationFile&v=2 and (in Swedish) at https://bundesfinanzministerium.de/Content/DE/Standardartikel/Themen/Steuern/Internationales_Steuerrecht/Staatenbezogene_Informationen/Laender_A_Z/Schweden/2023-01-18-Schweden-Abkommen-DBA-Aenderungsprotokoll-schwedische-Fassung.pdf?__blob=publicationFile&v=1 (accessed 15 Jan. 2024).

### 4.4.3 The German-Austrian Clause: Making Use of Article 273 TFEU

One (until now) unique decision system deserves special consideration because it came to the fore with the CJEU's decision in *Austria v. Germany* (C-648/15):[216] the arbitration clause in Article 25(5) of the Austria-Germany Income and Capital Tax Treaty (2000) allows for taxpayers to propose arbitration pursuant to Article 239 of the EC Treaty (now Article 273 of the Treaty on the Functioning of the European Union, TFEU). This reference appears remarkable because one key criterion of Article 273 of the TFEU is that the dispute at stake *relates to the subject matter of the Treaties*. A relationship to the Treaties of the European Union might be doubted as conflicts usually arise from difficulties or doubts regarding the interpretation or application[217] of a tax treaty in general and the Austria-Germany treaty in particular since these are conflicts of common international law rather than of EU law.

In his opinion in *Austria v. Germany*, the Advocate General defined the relationship required by Article 273 of the TFEU as given if there is a sufficient and objectively identifiable link between the dispute and the action or objectives of the European Union.[218] The CJEU followed this approach[219] and stated that this link was given in the light of the beneficial effect of the mitigation of double taxation on the functioning of the internal market.[220] This interpretation of Article 273 TFEU has been criticised, not only regarding the link between EU law and the interpretation of tax treaties but also in the light of previous CJEU case law.[221]

The reasoning of the CJEU is easier to understand, however, when one takes into account the historical context:[222] Article 293 of the EC Treaty stated that:

> Member States shall, so far as is necessary, enter into negotiations with each other with a view to securing for the benefit of their nationals: [...] the abolition of double taxation within the Community [...].

This shows that the negotiation and application of tax treaties were seen as a subject matter related to the EC Treaty by the Member States.[223] However, the rule

216. CJEU, Judgment (Grand Chamber) of 12 Sep. 2017, *Republic of Austria v. Federal Republic of Germany*, C-648/15, ECLI:EU:C:2017:664. *See also M. Lang*, DBA-Interpretation durch den EuGH, 27 SWI 10, pp. 507 ff. (2017); *N. Strotkemper*, Schiedsgerichtsurteil des EuGH v. 12.9.2017 in Sachen Republik Österreich/Bundesrepublik Deutschland: Kritische Analyse und Folgen für die Praxis, 28 IStR 7, pp. 235 ff. (2019).
217. As mentioned in Art. 25(5) of the Austrian-German tax treaty.
218. AG Mengozzi, Opinion of 27 Apr. 2017, *Republic of Austria v. Federal Republic of Germany*, Case C-648/15.
219. CJEU, *Republic of Austria v. Federal Republic of Germany* (C-648/15, *supra* n. 216), m.no. 25.
220. CJEU, *Republic of Austria v. Federal Republic of Germany* (C-648/15, *supra* n. 216), m.no. 26.
221. *B. Michel*, Austria v. Germany (Case C-648/15): The ECJ and Its New Tax Treaty Arbitration Hat, 58 ET 1, pp. 4 f. (2018).
222. Stressing this aspect as well *A. Cloer/N. Niemeyer*, EuGH mit Entscheidungsbefugnis durch DBA-Schiedsklausel – Vorbildcharakter für die Streitbeilegung innerhalb der EU?, FR, p. 675 (2018).
223. *M. Züger*, The ECJ as Arbitration Court for the New Austria–Germany Tax Treaty, 40 ET 3, p. 102 (2000); *Züger*, *supra* n. 214, at pp. 112 f.; *M. Züger*, Schiedsverfahren für Doppelbesteuerungsabkommen: *Möglichkeiten zur Verbesserung des Rechtsschutzes im internationalen Steuerrecht*, pp. 123 f. (Linde 2001).

under Article 293 of the EC Treaty was abolished under the Lisbon Treaty and does not find a successor in the TFEU[224] – which might pose a problem in the light of the principle of conferral,[225] but does not justify the conclusion that the Member States wanted to express that there is no relationship between (the elimination of) double taxation and the subject matter of the Treaties.[226]

Consequently, it is possible for international tax disputes to be arbitrated by the CJEU, making use of Article 273 TFEU. This option could also be made use of by EU Member States under Article 25(5) OECD-MC because all Article 273 TFEU requires is a *special agreement between the parties*; this does not necessarily need to be a treaty but might as well be a mutual agreement between the states[227] that could be concluded when agreeing on the procedural rules under Article 25(5) OECD-MC.

Once the CJEU is mandated as an arbitrator, the CJEU's procedural law applies.[228] Consequently, the parties are both involved states,[229] whereas taxpayers might only be heard as witnesses.[230]

In sum, the clause also uses an institutionalised mechanism and has proven to be successful in one case. It appears to be efficient to make use of the CJEU's infrastructure and procedural rules, and it is beneficial for the public that the CJEU's arbitration decision is published.[231] Taxpayers, however, still only have a limited standing under the clause.

## 4.5 THE ARBITRATION CONVENTION

The Convention on the elimination of double taxation in connection with the adjustment of profits of associated enterprises[232] (Arbitration Convention, AC) was established as a multilateral convention with the signature of all EEC Member States on 23 July 1990. It is based on the proposal of a directive which had been introduced as early as 1976.[233]

224. *D. Dürrschmidt*, 'Europäisches Steuerrecht' nach Lissabon, 63 NJW 29, p. 2089 (2010)
225. *M. Lehner*, Beseitigt die neue Verfassung für Europa die Verpflichtung der Mitgliedstaaten zur Vermeidung der Doppelbesteuerung?, 14 IStR 12, p. 398 (2005).
226. *J. Luts/C. Kempeneers*, Case C-648/15 Austria v. Germany: Jurisdiction and Powers of the CJ to Settle Tax Treaty Disputes Under Article 273 TFEU, 27 EC Tax Review 1, p. 10 (2018).
227. *W. Cremer*, Art. 273 AEUV m.no. 2 (C. Calliess/M. Ruffert eds, C.H. Beck 2016).
228. In detail *Züger*, *supra* n. 214, in sections 4.4.1. and 4.4.2.
229. *Strotkemper*, *supra* n. 18, at pp. 238 f.
230. *Strotkemper*, *supra* n. 18, at pp. 270 f.
231. It is especially clear that an academic debate is possible after the publication of the decision – *see* the publications mentioned in n. 216.
232. 90/463/EEC.
233. *See* OJ C 301 of 21 Dec. 1976, p. 4. Extensively on this proposal *M. Lehner*, Möglichkeiten zur Verbesserung des Verständigungsverfahrens auf der Grundlage des EWG-Vertrages: *Dargestellt anhand eines Richtlinienvorschlages der EG-Kommission zur Vermeidung der Doppelbesteuerung im Fall der Gewinnberichtigung zwischen verbundenen Unternehmen* (C.H. Beck 1982). In greater detail on the history of the Arbitration Convention *H.M. Pit*, Dispute Resolution in the EU, pp. 32 ff. (2018). Stating that the OECD Transfer Pricing Guidelines need to be considered in cases under the AC *J.-P. van West/C. Zöhrer*, The EU Arbitration Convention and Directive: *Chapter 10*, 866 (M. Lang et al. eds, Linde 2018).

Compared to the mechanisms I have analysed so far, the Arbitration Convention is characterised by the features that:

(1) it is limited in scope to intra-group transactions of enterprises situated in signatory states and subject to income tax (Articles 1 and 2 AC); and
(2) it contains its own material rule on the attribution of profits (Article 4 AC), which is equivalent to the arm's-length principle in Article 9 OECD-MC (for associated enterprises as in Article 4(1) AC) and Article 7(2) OECD-MC (for permanent establishments as in Article 4(2) AC).[234]

In the event of a profit adjustment, a state shall inform the affected enterprise and enable it to inform the other enterprise which in turn can inform its state about the envisaged profit adjustment and ask for a counter-adjustment (Article 5(1) AC).[235] If there is a disagreement, the AC offers a dispute resolution mechanism. This mechanism provides for a MAP (Article 6 AC) and a subsequent arbitration phase (Articles 7 through 14 AC).

### 4.5.1 Exclusion of Cases

Pursuant to Article 8 AC, access to the dispute resolution mechanism can be denied to enterprises if *legal or administrative proceedings have resulted in a final ruling that by actions giving rise to an adjustment of transfers of profits under Article 4, one of the enterprises concerned is liable to a serious penalty*.[236] Even though the Revised Code of Conduct of the Council of the European Union[237] in paragraph 3 proclaims that these *serious penalties* should only include exceptional cases like fraud, some states have in their unilateral declarations already declared cases in which administrative penalties have been imposed – for instance, for the refusal to supply documents to tax authorities – to be covered by the excluding provision.[238]

### 4.5.2 The Mutual Agreement Phase

The MAP is initiated by an affected enterprise that considers that the rule in Article 4 AC has not been observed (Article 6(1) AC). Within a deadline of three years that starts with the *first notification of the action which results or is likely to result in double*

234. *G. Kofler/P. Pistone*, Seminar J: Ist die positive Integration im EU-Steuerrecht wieder auf Schiene? *Gedanken in Vorbereitung auf den 71. IFA Kongress in Rio de Janeiro*, 26 IStR 16, p. 705 (2017) consider this rule to be part of the European Union's *acquis communautaire*.
235. In detail on this procedural step *H. Schaumburg*, Schiedsverfahrenskonvention zu Verrechnungspreiskorrekturen, 23.11-23.12 (H. Schaumburg/J. Englisch eds, Otto Schmidt 2020).
236. In detail and critical *L. Hinnekens*, The European Tax Arbitration Convention and Its Legal Framework: *Part 2*, B.T.R. 3, p. 283 (1996).
237. OJ C 322 of 30 Dec. 2009, p. 3.
238. *See*, for example, the statement of Romania of 17 Jun. 2008, Interinstitutional File 2007/0283 (CNS), p. 2. A good overview of the states' unilateral definitions is provided by *Pit, supra* n. 233, at pp. 1623 ff.

*taxation*, the enterprise may present the case to the CA of its state of residence or the state in which a permanent establishment is situated.

The CA shall notify the CAs of other concerned states *without delay*. If no unilateral relief is possible, the CAs *shall endeavour to resolve the case by mutual agreement* (Article 6(2) AC).

The maximum timespan for a MAP is two years from the submission of the case to the first CA on (Article 7(1) AC). However, paragraph 5(b) of the Code of Conduct states that the two-year period shall not begin before the date of the actual tax assessment notice. With the agreement of the enterprise concerned, the deadline can furthermore be waived pursuant to Article 7(4) AC.

### 4.5.3 The Arbitration Phase

There is no option for the concerned enterprise to start the arbitration phase with an application. The arbitration phase is instead designed to start automatically: pursuant to Article 7(1) AC, the CAs shall set up an arbitration panel (called 'Advisory Commission') to deliver an opinion on the elimination of the double taxation in question if they fail to reach an agreement within the time frame of two years (or a possible extension pursuant to Article 7(4) AC).

Other than under the OECD/UN-MC, the entire case is under review in the arbitration phase – it is not limited to unresolved issues.[239] This can be read from Article 7(2) AC which mentions the *submission of the case* compared to *any unresolved issues* in Article 25(5) OECD-MC.

#### *4.5.3.1 Composition of the Panel*

The arbitration panel under the AC is called *Advisory Commission* (Article 7(1) AC). A special feature of the AC is that representatives of the CAs are members of the Advisory Commission: pursuant to Article 9(1) AC, two representatives of each CA shall be appointed as panel members. If the CAs agree, this number may be reduced to one per state. The effectiveness of this feature is doubted by some.[240] *Lodin*, for example, reports from his experience as a panel member that the representatives mostly stick to their original position.[241] Thus, he calls into question whether they should be granted voting power. I would go one step further and question whether they should be part of the panel at all.[242]

Furthermore, *an even number of independent persons* shall be part of the Advisory Commission. Therefore, each signatory shall – pursuant to Article 9(4) AC – nominate five persons who appear on a list of independent persons that is maintained

239. *M. de Ruiter*, Supplementary Dispute Resolution, 48 ET 9, p. 496 (2008).
240. *See*, for example, *Park/Tillinghast, supra* n. 24, at p. 32. Differentiated *Pit, supra* n. 233, at pp. 657 ff.
241. *S.-O. Lodin*, The Arbitration Convention in Practice – Experiences, 42 Intertax 3, p. 173 (2014) DOI: 10.54648/taxi2014019.
242. In detail *see* section 5.3.2. Also critical in this regard *Park/Tillinghast, supra* n. 24, at p. 32.

by the Council of the European Union.[243] To qualify as an independent person, one must be a national of a signatory state and a resident in the territory to which the AC applies. The professional requirements are fulfilled by being competent and independent (Article 9(4)(2) AC).

The independent persons are to be appointed by mutual agreement of the CAs. If the CAs fail to agree on independent persons, they shall draw lots from the entire list.[244] Pursuant to Article 9(3) AC, the CAs may object to the appointment of an independent person who has been drawn by lot *in any circumstance agreed* upon *in advance* between the CAs, as well as for one of these three reasons:

(1) The person belongs to or is working on behalf of one of the tax administrations concerned.
(2) The person is related to one or each of the associated enterprises by:
   a. having – or having had – a *large holding*
   b. being – or having been – an employee
   c. being – or having been – an advisor.
(3) The person does not offer a sufficient guarantee of objectivity for the settlement of the case.

There is no defined consequence for such an objection. Thus, it is to be assumed that the persons are excluded without the option of the other CA countering the objection.[245]

Together, the appointed independent persons and the representatives of the CAs elect a chairperson from the list of independent persons. The qualification requirements for the chairperson are stricter than those for other independent panel members: pursuant to Article 9(5)(2) AC, the chairperson *must possess the qualifications required for appointment to the highest judicial offices in* their country or *be a jurisconsult of recognised competence*. To assist the assessment of these qualifications, the states can already point out whether a person is eligible to serve as chair if they appoint them.[246] This is mentioned in the list.

Regarding the composition of the panel, it can be stated that the panel consists of at least 5 persons (2 representatives of the CAs, 2 independent persons and 1 chairperson) and is not limited upwards because the number of independent persons only needs to be even.[247] Thus, the only limiting factor is the list of independent

243. The list can be accessed at https://www.consilium.europa.eu/en/documents-publications/treaties-agreements/agreement/?id = 1990093 (accessed 15 Jan. 2024).
244. *Züger* also interprets the provision in the way that all of the members on the list form a pool, *see Züger, supra* n. 214, at p. 83.
245. *Pit* comes to the same conclusion and thus points out that it is a veto rather than an objection, *see Pit, supra* n. 233, at p. 669.
246. This is proposed in section 7.1 lit. c of the Revised Code of Conduct for the effective implementation of the Convention on the elimination of double taxation in connection with the adjustment of profits of associated enterprises, OJ C 322, p. 7.
247. *See also G.T. Joseph*, Transfer Pricing: The EC Arbitration Convention as a Dispute Resolution Mechanism, 28 Int'l Tax J. 37, p. 52 (2002).

persons, which allows for a panel of 116 persons.[248] Apart from this hypothetical case, however, a rather questionable composition of 4 CA representatives (or even more in multilateral cases), 2 independent persons and 1 chairperson is conceivable.[249] I seriously doubt whether such a body is beneficial to efficient decision-making.

Article 9(6) AC obliges the panel members to maintain secrecy about everything they learn during the proceedings. Therefore, the signatories are requested to *adopt appropriate provisions to penalise any breach of secrecy obligations*. The measures shall be communicated to the Commission which thereafter shall report them to the other signatory states.[250] To my knowledge, there is no information available to the public about these measures. Thus, there is a uniform (yet vague) material standard regarding what is to be kept secret but no uniform legal consequence in the case of a breach. Especially in the case of independent persons, it remains unclear which state's secrecy violation rule is applicable.[251]

#### *4.5.3.2 Finding and Implementing a Decision*

The panel shall find its decision based on Article 4 AC within six months (Article 11(1) AC) after the case was referred to it. The decision is adopted by a simple majority of the board members (Article 11(2) AC). Further, procedural rules may be agreed upon by the CAs (Article 11(2) second sentence AC).

The panel's decision is not immediately binding – that is why the AC calls it an 'opinion' (Article 11(1) AC). Instead, even after the 'opinion' has been expressed, the authorities remain free to take their own different decision within six months (Article 12(1) AC).[252] However, this decision is required to eliminate double taxation. As clarified in Article 14 AC, this may be achieved in one of two ways: either the profits are taxed by one state only or the tax chargeable in one state is reduced by an amount equal to the tax chargeable in the other.

If the CAs are not able to agree on their own solution within six months, the advisory committee's 'opinion' becomes binding – pursuant to Article 12(1)(2) second sentence AC, the CAs *shall be obliged to act in accordance with that opinion*.

---

248. There are 118 entries in the list. Hypothetically, the maximum number would be 134 independent persons because every one of the 27 signatories is allowed to nominate 5 persons. However, Croatia, Latvia and Lithuania have not (yet, as of March 2021) made use of this right and others (like Portugal or Slovenia) have appointed fewer than 5 persons. Thus, the list can contain up to 135 listings, but the chairperson is also to be selected from the list, which is why not all nominated persons can be independent persons.
249. Pointing this out as well *Strotkemper, supra* n. 18, at 260 n. 629.
250. Many states consider their existing domestic provisions to be sufficient, e.g., Germany – *see J. Förster,* Das EG-Schiedsübereinkommen, 45 BFuP 5, 493 n. 23 (1993).
251. This is also pointed out by *Pit, supra* n. 233, at p. 717.
252. Very critical and mainly seeing an unnecessary delay in this option *Strotkemper, supra* n. 18, at p. 417.

#### 4.5.3.3 *Participation of Affected Enterprises*

In comparison to other dispute resolution mechanisms, the Arbitration Convention offers affected enterprises the most far-reaching opportunities to participate in the proceedings: pursuant to Article 10 AC, the associated enterprises concerned *may provide any information, evidence or documents* to the arbitration panel which seem of use for its decision.[253] Furthermore, they may, at their request, appear or be represented before the Advisory Commission. This unlimited right to be heard is unique among all dispute resolution mechanisms.

However, affected enterprises and CAs are obliged to provide information, evidence or documents at the request of the Advisory Commission. As regards the CAs, this obligation does not include measures that are *at variance* with domestic law or administrative practice as well as the supply of information that either cannot be obtained under domestic law or administrative practice or would disclose *any trade, business, industrial or professional secret or trade process* or would be contrary to the *ordre public*. Furthermore, the associated enterprises are obliged to appear or be represented before the Advisory Commission on request.

#### 4.5.3.4 *Publication of Decisions*

Pursuant to Article 12(2) AC, the final decision may be published if the CAs agree and the affected enterprises consent to it.

#### 4.5.3.5 *Costs*

Article 11(3) AC provides that affected enterprises bear their own costs while the remaining costs of the arbitration procedure are shared equally by the participating states. The remuneration of arbitrators is not mentioned in the Arbitration Convention itself. The Code of Conduct, however, addresses the remuneration from two directions: (1) it is limited to the usual reimbursement for *high ranking civil servants* of the state which started establishing the Advisory Commission, and (2) the fees of independent persons are fixed at EUR 1,000 per person per meeting day of the Advisory Commission – only the chairperson receives a 10% surcharge.[254] Especially the sum in the second element has served as a model for other dispute resolution mechanisms, presumably due to an anchoring effect.[255]

253. *See also E. Frink*, Verständigungs- und Schiedsverfahren im Internationalen Steuerrecht, p. 118 (Peter Lang 2015).
254. Section 7.3 lit. f of the Revised Code of Conduct for the effective implementation of the Convention on the elimination of double taxation in connection with the adjustment of profits of associated enterprises, OJ C 322, p. 9.
255. On this, *see Rüll, supra* n. 150, at p. 355 n. 79.

### 4.5.4 Relationship to Other Remedies

In general, domestic remedies can be pursued simultaneously with the AC's mechanism (Article 6(1) AC). However, if there are parallel domestic proceedings during which the case *has been submitted to a court or tribunal*, Article 7(1)(2) second half-sentence AC stipulates that the final decision shall be awaited and the two-year term for the MAP shall start thereafter. Thus, it might be advisable for affected enterprises to make use of domestic administrative remedies to prevent national deadlines from elapsing but to suspend the proceedings thereafter to allow for the AC's mechanism to be conducted first. This should be possible in my view because these administrative proceedings do not imply the submission to a *court or tribunal* - this would only be the case if the administrative decision is appealed against.[256] However, this view is not shared by all signatories to the AC - some already count the tax administration as a *court or tribunal*, which would not allow for a suspension of the domestic remedy.[257]

Furthermore, if there has been a final decision, arbitration can only be entered into if the CAs are able to deviate from this decision (Article 7(3) AC).

The relationship with other international dispute resolution mechanisms is alluded to in Article 15 AC - the AC does not intend to:

> affect the fulfilment of wider obligations with respect to the elimination of double taxation in the case of an adjustment of profits of associated enterprises resulting [...] from other conventions.

The term *wider obligations* - which is also used in Article 26(3) of the MLI - is rather vague. A possible reference point for the *width* of obligations of the contracting states seems to be the intensity of legal protection for the affected enterprise. This criterion, however, still carries the risk of ambiguity: a mechanism might grant intense legal protection by setting strict terms for the actions of CAs and arbitrators but might not allow for a personal appearance of the affected person in front of the arbitration panel. Does this mechanism imply wider obligations than one which does not set strict deadlines but allows for the personal appearance of affected persons?[258] In view of these ambiguities, a pragmatic approach is to see mechanisms providing for mandatory arbitration as equivalent alternatives and to leave it to the affected enterprises to choose one.[259]

256. Sharing this view *L. Meeus*, Settlement of Disputes in Belgian Tax Treaty Law, p. 119 (M. Lang/M. Züger eds, Kluwer Law International 2003).
257. This is explained and criticised by *Pit, supra* n. 233, at pp. 836 ff.
258. Attempting to classify different tax treaties and the MLI as to whether they contain wider obligations than the AC *Pit, supra* n. 233, at pp. 230 ff.
259. This approach is, for example, taken by France and the Netherlands - as reported by *Pit, supra* n. 233, at p. 830. *See also Ismer/Piotrowski, supra* n. 88, at m.no. 358.

### 4.5.5 The Resolution of Multilateral Cases under the Arbitration Convention

The wording of the Arbitration Convention allows for the solution of multilateral cases: for instance, Article 6(1)(2) AC mentions *other contracting states*.[260] However, the Arbitration Convention itself does not contain procedural rules on how to deal with multilateral cases.

This issue is addressed in paragraph 6.3 of the Code of Conduct, where a truly multilateral procedure with full participation of all states involved is recommended. This also implies that all states are bound to the result of the procedure. As an alternative, the Code of Conduct proposes to conduct multiple bilateral procedures in which the respective non-party states may have an observer status.

### 4.5.6 Statistics

The EU Joint Transfer Pricing Forum publishes statistics on cases under the AC.[261] These statistics detail an inventory of cases as well as reasons why cases were not concluded within two years of initiation.

In Figures 4.7 and 4.8, the accessible statistics are compiled.

*Figure 4.7 Cases under the Arbitration Convention*

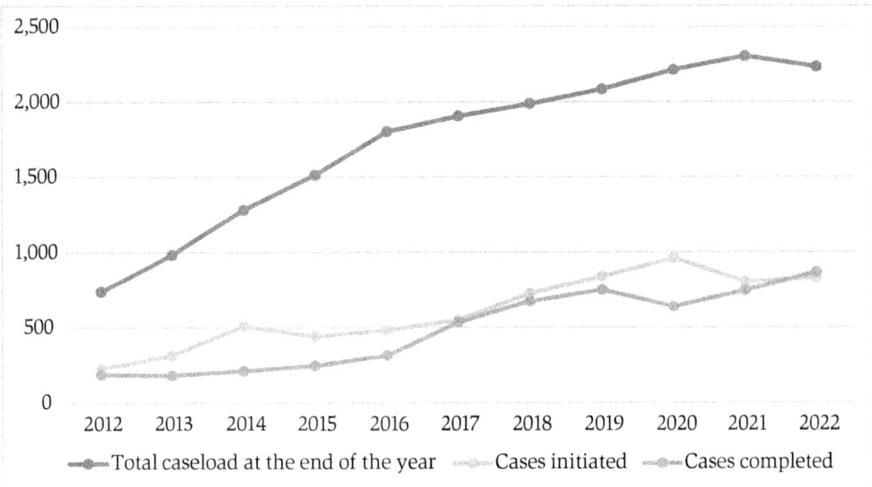


260. With the same interpretation *M. Hendricks,* Internationale Verfahren, 8.104 (H. Schaumburg/M. Hendricks eds, Verlag Dr. Otto Schmidt 2018); *A. Bödefeld/N. Kuntschik,* Der Überarbeitete Verhaltenskodex zur Anwendung des EU-Schiedsübereinkommens, 19 IStR 13, p. 475 (2010).

261. *See* https://ec.europa.eu/taxation_customs/news/statistics-apas-and-maps-eu_en (accessed 15 Jan. 2024).

*Figure 4.8 Cases Pending for More Than Two Years*

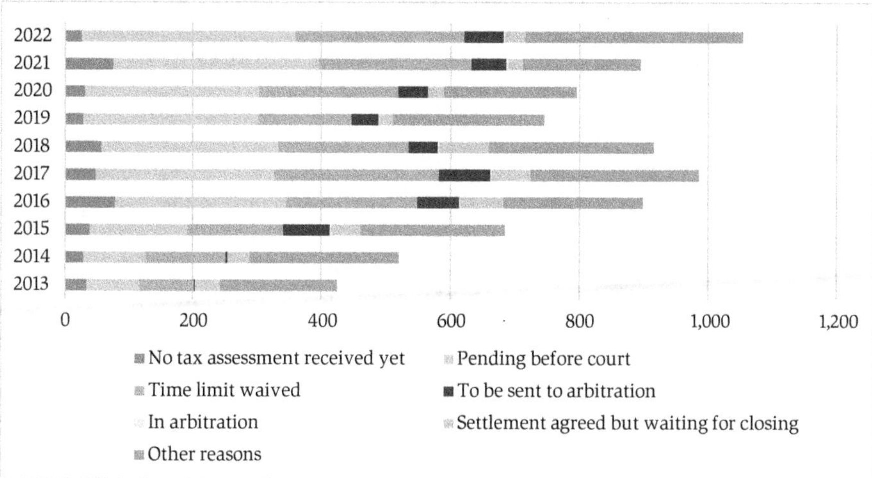


The figures show, comparable to those of the OECD statistics,[262] a steady increase of cases that the CAs in most years were not able to process fully. Figure 4.8 indicates that the arbitration mechanism of the AC is dysfunctional:[263] from up to nearly 1,000 cases that were pending longer than the two years after which the arbitration phase is designed to start automatically, not even a handful ever actually reaches the arbitration phase. This proves that the automatic start of the arbitration phase does not work. In 2017, only 80 cases were reported to proceed to the arbitration stage. In the following year, however, it appears that no cases proceeded to arbitration because the number of cases that are actually in arbitration did not increase accordingly. A staggering number of (since 2014) more than two hundred cases each year had been pending longer than two years without any reasons mentioned.

## 4.6 THE DISPUTE RESOLUTION DIRECTIVE

Following a relatively fast legislative procedure, Council Directive 2017/1852/EU on tax dispute resolution mechanisms in the European Union[264] (Dispute Resolution Directive, DRD) was adopted on 10 October 2017.[265] The Member States had to implement the Directive in accordance with Article 22(1) DRD by 30 June 2019.[266]

262. *See* section 4.1.3.
263. This, sadly, proves the assumption of the AC being an *unqualified success* in its early years by *van Raad, supra* n. 17, at p. 226 wrong.
264. OJ L 265, 14 Oct. 2017, p. 1.
265. On the genesis of the DRD, *see Pit, supra* n. 233, at pp. 1149 ff.
266. For detailed information on the different states' implementation laws, *see* either the IBFD's overview at https://research.ibfd.org/home/content/tax-dispute-resolution (accessed 27 Nov. 2020) or the one on EUR-Lex at https://eur-lex.europa.eu/legal-content/EN/NIM/?uri=

In the following, I will analyse the scope of the Directive (4.6.1.), portray the dispute resolution mechanism (4.6.2.), examine whether the CJEU has jurisdiction to interpret the Directive (4.6.3.), assess whether the Directive complies with European Fundamental Rights (4.6.4.) and, finally, highlight future design options, especially with regard to the establishment of a Standing Committee (4.6.5.).

### 4.6.1 Scope of the Directive

The touchstone for the application of the Directive is a dispute arising from the interpretation or application of an agreement or convention to eliminate double taxation of income and – where applicable – capital (legally defined as a *question in dispute* in Article 1 DRD). Thus, the existence of double taxation is not a mandatory precondition for the existence of a dispute.[267] However, pursuant to Article 16(7) DRD, a Member State may refuse access to the arbitration phase in individual cases if the dispute does not involve double taxation (what exactly amounts to double taxation is defined in Article 1(1) lit. c DRD).[268] From this provision can be concluded that a MAP must nevertheless be carried out in such cases.

Any *affected person*, i.e., a legal or natural person who is resident for tax purposes in a Member State[269] and whose taxation is directly affected by the dispute, is entitled to make use of the dispute resolution mechanism pursuant to Article 2(1) lit. d DRD.

Compared to the Arbitration Convention, this results in two major advances and extensions: on the one hand, the dispute resolution mechanism of the DRD objectively applies to all disputes arising out of tax treaties within the European Union and is no

CELEX:32017L1852 (accessed 15 Jan. 2024). On the German implementation *D. Rüll*, Die Streitbeilegungsrichtlinie und ihre Umsetzung in Deutschland, 28 IStR 18 (2019); *K. Flüchter*, Das 'EU-Doppelbesteuerungs-Streitbeilegungsgesetz' ist in Kraft, 9 ISR 2 (2020); *T. Jansen/A. Mammen*, Kritische Analyse des EU-Doppelbesteuerungsabkommen-Streitbeilegungsgesetzes, 58 DStR 10, 465 (2020). On the Spanish implementation *G.M. Luchena Mozo*, Pros and Cons of the New European Tax Dispute Resolution System and the Spanish Attempt at Transposition, 60 ET 4, p. 141 (2020) DOI: 10.59403/2edjfam.

267. Likewise *F. Debelva/J. Luts*, Directive on Tax Dispute Resolution Mechanisms in the EU, 89 Tax Notes Int'l 1, p. 73 (2018). Different *S.M. Ronco*, Chapter 17: The EU Directive on Tax Dispute Resolution Mechanisms in the European Union: A Flexible but still Perfectible Tool for Resolving International Tax Disputes, p. 357 (P. Pistone/J.J. de Goede eds, IBFD 2021); *T. Zinowsky/J. Schönfeld*, Verfahren zur Beilegung von Streitigkeiten in Doppelbesteuerungssituationen – Überblick über die neue EU-Richtlinie, 6 ISR 3, p. 8 (2017).
268. Criticising this provision *P. Pistone/J.J. de Goede*, Chapter 19: The Flexible Multi-Tier Dispute Resolution Framework and Our Final Conclusions and Recommendations, p. 521 (P. Pistone/J.J. de Goede eds, IBFD 2021).
269. Critical regarding this requirement *Debelva/Luts*, *supra* n. 267, 89 Tax Notes Int'l 1 (2018), at p. 74.

longer limited to transfer pricing/allocation of profits disputes.[270] The DRD does not contain its own substantive provisions on taxation but is linked to other agreements – including expressly the Arbitration Convention (*see* Recital 1 DRD). On the other hand, the Directive covers not only enterprises but also natural persons.[271]

Not only bilateral but also multilateral procedures are (still) possible, provided that all the states involved are EU Member States. Although this is not explicitly mentioned in the DRD, it can be seen from the fact that in most cases, the open wording of *the Member States concerned* and in Article 7(1)(3) DRD of *all Member States concerned* (instead of *both*) is used. Moreover, pursuant to Article 3(1) sentence 3 DRD, the complaint must indicate *which other Member States* are concerned.

### 4.6.2 The Dispute Resolution Mechanism

The dispute resolution mechanism essentially resembles the 'classic' two-stage system of international tax dispute resolution mechanisms:[272] it first provides for a MAP phase and – in the event the parties are unable to resolve their dispute during this phase – for a mandatory resolution of the dispute. In this respect, the Arbitration Convention served as the basis for the mechanism of the Directive (cf. Recital 7 DRD).

The DRD, however, has a special feature in the differentiated regulation of the complaint stage: it not only serves as a basic admissibility station for the MAP but also allows unilateral measures of relief or even, under certain circumstances, an immediate transition to the arbitration phase. For this reason, the Directive's mechanism can be understood as a three-stage[273] procedure and be divided into the complaint stage, the MAP and arbitration either by an Advisory Commission or by an Alternative Dispute Resolution Commission (Figure 4.9).

270. *See also J. Kokott,* Das Steuerrecht der Europäischen Union, § 11 m.no. 43 (C.H. Beck 2018).
271. The Commission proposal of 25 Oct. 2016 (COM(2016) 686 final) still provided for a limitation to enterprises, which may have been due to the fact that it came in a package with a proposal regarding the CCCTB. Regarding the Commission's proposal already *N. Strotkemper,* Reformiertes Streitbeilegungsverfahren für Doppelbesteuerungskonflikte in der EU: *Überblick zum Richtlinienvorschlag vom 25.10.2016,* IWB 2 (2017).
272. *See also Ronco, supra* n. 267, at p. 354; *Luchena Mozo, supra* n. 195, 58 ET 1 (2018), in section 1.
273. For a three-stage understanding as well *Govind/Turcan, supra* n. 55, 19 DFI 5 (2017), in section 2.2.2.; *K. Hafner/M. Stiastny,* Die EU-Streitbeilegungsrichtlinie – eine Vorstellung, SWI, p. 13 (2018); *M. Vock/P. Spanböchl,* Das EU-Besteuerungsstreitbeilegungsgesetz im Überblick, RdW 3 (2019). *Pit* even understands the procedure as a five-stage one, in that he separates the step of the unilateral examination from the complaint stage and, at the end, sees the path to the final decision and its implementation as a separate procedural step, *see Pit, supra* n. 233, at 1289 ff., 1501 ff.

*Figure 4.9 Overview of the Procedure under the Dispute Resolution Directive*

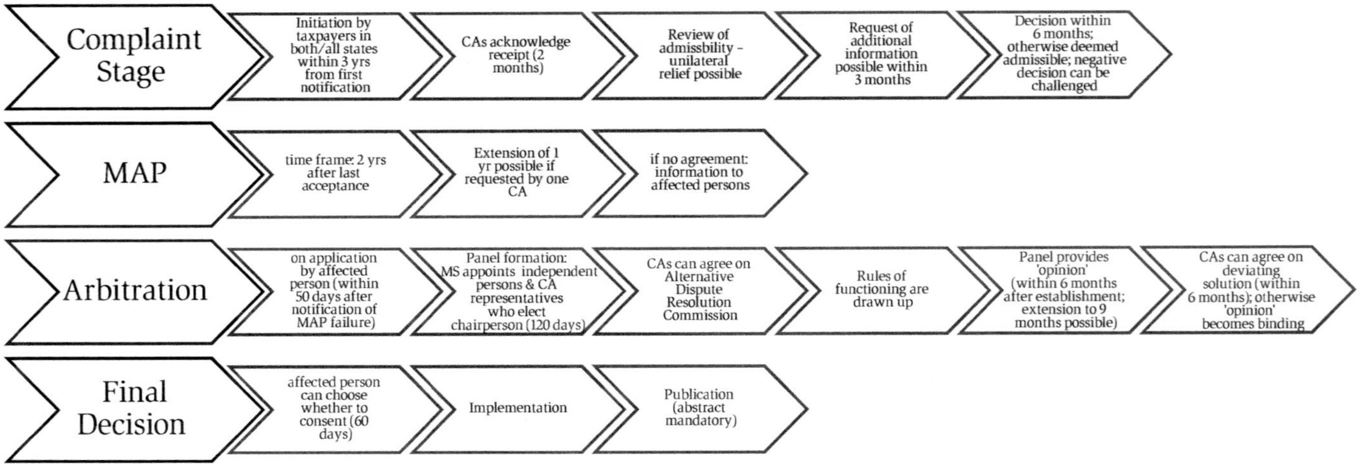

### 4.6.2.1 *The Complaint Stage*

#### *4.6.2.1.1 Submitting the Complaint*

The procedure is initiated by the application (*complaint*) of an affected person pursuant to Article 3(1) DRD. The complaint must contain the information listed in Article 3(3) lit. a through e DRD. This includes information necessary to identify the affected person, precise information on the facts of the case (tax periods concerned, description of the economic background and tax measures) as well as on the relevant standards of national and treaty law, evidence of the statements and information made and a statement of the affected person.

Pursuant to Article 3(1) sentence 2 DRD, the application deadline is three years *from the receipt of the first notification of the action resulting in, or that will result in, the question in dispute*. It was up to the Member States to specify in their implementation legislation which measure qualifies as an action in this sense.[274]

The complaint has to be addressed to the CAs of the Member States concerned. In principle, the complaint must be addressed to the authorities of all the Member States concerned at the same time.[275] Article 17 DRD provides for an exception for natural persons and companies which are not large within the meaning of Article 3(4) of the Accounting Directive[276] and are not part of a large group within the meaning of Article 3(7) of the Accounting Directive. They may also solely address the complaint to the CA of their state of residence.

With the filing of the complaint, all other MAP or arbitration proceedings on the same issue, which the affected person has brought under a tax treaty, end automatically in accordance with Article 16(5) DRD.[277]

The authorities must acknowledge receipt of the complaint to the affected person within two months and inform each other, as well as determine the language of the proceedings (Article 3(2) DRD).

#### *4.6.2.1.2 Review of Admissibility*

A decision will then have to be taken as to whether the complaint is admissible. The time limit for this is six months from the receipt of the complaint and all further

274. Critical regarding the drafted German implementation legislation *Rüll, supra* n. 266, 28 IStR 18 (2019), at p. 731; *J. Förster*, Vermehrte Streitschlichtung durch Schiedsverfahren - eine 'Konkurrenz' für die nationale Finanzgerichtsbarkeit?, p. 147 (D. Gosch et al. eds, C.H.Beck 2019).
275. This mechanism is appreciated by *P. Pistone*, Chapter 8: *EU Cross-Border Tax Disputes Settlement*, section 8.6.1.2. (P.J. Wattel et al. eds, Wolters Kluwer 2018) and *Ronco, supra* n. 267, at p. 373, who highlights the opportunity of cooperation between authorities.
276. Directive 2013/34/EU of the European Parliament and of the Council of 26 Jun. 2013, OJ L 182, 29 Jun. 2013, p. 19.
277. On the relation of the DRD with other international dispute resolution mechanisms *see also S. Govind*, The New Face of International Tax Dispute Resolution: Comparing the OECD Multilateral Instrument with the EU Dispute Resolution Directive, 27 EC Tax Review 6, p. 322 (2018) DOI: 10.54648/ecta2018034; *Ronco, supra* n. 267, at p. 366.

information requested by the CAs (cf. Article 3(5) DRD). For requests for information at the beginning of the MAP, Article 3(4) DRD gives the authorities three months from the receipt of the complaint, without excluding further requests for information after the acceptance of the complaint. The affected person must provide the information within three months of the receipt of the request (Article 3(4)(2) DRD).

Within the time limit for the decision on the admissibility of the complaint, the CAs are free to solve the case unilaterally (Article 3(5)(2) DRD).

Pursuant to Article 5(1) DRD, the rejection of a complaint can only be based on the following grounds:

(1) the complaint does not contain the information required under Article 3(3) DRD or the information requested has not been provided or has not been provided in due time;
(2) there is no question in dispute;[278] or
(3) the complaint is time-barred.

If no decision on the admissibility of the appeal is taken in due time, it shall be deemed admissible pursuant to Article 5(2) DRD.

#### *4.6.2.1.3 Appeals Against the Rejection of the Complaint*

In accordance with Article 5(3) DRD, taxpayers must be given the opportunity to appeal a negative decision by both (or in multilateral proceedings by all) CAs in accordance with national regulations. In addition, taxpayers may also request an Advisory Commission to be set up to decide on the admissibility of the complaint (*see* section 4.6.2.3.1. for more details).

The text of the directive is somewhat misleading at this point: the application is directly admissible pursuant to Article 6(1)(1) lit. a DRD if the complaint has been *rejected by at least one, but not all of the competent authorities.*[279] In addition, it must be concluded from Article 5(3) sentences 2 and 3 DRD that an application is also possible in the case of a rejection by all CAs if the national appeal procedures have been exhausted in at least one state and if the courts or authorities in at least one Member State have granted approval while – in case of disapproval in another state – the constitution of the disapproving state permits deviations from decisions of its courts or judicial authorities.[280] This rule only requires an appeal in at least one state and does not require an appeal in all states that denied access to the procedure; this allows for

278. This would be the case, for example, in a dispute involving a country that is not an EU Member State, *see P. Spanböchl/L. Turcan,* Das neue EU-Besteuerungsstreitbeilegungsgesetz (EU-BStbG), SWI, p. 190 (2019).
279. *See also Ronco, supra* n. 267, at p. 374.
280. *See also Hafner/Stiastny, supra* n. 273, SWI (2018), at p. 15; *Ronco, supra* n. 267, at p. 380. Differing – for an end to the procedure immediately after both Member States have rejected the complaint as inadmissible *M.J. Chwalek/L. Bühl,* Obligatorisches Verfahren zur Beilegung von Doppelbesteuerungsstreitigkeiten in der EU ab 2019, IWB 6, p. 215 (2018). On the question of whether deviations are possible in various jurisdictions *see* already n. 150.

'forum shopping'[281] by taxpayers (especially with regard to the question of whether a deviation from final decisions is constitutionally possible in the respective state). If all national appeal procedures are unsuccessful, however, the Advisory Commission is not allowed to consider the admissibility of the complaint pursuant to Article 6(1)(1) lit. a DRD.

#### *4.6.2.2 MAP*

After the complaint has been admitted, Article 4(1)(1) DRD requires the CAs to resolve the dispute within two years from the last decision on the acceptance. They may agree on an extension of one year - provided that the application and a written statement of reasons are submitted by a CA (Article 4(1)(2) DRD); there are no further requirements stated regarding the justification and the extension does not - as under Article 7(4) AC - depend on the affected person's consent.[282]

If the CAs reach an agreement within this period, it can be enforced by the affected person in the respective states, provided that the affected person agrees to the decision and waives other remedies. If they have already filed other national appeals, they shall endeavour to terminate the proceedings and shall provide proof thereof within 60 days of the receipt of the notification of agreement by the CAs (Article 4(2) DRD).

If it becomes apparent towards the end of the mutual agreement procedure that the CAs will not reach an agreement on their own, they should be encouraged to seek assistance in the form of alternative dispute resolution (ADR) options such as mediation or conciliation pursuant to the third sentence of Recital 6 of the Directive.

If the CAs do not reach an agreement in due time, they must inform the affected person in accordance with Article 4(3) DRD of *the general reasons for the failure to reach agreement*. This is an improvement compared to the previous rules on the mutual agreement procedure in the Arbitration Convention (as well as under the UN/OECD-MC).

The affected person's involvement in the MAP is not addressed in the provision. Consequently, there is no right to be heard in the MAP phase.[283]

#### *4.6.2.3 The Arbitration Phase*

As is already the case under the Arbitration Convention (*see* Article 7 AC), a so-called *Advisory Commission* can be considered as the arbitration body. The DRD introduced a new second option, an *Alternative Dispute Resolution Commission* under Article 10.

---

281. *See also Ronco, supra* n. 267, at p. 379.
282. Criticising this option as *a possible step back in the acquis of the Union Pistone, supra* n. 275, in section 8.6.1.4. This is partly true; however, the limitation to an extension of one year still is an improvement compared to the complete waiver under Art. 7(4) AC. Critical as well *Cloer/Niemeyer, supra* n. 222, FR (2018), at p. 676.
283. *See also Ronco, supra* n. 267, at p. 383; *Govind, supra* n. 277, 27 EC Tax Review 6 (2018), at p. 314.

#### *4.6.2.3.1 The Advisory Commission*

The Advisory Commission is set up in accordance with Article 6(1) DRD at the written request of the affected person – either after their complaint has been rejected (*see* section 4.6.2.1.3.) or after no agreement has been reached in the MAP. This application requirement seems to result from a lesson learned from the Arbitration Convention, in which the transition to the arbitration phase should be carried out 'automatically' after two years following an unsuccessful MAP pursuant to Article 7(1) AC. This provision does not work in practice, as analysed in section 4.5.6. In contrast, the Model Conventions already provide for an application requirement. However, Article 6(1)(3) DRD contains an innovation regarding the application too, in that it is bound by a time limit: it must be filed within 50 days of receipt of notification of the failure of the MAP.

Access to the dispute resolution procedure may be denied to the affected person by a Member State pursuant to Article 16(6) sentence 1 DRD if, in connection with the adjusted income or assets, penalties for *tax fraud, wilful default and gross negligence* have been imposed in that state. If a procedure within the meaning of Article 16(6) sentence 1 DRD is pending, the arbitration procedure may be suspended pursuant to sentence 2 after it has been admitted, until there is a final decision on the allegation. Furthermore, there is, as already mentioned, the option for Member States to deny access to the arbitration stage pursuant to Article 16(7) DRD *on a case-by-case basis* if the question in dispute *does not involve double taxation* as defined in Article 1(1) lit. c DRD.

In accordance with Article 8 DRD, the Advisory Commission is composed of a chairperson, one representative of each CA concerned (the number may be increased to two by mutual agreement) and one independent person per Member State (this number may also be increased to two by mutual agreement). The independent persons shall be selected from lists drawn up by the Member States and maintained by the Commission.[284] In accordance with Article 9(1) DRD, each Member State must designate at least three *competent and independent individuals who can act with impartiality and integrity*. In accordance with Article 9(2) DRD, the nomination must also include information on the person's professional and academic background, as well as on their competence and expertise. It may also already be indicated whether, from the point of view of the Member State, the person may be considered to be appointed as a chair. Should any conflicts of interest emerge, details must also be provided.

According to Article 9(3)(3) DRD, doubts about the independence of the designated persons entitle other Member States to express their objections with evidence to the Commission. The Commission shall then forward the objections and the supporting documents to the state which has designated the person. This state has six months to decide whether to leave the person on the list or to remove them.

284. This list is provided at https://ec.europa.eu/taxation_customs/business/company-tax/resolution-double-taxation-disputes_en_en (accessed 15 Jan. 2024).

In addition to this refusal based on an entry in the list, a refusal in a specific case is also possible if the independent person has not been nominated by a court. Pursuant to Article 8(4) DRD, in addition to reasons possibly agreed in advance by the CAs, four listed reasons may be considered:

(1) working for or belonging to one of the tax administrations involved within the last three years;
(2) proximity to the affected person, either through a material holding or a holding conferring the right to vote or through an activity as an employee or consultant in the last five years;
(3) the lack of sufficient guarantee of impartiality for other reasons; and
(4) work in a tax advisory profession in the last three years, whether as an employee in a consulting firm or in another professional capacity – even without any reference to a party or affected person to the proceedings.

The fourth reason for exclusion appears to be very strict since all professionals who are or have been tax consultants in any way can be excluded if a CA objects to their appointment. This could affect not only persons who are full-time tax advisors but also, for example, professors who are part-time tax advisors, provided that the clause is not interpreted restrictively. (Tax court) judges are therefore primarily considered as arbitrators. The wording can be traced back to Article 8(4) lit. d of the compromise proposal of the Council Presidency of 12 May 2017.

The rules for the appointment of independent persons and their deputies shall be made by mutual agreement pursuant to Article 8(2) DRD. If the authorities are unable to determine a procedure, the decision shall be taken by lot in accordance with Article 8(3) DRD.

The appointed independent persons, together with the representatives of the authorities who are part of the Advisory Commission, shall elect a chairperson from the list of independent persons in accordance with Article 8(6) DRD. Unless the CAs agree otherwise, the chair shall be a judge.

The establishment of the Advisory Commission is also subject to a time limit: pursuant to Article 6(1)(3) sentence 2 DRD, it must take place within 120 days. A major innovation of the Directive is that the affected persons can themselves initiate the setting up of the Advisory Commission if this time limit elapses. Article 7(1) DRD sets out that Member States shall provide that the affected person may apply either to a court or to any other designated body which appoints the independent person(s) from the list if a state fails to appoint at least one independent person and one substitute (Article 7(1)(2) DRD). If none of the CAs fulfils their obligation to appoint within the prescribed period, the affected person must request the court or designated body of each Member State to appoint the independent person (and probably also a substitute) in accordance with Article 7(1)(3) DRD. They only have to apply to the courts or designated authorities of their country of residence if two or more affected persons are involved (Article 7(1)(4) DRD). In accordance with Article 7(3) sentence 2 of the DRD, the rules for the appointment procedure are to be modelled on those for arbitration proceedings in civil and commercial matters in which the parties could not agree on the appointment of arbitrators.

If all independent persons have been appointed by courts or other nominating bodies, they shall not appoint the chair of the Advisory Commission pursuant to Article 8(6) DRD in consultation with the representatives of the authorities, but in accordance with Article 7(1)(3) DRD by lot. The CA which has failed to appoint independent persons in due time may, in accordance with Article 7(3) sentence 4 DRD, take action against the appointment decision in the respective Member State if it is entitled to do so under national law.

Where the affected person's request for the Advisory Commission to be set up is made after the complaint has been rejected by a CA, the Advisory Commission shall initially decide on the admissibility of the complaint within six months. If it admits the complaint, the authorities are given the opportunity, pursuant to Article 6(2)(2) and (3) DRD, to request the initiation of a MAP within 60 days. If they allow this period to elapse, the arbitration proceedings shall commence immediately.

#### *4.6.2.3.2 The Alternative Dispute Resolution Commission*

The rules on the Alternative Dispute Resolution Commission (ADRC) are not particularly detailed. This Commission may be set up in lieu of the Advisory Commission if the CAs so agree (Article 10(1) sentence 1 DRD). Therefore, the affected person has no influence over whether an Advisory Commission or an ADRC is set up if the CAs set up one of the two commissions within the respective time limits.

Article 10(2)(1) DRD allows deviations, initially regarding the composition and form of the arbitration body, provided that the strict independence provisions of Article 8(4) and (5) DRD are complied with. Beyond that, the DRD offers a lot of flexibility when it comes to the procedure. Pursuant to Article 10(2)(2) DRD, the Commission shall be entitled to use any procedures or techniques for binding dispute resolution. The use of *final-offer arbitration* is explicitly mentioned as an alternative to the *independent opinion arbitration* of the Advisory Commission.

According to Article 10(1) sentence 2 DRD, the ad hoc concept of the Advisory Commission may also be deviated from, and an ADRC can be set up as a so-called *Standing Committee* by the CAs of the Member States. *Vock* and *Spanböchl* interpret this provision as meaning that an existing institution such as the CJEU or the ICJ can also be entrusted with the task of an arbitration body.[285] I would like to endorse this view: admittedly, the wording to *set up* argues in favour of an active selection decision regarding the individual arbitrators, which cannot be guaranteed in the case of the assignment of an institution. Nevertheless, the systematic-teleological consideration that Article 10 of the Directive seeks a high degree of openness for future developments (in particular Article 10(2)(2) DRD) justifies the conclusion that the wording of Article 10(1) sentence 2 DRD should not prevent the transfer of responsibility to an

285. *Vock/Spanböchl, supra* n. 273, RdW 3 (2019), at p. 194. Detailed information on the involvement of the CJEU is provided by *Pit, supra* n. 233, at pp. 1386 f.

established body – such as a specialised body for the resolution of international tax conflicts which may have to be created in the future. In my opinion, if the CJEU was assigned, the agreement of the CAs pursuant to Article 10(1) sentence 2 DRD would constitute a *special agreement* within the meaning of Article 273 TFEU and thus establish the jurisdiction of the CJEU according to this provision.[286]

Additionally, however, apart from a mandate for already existing institutions, Article 10(1) second sentence DRD allows for new *Standing Committees* to be established. This power lies with the CAs of the Member States. From this, I infer that CAs of two or more Member States can set up permanent committees that deal with all, only with specifically assigned or with all cases of a certain subject matter that occur in their relation. Thereby, CAs enjoy great freedom in how to shape these committees.

The options to fill the concept of an ADRC – including the establishment of a *Standing Committee* – with life were also elaborated by a Fiscalis Project Group[287] that met six times between October 2018 and July 2019,[288] and published a report in August 2019.[289] The group discussed four potential forms of an ADRC:

(1) one with full-time arbitrators,
(2) one with part-time arbitrators,
(3) one with a roster system and
(4) one without deviation from default.[290]

For a Standing Committee with full-time arbitrators, they deemed having a permanent secretariat as beneficial and contemplated the option to set up separate panels for different questions in dispute (such as transfer pricing and other DTA questions).[291] The same ideas applied to a Standing Committee with part-time arbitrators who meet and are compensated for a fixed amount of meetings per month (two were given as an example) that was considered as a starting point for a Standing Committee.[292]

The roster system was suggested as an option for an automatic and predetermined assignment of arbitrators for a specific period. The system should also be administered by a secretariat which could also take the arbitrators' specific expertise into account and thus ensure a reasonable panel composition.[293]

---

286. The CJEU could also be set up on an ad hoc basis with an agreement pursuant to Art. 10(1) sentence 1 of the Directive.
287. Consisting of experts from Austria, Belgium, the Czech Republic, Finland, France, Germany, Italy, the Netherlands, Poland, the Slovak Republic, Spain, Sweden and the United Kingdom.
288. As reported at the Commission's webpage at https://ec.europa.eu/taxation_customs/business/company-tax/resolution-double-taxation-disputes_en_en (accessed 15 Jan. 2024).
289. *See* Fiscalis Project Group (FPG) 093, Working Paper on the Implementation of Art. 10 of Directive (EU) 2017/1852 on Tax Dispute Resolution Mechanisms in the European Union, https://taxation-customs.ec.europa.eu/system/files/2019-10/2019-tax-dispute-resolution-fiscalis-project-group-report.pdf (accessed 15 Jan. 2024).
290. Fiscalis Project Group (FPG) 093, *supra* n. 289, at pp. 15 ff.
291. Fiscalis Project Group (FPG) 093, *supra* n. 289, at p. 15.
292. Fiscalis Project Group (FPG) 093, *supra* n. 289, at p. 16.
293. Fiscalis Project Group (FPG) 093, *supra* n. 289, at pp. 16 f.

Finally, they pointed out that an ADRC might still follow the standard form of an Advisory Commission but might be used to deviate from the directive's standard procedure in other aspects such as the dispute resolution method or the composition of the Commission.[294]

#### 4.6.2.3.3 *The Arbitration Procedure*

The arbitration procedure consists of the arbitration panel submitting a so-called *opinion* within six months of its establishment – or after an extension of the deadline to be decided by it after nine months. At the beginning of the arbitration proceedings, rules on the functioning of the arbitration panel shall be drawn up, signed by the CAs and communicated to the affected person (Article 11 DRD). The rules of functioning shall describe, *inter alia*, the subject at issue and its characteristics, as well as the legal and factual issues on which the CAs have agreed. Information shall also be provided regarding the arbitration panel, including whether it is an Advisory Commission or an ADRC, the composition of the arbitration panel, the type of procedure to be followed and the time frame for the arbitration phase. On 24 April 2019, the European Commission – based on Article 11(3) of the Directive – issued a standard set of rules of functioning[295] within the framework of an implementing regulation,[296] which applies in accordance with Article 11(3) sentence 2 DRD if the rules of functioning are incomplete or have not been communicated to the affected person.

Unlike under the Arbitration Convention (*see* its Article 11(2) sentence 1), the affected person no longer enjoys an unrestricted right to be heard. Both submitting information, evidence and documents (Article 13(1) sentence 1 DRD) and appearing before the arbitration panel (Article 13(2) sentence 1 DRD) are now subject to the approval of the CAs.[297] This is a regrettable step backwards. The affected person still has to submit information or appear at the request of the arbitration panel.

The opinion to be formulated in the case of an Advisory Commission constitutes an arbitration decision to be taken by way of *independent opinion arbitration*. The ADRC is also required to deliver an opinion. The title *opinion* already indicates that this decision is not yet binding. Rather, the CAs are granted six months after the submission of the opinion in accordance with Article 15(1) and (2) DRD in order to find a different solution to the dispute. Only if they do not reach another agreement are they bound by the opinion (Article 15(2) DRD).

The final decision – whether in the form of a solution by the CAs that deviates from the opinion or in the form of a binding opinion – must then be communicated to

294. Fiscalis Project Group (FPG) 093, *supra* n. 289, at p. 17.
295. The Standard Rules of Procedure constitute Part 1 of Annex I to the Implementing Regulation, OJ L 110, 25.04.2019, pp. 28 to 32.
296. Commission Implementing Regulation (EU) 2019/652 of 24 Apr. 2019 laying down standard Rules of Functioning for the Advisory Commission or Alternative Dispute Resolution Commission and a standard form for the communication of information concerning publicity of the final decision in accordance with Council Directive (EU) 2017/1852, OJ L 110, 25 Apr. 2019, p. 26.
297. Criticising this approach *Förster, supra* n. 274, at p. 153.

the affected person within 30 days. Failure to do so means that the affected person has a right to information pursuant to Article 15(3) DRD, which they can enforce by means of the national law of their country of residence.[298]

The decision is implemented if the affected person agrees within 60 days of becoming aware of it and – if they still have the right to do so – waives domestic remedies (Article 15(4)(1) sentence 2 DRD). If the decision is not implemented, the affected person is entitled to an appeal. The final decision can only be challenged under national procedural law if there are doubts as to the independence of the arbitration body (Article 15(4)(2) DRD).[299]

#### 4.6.2.4 *Publication of the Final Decision*

The decision must be published by the CAs in an abstract (Article 18(3) DRD), which is also a welcome novelty of the DRD because it guarantees that some basic information becomes public. As under the Arbitration Convention, full publication is only possible with the consent of the CAs and the affected person. In addition to information on the date, the tax periods concerned, the legal basis and the industry sector, the abstract shall also contain a description of the facts and the subject matter of the dispute as well as a *short description of the final outcome*. The last term is still quite vague. It is often stressed in the procedural rules of established mechanisms that arbitration decisions should not set a precedent – Article 15(4) sentence 1 DRD expresses this once again. Accordingly, it seems likely that the CAs will try to keep this short description as brief as possible. The Commission's implementing regulation contains – based on Article 18(4) of the Directive – a template form for the transmission of information for the publication of the decision.[300] There is reason to fear that the form character will contribute to a very laconic diction. This would in particular complicate the academic examination of the cases. Before publication, the abstract of the decision shall be forwarded to the affected person, who within 60 days may object to the publication of individual items of information by invoking trade, business, industrial or professional secrets or public order. Publication shall take place in accordance with Article 19(3) DRD in a central register maintained by the Commission.

#### 4.6.2.5 *Costs*

Article 12 DRD contains a cost regulation that is slightly different from the previously widespread regulations: so far, it has been common for each state and each affected person to bear their own costs. In addition, the costs of the arbitration procedure were mostly borne equally by the states concerned. Article 12(2) DRD, however, allows for the affected person, with the consent of the CAs, to be ordered to pay the procedural

298. *Ronco, supra* n. 267, at p. 411 points out that this right faces the practical difficulty that affected persons need to know that there has been a decision at all.
299. Critical on this option *J. Voje*, EU Tax Dispute Resolution Directive (2017/1852): Paving the Path Toward a European Tax Court?, 58 ET 7, section 2.6. (2018) DOI: 10.59403/1d77xbs.
300. Annex II to the Implementing Regulation, OJ L 110, 25 Apr. 2019, p. 33.

costs if the affected person either withdraws their complaint in accordance with Article 3(6) DRD or if the Advisory Commission has definitively rejected their complaint.

The remuneration of the arbitrators amounts – as already within the framework of the Arbitration Convention[301] – up to EUR 1,000 per meeting day pursuant to Article 12(1) sentence 1 lit. b DRD. There is no surcharge for chairpersons (as provided for by the Code of Conduct for the Arbitration Convention).

#### 4.6.2.6 *Interaction with National Remedies*

National remedies can generally be pursued simultaneously with the use of the DRD's mechanism (Article 16(3) first sentence DRD). The DRD's mechanism is, however, at least with regard to the time limits, suspended until there is a final national decision (as can be concluded from Article 16(3) second sentence DRD).[302] Furthermore, Article 16(4) DRD allows Member States to provide for a rule which terminates proceedings under the DRD's mechanism at different stages where a national court or judicial authority has taken a decision which cannot be deviated from under national law.[303]

### 4.6.3 Interpretation of the Directive by the CJEU

Since the DRD is an EU directive, it may also – unlike the Arbitration Convention[304] – be interpreted by the Court of Justice of the European Union.[305] Questions of interpretation could be brought before the CJEU in the context of preliminary ruling proceedings pursuant to Article 267 TFEU. While the competence of national courts involved in the proceedings to refer questions to the Court does not raise major questions, it is necessary to examine whether the arbitration panels under Articles 8 and 10 DRD are entitled to do so as well.

According to Article 267(1)(2) TFEU, a *court or tribunal of a Member State* is entitled to make a reference. The link with *a* Member State seems to be an initial argument against granting the right to refer to an arbitration panel set up by several Member States. In its case law, however, the CJEU has also accepted submissions from joint courts of several Member States.[306] In the *Achmea* case, although, the CJEU drew a line and demanded – concluding this criterion from the previous decision in *Christian Dior* – *links with the judicial systems of the Member States*.[307] While the CJEU did not

301. *See* section 4.5.3.5.
302. *See also Pistone, supra* n. 275, in section 8.7.
303. On whether states allow for deviations from national decisions *see* n. 150.
304. The EU Arbitration Convention is a multilateral agreement under international law, although the Commission proposed it as a directive in 1976 (*see* OJ C 301, 21.12.1976, p. 4) – *see also* section 4.5.
305. *See also* (even though without further details or arguments) *Ronco, supra* n. 267, at p. 364.
306. CJEU, Judgment of 4 Nov. 1997, *Parfums Christian Dior SA & Parfums Christian Dior BV/ Evora BV*, C-337/95, 20 et seq.
307. CJEU, Judgment of 6 Mar. 2018, *Slovak Republic v. Achmea BV*, C-248/16, ECLI:EU:C:2018:158, m.no. 48. The CJEU thereby also refers to CJEU, Judgment of 14 Jun. 2011, *Paul Miles and Others v. European Schools*, C-196/09, ECLI:EU:C:2011:388, m.no. 41.

see this criterion fulfilled for an arbitral tribunal constituted pursuant to a BIT, this is – as I see it – the case for arbitration panels under the DRD. These tribunals form part of the European Union's and thus of the Member States' judicial system, as their legal framework is based on a directive which is to be implemented by the Member States and thereafter part of their national law. Not least, national courts are involved in the procedure (functioning, however, rather as procedural safeguards than assessing substantive legal questions).[308]

Furthermore, it is to be examined whether the arbitration panel is a *court or tribunal* within the meaning of Article 267(1) and (2) TFEU. The list of criteria which the CJEU regularly applies to a court or tribunal in this sense includes the following characteristics: it must be established on a legal basis, have a permanent character, exercise compulsory jurisdiction, apply rules of law (and not merely take decisions of equity) as well as an *inter partes* procedure and be independent.[309]

The DRD and the respective implementing laws provide a legal basis,[310] and there are rather strict rules for the independence of the arbitration panel. However, it should be borne in mind that, at least in the Advisory Commission, representatives of public authorities are still involved and their independence may be called into question.[311] In my view, it is still justifiable to regard the majority of the panel as independent, given that at least three independent persons are involved and considering the fact that the Member States involved send the same number of representatives of the authorities to the panel.[312] This is only the case though as long as the option in Article 8(1)(b) DRD to increase the number of CA representatives to two per state is not made use of without increasing the number of independent persons pursuant to Article 8(1)(c) DRD.

The procedure can be described as an *inter partes* procedure. For this criterion, it is not decisive whether the affected persons can be regarded as an actual party to the

308. Arguing in a similar direction *S. Piotrowski et al.*, Towards a Standing Committee Pursuant to Article 10 of the EU Tax Dispute Resolution Directive: A Proposal for Implementation, 47 Intertax 8/9, p. 683 (2019) DOI: 10.54648/taxi2019068.
309. Cf. CJEU, Judgment of 30 Jun. 1966, *G. Vaassen (née Göbbels) v. Managment of the Beambtenfonds voor het Mijnbedrijf*, 61/65, ECLI:EU:C:1966:39; CJEU, Judgment of 17 Sep. 1997, *Dorsch Consult Ingenieurgesellschaft mbH*, C-54/96, ECLI:EU:C:1997:413, m.no. 23; CJEU, Judgment of 2 Mar. 1999, *Nour Eddline El-Yassini*, C-416/96, m.no. 17; CJEU, Judgment of 30 Mar. 2006, *Elizabeth Florence Emanuel/ Continental Shelf 128 Ltd*, C-259/04, m.no. 19; CJEU, Judgment of 18 Jun. 2002, *Hospital Ingenieure Krankenhaustechnik Planungs-Gesellschaft mbH (HI)/ Stadt Wien*, C-92/00, m.no. 25; CJEU, Judgment of 31 Jan. 2013, *Valeri Hariev Belov v. CHEZ Elektro Balgaria AD et al.*, C-394/11, ECLI:EU:C:2013:48, m.no. 38; CJEU, Judgment of 12 Jun. 2014, *Ascendi Beiras Litoral e Alta, Auto Estradas das Beiras Litoral e Alta SA v. Autoridade Tributária e Aduaneira*, C-377/13, ECLI:EU:C:2014:1754, m.no. 23; *U. Ehricke*, Art. 267 AEUV m.no. 29 (R. Streinz ed., C.H. Beck 2018).
310. *J. Monsenego*, Does the Achmea Case Prevent the Resolution of Tax Treaty Disputes Through Arbitration?, 47 Intertax 8/9, p. 735 (2019) DOI: 10.54648/taxi2019071, however, stresses that single panels are established by agreements and thus does not see this criterion fulfilled. I do not share this view, not least in the light of the elaborate rules for panels in the directive.
311. So *Monsenego*, *supra* n. 310, 47 Intertax 8/9 (2019), at p. 734.
312. *See also D. de Carolis*, The EU Dispute Resolution Directive (2017/1852) and Fair Trial Protection under Article 47 of the EU Charter of Fundamental Rights, 58 ET 11, p. 504 (2018) DOI: 10.59403/33kz8jz; *Piotrowski et al.*, *supra* n. 308, 47 Intertax 8/9 (2019), at p. 684.

procedure.[313] Instead, it is necessary and sufficient that there really is a legal dispute (rather than an administrative decision) that two parties (even if these are states) take part in.[314]

The arbitration bodies provided for by the Directive can be regarded as *mandatory*.[315] Unlike with private arbitral tribunals, no further agreement is required in order to use them, only the application of the affected person pursuant to Article 6(1) of the Directive. However, it is doubtful whether the panel is also a *permanent* one and whether legal norms are applied, especially in the case of an ADRC which applies *final-offer arbitration*. If the criterion of *permanence* were to be taken seriously, only a Standing Committee under the second sentence of Article 10(1) DRD might be able to fulfil it.[316] Yet, the CJEU does not always seem to consider the criterion that the court must be a *permanent* one to be decisive in its case law. For example, it has already once granted the right to make a reference to a Danish Industrial Arbitration Board whose members were to be appointed by the parties.[317] Furthermore, the CJEU has seen Portuguese Tax Arbitration Tribunals (*Tribunais Arbitrais Tributários*) as *permanent in nature* even though the 'composition of trial formations' was 'ephemeral and their activity ends once they have made their ruling'.[318] The same logic can apply to the arbitration bodies under the DRD: the assumption of *permanence* could be based on the fact that the number of eligible arbitrators is limited by the list the Member States have drawn up and that the nomination for the list equals an *appointment* by the states for a considerable period that can be made use of ad hoc but which can in itself be regarded as *permanent*.

With regard to the question of whether the arbitration panel applies legal norms, it could also be argued in the case of *final-offer arbitration* that the arbitration panel does not render a decision based on equity, but typically subsumes the case – at least in the course of a summary plausibility check – under the legal provisions and only then decides on one of the solutions proposed by the authorities involved.

Finally, it should not hinder the qualification of the arbitration panel as a *court or tribunal* that the CAs, in accordance with Article 15(1) DRD, are allowed to derogate within six months from the 'opinion' of the arbitration panel because it becomes binding if the authorities are unable to agree on another solution.[319]

---

313. Examining this point – at least for the MAP – *Carolis, supra* n. 312, 58 ET 11 (2018), at p. 500.
314. *See*, for example, CJEU, Judgment of 15 Jan. 2002, *Lutz GmbH and Others*, C-182/00, ECLI:EU:C:1994:195, m.no. 12; CJEU, Judgment of 30 Jun. 2005, *Mathias Längst*, C-165/03, ECLI:EU:C:2005:412, m.no. 25. Apart from this, the CJEU stated that *the requirement that the procedure before the hearing body concerned must be inter partes is not an absolute criterion, see* CJEU, *Dorsch Consult Ingenieurgesellschaft mbH* (C-54/96, *supra* n. 309), m.no. 31.
315. In detail regarding this criterion *S. Kaufmann*, P. II. Vorabentscheidungsverfahren, 75-77 (M.A. Dauses/M. Ludwigs eds, C.H. Beck) with further references.
316. So *Monsenego, supra* n. 310, 47 Intertax 8/9 (2019), at p. 734.
317. CJEU, Judgment of 17 Oct. 1989, *Handels- og Kontorfunktionaerernes Forbund/ Danfoss*, C-109/88, EU:C:1989:383 [7-8].
318. CJEU, *Ascendi Beiras Litoral e Alta, Auto Estradas das Beiras Litoral e Alta SA v. Autoridade Tributária e Aduaneira* (C-377/13, *supra* n. 309), m.no. 26.
319. *See* the decision on the Italian *Consiglio di Stato*: CJEU, Judgment of 16 Oct. 1997, *Garofalo*, C-69/96-C-79/96, 19 et seq. Different, however, *Monsenego, supra* n. 310, 47 Intertax 8/9 (2019), at p. 735.

Overall, it is in line with the CJEU case law to award an arbitration panel pursuant to Article 8 or 10 DRD the right to make a reference within the meaning of Article 267(1) TFEU.[320] It should also be borne in mind in this context that the CJEU does not apply its criteria schematically but assesses them on a case-by-case basis.[321]

### 4.6.4 Compatibility of the Directive with European Fundamental Rights

As with all other dispute resolution procedures under treaty law or the Arbitration Convention, the procedure of the DRD is described as being one between the participating states in which the affected persons are not formally a party.[322] Nevertheless, tax claims against them are at issue, and they have a strong interest in the outcome of the proceedings. In addition, they can influence the course of the proceedings in a unique way: not only do they make the request to initiate the MAP or later the arbitration phase and decide whether they agree with the result but also they can advance the individual procedural steps by involving national courts.[323] In my view, this is the most important innovation of the DRD, as for the first time it gives the affected persons the right to take action against a possible abandoning of the procedure by the CAs.

As regards the status in the proceedings, however, the DRD at the same time takes a step backwards in that it leaves the admissibility of written submissions and appearance before the arbitration panel in the arbitration phase at the discretion of the authorities involved. This step is astonishing, not least in view of the explicit reference to the Charter of Fundamental Rights and the right to a fair trial in Recital 9 of the Directive.[324]

This gives rise to an examination of whether the Charter of Fundamental Rights (CFR) provides for rules that demand a higher degree of participation rights. In its Article 47, the CFR grants a right to an effective remedy and to a fair trial. The latter implies the entitlement to a *fair and public hearing within a reasonable time by an independent and impartial tribunal previously established by law* as well as the right to be advised, defended and represented (Article 47(2) CFR). Furthermore, Article 41(2) lit. a CFR guarantees a right to be heard in the context of the right to good administration.

---

320. *See also Ismer/Piotrowski, supra* n. 88, at m.no. 340; *Rüll, supra* n. 266, 28 IStR 18 (2019), at p. 734. For the Standing Committee *see Piotrowski et al., supra* n. 308, 47 Intertax 8/9 (2019), at pp. 683 f.
321. *Ehricke, supra* n. 309, at m.no. 29; AG Ruiz-Jarabo Colomer, Opinion of 28 Jun. 2001, *François De Coster v. Collège des bourgmestre et échevins de Watermael-Boitsfort*, ECLI:EU:C:2001:366, m.no. 14; *Monsenego, supra* n. 310, 47 Intertax 8/9 (2019), at p. 733.
322. *See J. Voje*, The Limits to the Participation of the Taxpayer in Tax Dispute Resolution Procedure Under the Dispute Resolution Directive, 48 Intertax 2, pp. 159 f. (2020) DOI: 10.54648/taxi20 20015.
323. *See also G.A. Corciulo*, Arbitration under the Dispute Resolution Directive: *Does the Directive Solve the Problems Encountered with the EU Arbitration Convention?*, p. 463 (A. Majdanska/L. Turcan eds, Linde 2018).
324. Also critical *Debelva/Luts, supra* n. 267, 89 Tax Notes Int'l 1 (2018), at p. 78.

Finally, a right of more involvement of affected persons might also be derived from the Convention for the Protection of Human Rights and Fundamental Freedoms (ECHR) which, in Article 6(1) first sentence, states a right to be heard as well.

#### 4.6.4.1 *The Applicability of the CFR in General*

Pursuant to Article 51 CFR, the Charter in general applies to the EU institutions and thus also applied to the Council adopting the DRD. It further applies to the Member States implementing the directive into national law and – pursuant to the CJEU's jurisprudence – also when they act in the scope of EU law.[325] Thus, the dispute resolution mechanism established under the DRD and its implementation and application can be measured against the standards set out in the CFR. In this context, it is in my view misleading if *Voje* attempts to differentiate whether *substantive EU rules form the subject of the dispute* under Article 51 CFR.[326] The procedural rules themselves stem – other than in the cases she cites where the procedures were governed by purely domestic procedural law – from EU law and thus need to comply with it.

##### 4.6.4.1.1 *Article 47 CFR*

###### 4.6.4.1.1.1 Applicability

Article 47(1) CFR has its own application rule which includes *everyone whose rights and freedoms guaranteed by the law of the Union are violated*. Thus, Article 47 CFR is an accessory procedural guarantee that takes effect if there is a right or freedom out of the realms of European Union law in dispute.[327] This right or freedom does not need to stem from the CFR or even primary EU law; it is sufficient if it is *linked* to Union law.[328]

*Flüchter* and *Voje* as well as the Fiscalis Project Group 093's experts point out that the original disputes stem from the application and interpretation of tax treaties that do not amount to the *law of the Union* and thus conclude that Article 47 CFR does not apply.[329] While it is true that the substantive law in dispute is public international law, there may still be EU law implications on a case-by-case basis. Despite the fact that the

325. *See* CJEU, Judgment (Grand Chamber) of 26 Feb. 2013, *Åklagaren v. Hans Åkerberg Fransson*, C-617/10, ECLI:EU:C:2013:105, m.no. 17-19; CJEU, Judgment of 17 Dec. 2015, *WebMindLicenses Kft. v. Nemzeti Adó- és Vámhivatal Kiemelt Adó- és Vám Főigazgatóság*, C-419/14, ECLI:EU:C:2015:832, m.no. 66.
326. *Voje, supra* n. 322, 48 Intertax 2 (2020), at pp. 161 f.
327. Even though *Shelton* and *Ward* argue that there is *no special meaning for the term 'rights and freedoms guaranteed by EU law'* and thus the scope of Art. 47 CFR equals the scope of Art. 51 CFR, *see A. Ward*, Art. 47 47.01 (S. Peers et al. eds, Nomos; C.H.Beck; Hart 2014); *D. Shelton*, Art. 47 47.46 (S. Peers et al. eds, Nomos; C.H.Beck; Hart 2014).
328. *A. Eser/M. Kubiciel*, Art. 47 m.no. 18 (J. Meyer et al. eds, 2019); *H.D. Jarass*, Art. 47 m.no. 6 (H.D. Jarass ed., C.H. Beck 2016); *Shelton, supra* n. 327, at 47.45; *P. Voet van Vormizeele*, Art. 47 GRCh m.no. 5 (U. Becker et al. eds, Nomos 2019).
329. *K. Flüchter*, Streitbeilegungs-Richtlinie, 24.82 (H. Schaumburg/J. Englisch eds, Otto Schmidt 2020); *Voje, supra* n. 322, 48 Intertax 2 (2020), at pp. 163 ff.; Fiscalis Project Group (FPG) 093, *supra* n. 289, at p. 9.

CJEU in *Austria v. Germany* has affirmed a *relation* of tax treaties to a *subject matter of the Treaties* pursuant to Article 273 TFEU in the light of the beneficial effect of the mitigation of double taxation on the functioning of the internal market,[330] EU law does not as such prohibit double taxation between Member States.[331] In the absence of harmonised EU law, Member States are free to determine the allocation of taxing rights in international agreements.[332] In exercising these taxing rights, they are, however, bound by EU law – first and foremost, their actions need to be non-discriminatory.[333] There are a number of scenarios in which EU law may have an impact on the interpretation and application of tax treaties, from questions of residence and whether a treaty is applicable[334] – not only in the case of permanent establishments[335] but also in the case of partnerships[336] – over the applicability of anti-abuse provisions[337] to the choice of method for the elimination of double taxation[338] – to name a few examples[339].[340] Thus, Article 47 CFR is applicable in all such cases that have a connection with EU law.

330. CJEU, *Republic of Austria v. Federal Republic of Germany* (C-648/15, *supra* n. 216), m.no. 26. Thinking in the same direction *K. Perrou,* Taxpayer Rights and Taxpayer Participation in Procedures under the Dispute Resolution Directive, 47 Intertax 8/9, p. 722 (2019) DOI: 10.54648/taxi2019070; seeing the connection but arguing against the acceptance of a link *Flüchter, supra* n. 329, at footnote 3.
331. CJEU, Judgment of 15 Apr. 2010, *CIBA Speciality Chemicals Central and Eastern Europe Szolgáltató, Tanácsadó és Keresdedelmi kft v. Adó- és Pénzügyi Ellenőrzési Hivatal (APEH) Hatósági Főosztály,* C-96/08, ECLI:EU:C:2010:185, m.no. 27-29. *See,* however, *R. Wernsmann,* Internationale Doppelbesteuerung als unionsrechtliches Problem – am Beispiel grenzüberschreitender Erbschaften und Schenkungen, pp. 378 f. (J. Damrau/K. Muscheler eds, Verlag C.H. Beck 2012), who sees an interference with the guarantee of the free movement of capital.
332. CJEU, Judgment of 12 May 1998, *Mr and Mrs Gilly v. Directeur des services fiscaux du Bas-Rhin,* C-336/96, ECLI:EU:C:1998:221, m.no. 24.
333. CJEU, Judgment of 21 Sep. 1999, *Compagnie de Saint-Gobain, Zweigniederlassung Deutschland v. Finanzamt Aachen-Innenstadt,* C-307/97, ECLI:EU:C:1999:438, m.no. 58; CJEU, Judgment of 19 Jan. 2006, *Margaretha Bouanich v. Skatteverket,* C-265/04, ECLI:EU:C:2006:51, m.no. 50; *G. Kofler,* Doppelbesteuerungsabkommen und Europäisches Gemeinschaftsrecht, p. 441 (Linde 2007); *J. Schönfeld/N.D. Häck,* Systematik m.no. 138 (J. Schönfeld/X. Ditz eds, Verlag Dr. Otto Schmidt 2019). In detail on the interaction of tax treaties and Union law with reference to the CJEU's jurisprudence *J. Dombrowsky,* Die Einwirkungen des Unionsrechts auf Doppelbesteuerungsabkommen (Duncker & Humblot 2020).
334. *See* on these questions *Schönfeld/Häck, supra* n. 333, at m.no. 133; *Dombrowsky, supra* n. 333, at pp. 104 f.; *Kofler, supra* n. 333, at pp. 448 ff.
335. Very detailed *Dombrowsky, supra* n. 333, at pp. 106 ff.; in short *Schönfeld/Häck, supra* n. 333, at m.no. 134; *Kofler, supra* n. 333, at pp. 451 ff.
336. On this *Dombrowsky, supra* n. 333, at pp. 125 ff.
337. On limitation-on-benefits provisions *I. Oellerich,* DBA-Recht, 8.208-8.211 (H. Schaumburg/J. Englisch eds, Otto Schmidt 2020); *Dombrowsky, supra* n. 333, at pp. 319 ff.; *Kofler, supra* n. 333, at pp. 500 ff.; on switch-over clauses and activity tests *Oellerich, supra* n. 337, at 8.212-8.213; *Dombrowsky, supra* n. 333, at pp. 330 ff.; on subject-to-tax provisions *Schönfeld/Häck, supra* n. 333, at m.no. 149; *Oellerich, supra* n. 337, at 8.214.
338. In general *M. Keuthen,* Die Vermeidung der juristischen Doppelbesteuerung im EG-Binnenmarkt: *Die Vereinbarkeit der Anrechnungs- und der Freistellungsmethode mit den EG-Grundfreiheiten* (Duncker & Humblot 2009). Further *Dombrowsky, supra* n. 333, at pp. 241 ff.; *Kofler, supra* n. 333, at pp. 619 ff.
339. The impact of directives on tax treaties is also noteworthy, *see Dombrowsky, supra* n. 333, at pp. 377 ff.

*Flüchter* further argues against the application of Article 47 CFR that the affected persons have the option not to accept the final decision and that they can still make use of national remedies.[341] This is not a valid argument from my point of view. Since national remedies only allow for national decisions, they might grant extensive procedural rights but cannot assure a bilateral (or multilateral) solution and are thus inferior regarding the material legal protection of affected persons.[342] In this context, it seems rather sophistical to point out that affected persons still have the right not to accept a final decision if their choice is one between the devil and the deep blue sea.[343]

#### 4.6.4.1.1.2 Are the Requirements of Article 47 CFR Met?

After having established that Article 47 CFR is applicable to the dispute resolution mechanism of the DRD on a case-by-case basis if there is a connection with EU law, it needs to be examined whether the mechanism meets the requirements. While affected persons may only rely on Article 47 CFR in the aforementioned specific cases, the examination of the criteria is also relevant from a legal policy point of view because the DRD in Recital 9 claims, on the one hand, to *respect the fundamental rights* and to *observe the principles in particular by the* CFR and, on the other hand, to *seek to ensure full respect for the right to a fair trial.*

#### 4.6.4.1.1.2.1. Tribunal

The best starting point to answer this question seems to be the term *tribunal* in Article 47(1) CFR, which is further differentiated in the first sentence of paragraph 2: the criteria that have to be fulfilled by the *tribunal* include that it needs to be *independent* and *impartial* as well as *previously established by law.*[344] These requirements partly resemble those developed by the CJEU to define a *court or tribunal* under Article 267(2) TFEU, which include the questions of whether the body is established by law, whether it is permanent, whether its jurisdiction is compulsory, whether it applies rules of law and whether it is independent.[345] In *Wilson*, the CJEU held that this definition can be extended beyond the scope of Article 267(2) TFEU.[346]

---

340. *See also Monsenego, supra* n. 310, 47 Intertax 8/9 (2019), at pp. 729 f.; *M. Lehner,* Neue Regelungsebenen und Kompetenzen im Internationalen Steuerrecht, 28 IStR 8, pp. 278 f. (2019).
341. *Flüchter, supra* n. 329, at 24.82.
342. Very convincing in this regard in general also *K. Perrou,* Taxpayer Participation in Tax Treaty Dispute Resolution, p. 180 (IBFD 2014). *See also Pistone/Goede, supra* n. 268, at p. 486.
343. With similar considerations *J. Kokott,* Taxpayer's Rights, 60 ET 1, 6 right column (2020).
344. As *Voje, supra* n. 322, 48 Intertax 2 (2020), at p. 165 points out correctly, the question whether the panels established under the DRD form a *tribunal* pursuant to Art. 47(1) CFR does not regard the applicability of the provision (as assumed by *Carolis, supra* n. 312, 58 ET 11 (2018), at pp. 499 ff.).
345. Paraphrased after CJEU, *Ascendi Beiras Litoral e Alta, Auto Estradas das Beiras Litoral e Alta SA v. Autoridade Tributária e Aduaneira* (C-377/13, *supra* n. 309), m.no. 23.
346. CJEU, Judgment of 19 Sep. 2006, *Graham J. Wilson v. Ordre des avocats du barreau de Luxembourg,* C-506/04, ECLI:EU:C:2006:587, m.no. 48. Consenting *H.C. Hofmann,* Art. 47 47.52 (S. Peers et al. eds, Nomos; C.H.Beck; Hart 2014); *C. Nowak,* § 55 Recht auf effektiven gerichtlichen Rechtsschutz, 32 (F.S.M. Heselhaus/C. Nowak eds, C.H. Beck 2020).

In the preceding section 4.6.3, I have already examined whether the arbitration bodies under the DRD meet these criteria and have come to the conclusion that they do. From this, it follows that the criterion *previously established by law* that alludes to the questions of whether the tribunal is established by law (which is the case because it is established under a directive that is implemented in the national law of the Member States) and also whether it is permanent in nature (which is the case in the light of the CJEU's case law) are fulfilled by the arbitration bodies under the DRD. It should be noted here that I focus on the compatibility of the arbitration bodies with Article 47 CFR because the MAP stage clearly does not provide for a *tribunal* that complies with the criteria.[347] The question remains, however, whether an Advisory Commission under Article 8 DRD is also *independent and impartial* according to the standard of Article 47 CFR. This can be called into question because the Advisory Commission is composed of not only *independent persons* but also of CA representatives, whereas the CJEU's definition of independence implies that *an authority acting as a third party in relation to the authority which adopted the contested decision* is involved.[348] In relation to Article 267(2) TFEU, I have argued that the panel as a whole can still be regarded as independent as long as the number of independent persons (including the chair) exceeds the number of CA representatives.[349] Thus, from Article 47 CFR, the condition can be derived that the number of CA representatives, as is allowed under Article 8(1)(b) DRD, shall not be increased to two without increasing the number of independent persons accordingly (pursuant to Article 8(1)(c) DRD). If this condition is fulfilled, the entire panel can still be regarded as independent, even though the role of CA representatives can be questioned from a conceptual point of view.[350]

#### 4.6.4.1.1.2.2. Right to be Heard

The right to be heard forms part of the fair trial doctrine enshrined in Article 47(2) CFR.[351] Additionally, pursuant to Article 52(3) CFR, Article 47(2) CFR takes the material content of Article 6(1) ECHR as a minimum standard.[352]

The right to be heard contains three guarantees:[353]

(1) a right to be informed about all the material that is relevant for the tribunal's decision; this includes all documents or observations submitted to the tribunal for the purpose of influencing its decision;[354]

347. This is also addressed by *Carolis, supra* n. 312, 58 ET 11 (2018), at pp. 500 f.
348. CJEU, *Graham J. Wilson v. Ordre des avocats du barreau de Luxembourg* (C-506/04, *supra* n. 346), m.no. 49.
349. In the same direction *Piotrowski et al., supra* n. 308, 47 Intertax 8/9 (2019), at p. 684.
350. As for the Advisory Commission under the Arbitration Convention by *Lodin, supra* n. 241, 42 Intertax 3 (2014), who also reports from his experience as an arbitrator.
351. Calling it an *outstandingly important part C. Nowak,* § 57 Recht auf ein faires Verfahren, 36 (F.S.M. Heselhaus/C. Nowak eds, C.H. Beck 2020).
352. *See also D. Sayers,* Art. 47 47.196 (S. Peers et al. eds, Nomos; C.H.Beck; Hart 2014).
353. As described by *Jarass, supra* n. 328, at m.no. 32-35.
354. CJEU, Judgment of 4 Jun. 2013, *ZZ v. Secretary of State for the Home Department,* C-300/11, ECLI:EU:C:2013:363, m.no. 55.

(2) the right to comment on this material and to be able to debate and be heard on the matters of fact and of law which will determine the outcome of the proceedings;[355]
(3) these comments are to be considered by the tribunal (without it being bound by them).[356]

The dispute resolution mechanism established by the DRD does not fully comply with these guarantees:

(1) Both the DRD and the Standard Rules of Functioning[357] are tacit as to whether any material that is gathered by the tribunal is to be forwarded to affected persons – thus, there is no right of affected persons to be informed before they are notified of the final decision (which may even deviate from the panel's decision) pursuant to Article 15(3) DRD.
(2) As already elaborated above (in section 4.6.2.3.3), there is no unlimited right of affected persons to provide information to the panel or to appear in person (or by a representative), but these actions are, pursuant to Article 13(1) first sentence and (2) first sentence DRD, subject to the discretion of the CAs involved.

Consequently, the affected persons' right to be heard that is guaranteed in Article 47(2) CFR is limited. As Article 52(1) second sentence CFR states:

> Subject to the principle of proportionality, limitations may be made only if they are necessary and genuinely meet objectives of general interest recognised by the Union or the need to protect the rights and freedoms of others.

Thus, it is to be examined whether there is either an objective of general interest or any right of a third party that might be regarded as legitimate to be balanced against the affected persons' right to be heard under the principle of proportionality.

Even though it is not explicitly spelled out as a counterpart to the affected persons' right to be heard, it can be concluded from the directive's Recitals that the main objective in the design of the procedural rules was effectiveness: the term *effective* is mentioned six times in the 11 Recitals,[358] two times combined with the term *efficient*.[359] The pursuit of effectiveness and efficiency is also based on the lessons learned from the application of the Arbitration Convention.[360] The Arbitration Convention, in its Article 10, grants affected enterprises an unlimited right to be heard.[361]

---

355. CJEU, Judgment of 21 Feb. 2013, *Banif Plus Bank Zrt v. Csaba Csipai and Viktória Csipai*, C-472/11, ECLI:EU:C:2013:88, m.no. 30.
356. *H.-J. Blanke*, Art. 47 GRCh m.no. 14 (C. Calliess/M. Ruffert eds, C.H. Beck 2016); *Jarass, supra* n. 328, at m.no. 35.
357. Published as Part I of Annex I in the Commission Implementing Regulation (EU) 2019/652 of 24 Apr. 2019, OJ 2019 L 110, p. 26.
358. Recitals 2, 3, 4, 5, and 10.
359. Recitals 5 and 10.
360. *See* Recital 7.
361. On this, *see* section 4.5.3.3 above.

Hence, it is likely that this unlimited right was traded in the pursuit of effectiveness and efficiency.[362]

The objective of effectiveness, which, for example, is also expressed in the principle of procedural economy, is a recognised objective in procedural law.[363] The prioritisation of the objective of effectiveness over the affected persons' right to be heard needs, pursuant to Article 52(1) CFR, to comply with the principle of proportionality. The principle of proportionality requires that the measure is *appropriate* for attaining the objective pursued and does not go beyond what is *necessary* to achieve it.[364]

A measure is *appropriate* if it genuinely reflects a concern to attain the objective in a consistent and systematic manner.[365] The pursue of effectiveness without doubt is in every fibre of the DRD: it is consistently and systematically pursued – especially in comparison to the Arbitration Convention – by setting deadlines for every step of the procedure and establishing procedural safeguards to guarantee that these deadlines are adhered to. In this context, the limitations of the affected persons' right to be heard can be regarded as *appropriate* in the pursuit of the highest possible degree of effectiveness (if *effectiveness* is understood as the aim to arrive at a solution as rapidly as possible) because it simply might save time not to inform affected persons or to seek their opinion.

Furthermore, the arbitration panel is still able to obtain information from affected persons directly as they are obliged to provide information, evidence or documents upon request (Article 13(1) second sentence DRD) as well as to appear or be represented upon request (Article 13(2) second sentence DRD). Thus, it is to be asked whether it is also *necessary* to limit the right to be heard. A measure is *necessary* if, among several measures which are appropriate for meeting the objective pursued, it is the least onerous for the interest or legal right in question.[366] Striving for the shortest possible procedure does not necessarily need to affect the taxpayers' right to be heard – there are also options for streamlining that affect the interests of other actors, mainly such that affect the interests of CAs: for example, the period for an agreement on a final

362. Also seeing *celerity purposes* as the reason not to grant taxpayers participation rights *A.P. Dourado*, Editorial: *Post-BEPS International Tax Arbitration*, 47 Intertax 8/9, p. 671 (2019) DOI: 10.54648/taxi2019066.

363. For the principle of procedural economy *see*, for example, EGC, Judgment of 24 Mar. 1994, *Société Anonyme à Participation Ouvrière Compagnie Nationale Air France v. Commission of the European Communities*, T-3/93, ECLI:EU:T:1994:36, m.no. 67; CJEU, Judgment of 19 Mar. 2019, *Bashar Ibrahim and Others v. Bundesrepublik Deutschland and Bundesrepublik Deutschland v. Taus Magamadov*, C-297/17, C-318/17, C-319/17 and C-438/17, ECLI: EU:C:2019:219, m.no. 77.

364. CJEU, Judgment of 9 Nov. 2010, *Volker und Markus Schecke GbR (C-92/09) and Hartmut Eifert (C-93/09) v. Land Hessen*, C-92/09 and C-93/09, ECLI:EU:C:2010:662, m.no. 74; AG Trstenjak, Opinion of 14 Apr. 2010, *European Commission v. Federal Republic of Germany*, C-271/08, ECLI:EU:C:2010:183, m.no. 206.

365. CJEU, Judgment of 17 Nov. 2009, *Presidente del Consiglio dei Ministri v. Regione Sardegna*, C-169/08, ECLI:EU:C:2009:709, m.no. 42.

366. CJEU, Judgment of 11 Jul. 1989, *Hermann Schräder HS Kraftfutter GmbH & Co. KG v. Hauptzollamt Gronau*, 265/87, ECLI:EU:C:1989:303, m.no. 21; AG Trstenjak, *European Commission v. Federal Republic of Germany* (C-271/08, *supra* n. 364), m.no. 209.

decision that deviates from the *opinion* of the arbitration body might be shortened to three months instead of six;[367] these three months should be more than sufficient to allow for the affected persons' unlimited right to be heard. This example clearly shows that it is not *necessary* to curtail the affected persons' right to be heard in order to achieve an efficient procedure - it is merely a decision to prioritise effectiveness and the CAs' interests over the rights of affected persons.

For the sake of completeness, I also address the last requirement of the principle of proportionality: the disadvantages caused must not be disproportionate to the aims pursued.[368] Proportionality is not given, however, if affected persons have neither an unlimited right to be heard by the arbitration body nor any right to be informed or to participate in meetings during the arbitration procedure but if their participation is in the discretion of CAs. This limitation of the right to be heard pursuant to Article 47(2) CFR reaches as far as that - in accordance with Article 52(1) first sentence CFR - there is even reason to doubt whether the *essence* of this right is respected.

Thus, it can be concluded that the limitation of the affected persons' right to be heard cannot be justified under the principle of proportionality. Consequently, the right to be heard is violated. The DRD should constitute information rights for affected persons during the arbitration phase as well as the right to participate in hearings and to comment on the positions of other actors.

#### 4.6.4.1.1.2.3. Public Hearing

Article 47(2) CFR further demands a *public hearing*. The DRD only mentions *publicity* in the context of Article 18 regarding the publication of a final decision. There are no explicit rules governing the question of whether and how there shall be hearings and whether the public is allowed to attend them. The first two aspects of this question are to be addressed in every single dispute in the Rules of Functioning pursuant to Article 11 DRD. The Standard Rules of Functioning[369] thereby under paragraph 5 regarding the time frame for the dispute resolution procedure (as indicated in Article 11(2) lit. d DRD) provide for a field to mention 'scheduled dates and place of hearings (if any)'. This justifies the conclusion that the Commission interprets the DRD in the way that there does not necessarily need to be a hearing at all.

Thus, neither the *hearing* itself is mandatory under the DRD nor need such a hearing be *public*. As already examined, not even affected persons have a right to be present if the CAs and the arbitration tribunal meet.

The entitlement to a public hearing is stated in identical wording in Article 47(2) CFR and Article 6(1) ECHR; thus, the reference to the ECHR regarding the meaning in Article 52(3) CFR applies. The European Court of Human Rights (ECtHR) stresses the entitlement to a hearing and only sees a justification for its renunciation under

367. As provided for, for example, under the MLI.
368. CJEU, Judgment of 21 Jul. 2011, *Etimine SA v. Secretary of State for Work and Pensions*, C-15/10, ECLI:EU:C:2011:504, m.no. 124; CJEU, Judgment of 8 Jul. 2010, *Afton Chemical Limited v. Secretary of State for Transport*, C-343/09, ECLI:EU:C:2010:419, m.no. 45.
369. *Supra* n. 357.

*exceptional circumstances*.[370] Such *exceptional circumstances* have been accepted in cases *where proceedings concerned exclusively legal or highly technical questions*.[371] All these cases deal, however, with procedural rules that in general require a hearing or at least a right to apply for a hearing, with the court deciding on this application. There is no such right under the DRD – it is much more for the participating CAs to decide whether there will be any hearings while agreeing on the Rules of Functioning pursuant to Article 11(2) DRD. There is no option for affected persons to demand an amendment to the Rules of Functioning; they can only, pursuant to Article 11(4) DRD, demand them to be set up by a national court if neither the CAs nor the arbitration panel have managed to agree on Rules of Functioning. Otherwise, their only right is to receive the Rules pursuant to Article 11(1) lit. a DRD.

Thus, comparable to the analysis for the right to be heard, it needs to be stated that Article 47(2) CFR is also infringed in this regard: the complete disregard of a hearing is a violation of Article 47(2) CFR and gives rise to serious doubts as to whether the essence of the right to a hearing is being respected. This does not mean that there needs to be hearing in every single case – there may be good reasons not to have a hearing in a specific case. However, there needs to be a rule that allows, on the one hand, for an application of affected persons to demand a hearing and, on the other hand, for a right of the arbitration tribunal to decide whether to have a hearing or not.

The same thought applies to the question of whether such a hearing also needs to be public. Article 6(1) second sentence ECHR details exceptions from the rule of a *public* hearing:

> Judgment shall be pronounced publicly but the press and public may be excluded from all or part of the trial in the interests of morals, public order or national security in a democratic society, where the interests of juveniles or the protection of the private life of the parties so require, or to the extent strictly necessary in the opinion of the court in special circumstances where publicity would prejudice the interests of justice.

Even though Article 52(3) CFR states that it does not prevent Union law from providing more extensive protection, it can be assumed that the CJEU would consider the enlisted reasons for an exclusion of the public legitimate also under Article 47(2) CFR. The problem with the DRD's procedural rules also in this regard is the relationship between rule and exception: there might be cases that require the public to be excluded in the interest of national security or the affected persons' interest in secrecy.

370. ECtHR, Judgment of 26 Jan. 2006, *Brugger v. Austria*, 76293/01, ECLI:CE:ECHR:2006:0126JUD007629301, m.no. 21.

371. ECtHR, *Brugger v. Austria* (76293/01, *supra* n. 370), m.no. 21 with reference to ECtHR, Judgment of 24 Jun. 1993, *Schuler-Zraggen v. Switzerland*, 14518/89, ECLI:CE:ECHR:1993:0624JUD001451889, m.no. 58 (in this case, however, a hearing would have had to be set up on application of the applicant – thus, the court interpreted her non-application as an unequivocal waiver; only additionally, the court referred to the *highly technical* and *private* nature of the case); ECtHR, Decision of 25 Apr. 2002, *Varela Assalino v. Portugal*, 64336/01, ECLI:CE:ECHR:2002:0425DEC006433601 (no hearing necessary if facts not in dispute and questions of law *not unduly complicated*) and ECtHR, Decision of 5 Sep. 2002, *Speil v. Austria*, 42057/98, ECLI:CE:ECHR:2002:0905DEC004205798, m.no. 2 (same argument).

However, it is hardly conceivable that such cases are the norm. Consequently, the procedural rules would need to provide for public hearings as a rule and for the public to be excluded only under special circumstances. Above all, this question should be decided by the arbitration tribunal.

Finally, I would like to examine the requirement cited in Article 6(1) second sentence ECHR that judgments in any case need to be pronounced publicly. Under the DRD, there is no provision addressing the pronunciation of a *judgment* since the DRD refers to the panel's decision as an *opinion* but avoids calling the decision a *judgment*. There is, as already examined, a chance that affected persons might never get hold of this *opinion* if the CAs, pursuant to Article 15(1) and (2) first sentence DRD, manage to agree on a different solution within six months. Only if they do not agree on a different solution, does the *opinion* become, pursuant to Article 15(2) second sentence DRD, binding and has to be implemented by the CAs as a final decision. A publication is also only provided for regarding this final decision (even though the arbitration panels under the same heading *Publicity* in Article 18(1) DRD are required to issue their opinions in writing). In its entirety, a final decision is published according to Article 18(2) DRD only if the CAs agree and the affected persons consent. Otherwise, according to Article 18(3) DRD, only an abstract is published.

Even though this compulsory publication of an abstract constitutes a significant progress compared to other dispute resolution mechanisms, the system for publication still falls behind the standard the CFR sets: the panel's decision is neither pronounced publicly nor is it published in all cases.

#### 4.6.4.1.1.2.4. Full Control by a Judicial Body

In *Berlioz*,[372] the CJEU further defined the entitlement to a hearing by an independent and impartial tribunal in Article 47(2) CFR in this way:

> The decision of an administrative authority that does not itself satisfy the conditions of independence and impartiality must be subject to subsequent control by a judicial body, that must, in particular, have jurisdiction to consider all the relevant issues.[373]

Consequently, the procedure laid out in Article 4(2) DRD, due to which the dispute resolution procedure ends in the MAP stage if both CAs agree on a solution, does not comply with this standard because the MAP decision cannot be further challenged by the affected persons. They can only decide whether to accept it or not. There is no judicial body to review the decision with the jurisdiction to consider *all the relevant issues*: even if the MAP decision could be challenged in front of national courts, their jurisdiction would be limited to the reaction of one state only and would therefore not take *all relevant issues* into consideration.

Thus, to adhere to the standard expressed in *Berlioz*, affected persons should also be able to challenge MAP agreements if they do not agree with them. Under the current

372. CJEU, Judgment (Grand Chamber) of 16 May 2017, *Berlioz Investment Fund SA v. Directeur de l'administration des contributions directes*, C-682/15, ECLI:EU:C:2017:373, m.no. 55.
373. *Blanke*, *supra* n. 356, at m.no. 14; *Jarass*, *supra* n. 328, at m.no. 35.

dispute resolution procedure of the DRD, however, it might constitute a farce if affected persons are allowed to challenge MAP decisions, but CAs can still agree on another decision that deviates from the arbitration panel's *opinion*: in this scenario, they could easily adopt the contested agreement once again. Consequently, in such cases, the arbitration tribunal's decision should be binding immediately.

##### *4.6.4.1.2 Article 41 CFR*

Even though the right to good administration in Article 41 CFR is granted in relation between persons and *institutions, bodies, offices and agencies of the Union*, *Kokott* considers it to be possible that the element of a right to be heard *before any individual measure which would affect* them *adversely* (Article 41(2) lit. b CFR) might be held by the CJEU to be a general principle of EU law, and could thus also be invoked by affected persons beyond the limitations of Article 41(1) CFR.[374] Indeed, this seems likely, and I support such an approach, especially in consideration of the CJEU's case law stating that the right to be heard is a general principle of EU law that requires *addressees of decisions which significantly affect their interests* to be *placed in a position in which they can effectively make known their views as regards the information on which the authorities intend to base their decision*.[375]

Consequently, the affected persons' participation should already be possible in the MAP stage, not just in arbitration.

#### *4.6.4.2 Article 6 ECHR*

Other than Article 47(2) CFR, Article 6(1) first sentence ECHR limits the entitlement to a fair and public hearing within a reasonable time by an independent and impartial tribunal established by law to the determination of persons' civil rights and obligations and of criminal charges against them.

In its established case law, the ECtHR held tax disputes to be outside this scope.[376] Exceptions may only apply if there is a significant impact on civil

374. *Kokott*, *supra* n. 343, 60 ET 1 (2020), at p. 6. She thereby instances such an approach of the CJEU towards the right to have access to one's files as stated in Art. 41(2) lit. b CFR in CJEU, Judgment of 9 Nov. 2017, *Teodor & Anduța Ispas v. Direcția Generala a Finanțelor Publice Cluj*, C-298/16, ECLI:EU:C:2017:843.
375. CJEU, *WebMindLicenses Kft. v. Nemzeti Adó- és Vámhivatal Kiemelt Adó- és Vám Főigazgatóság* (C-419/14, *supra* n. 325), m.no. 84. A comparable statement can already be found in CJEU, Judgment of 23 Oct. 1974, *Transocean Marine Paint Association v. Commission of the European Communities*, 17/74, ECLI:EU:C:1974:106, m.no. 15.
376. ECtHR, Judgment of 12 Jul. 2001, *Ferrazzini v. Italy*, 44759/98, ECLI:CE:ECHR:2001:0712JUD004475998, m.no. 24-31; ECtHR, Decision of 13 Jan. 2005, *Emesa Sugar N.V. v. the Netherlands*, 62023/00, ECLI:CE:ECHR:2005:0113DEC006202300, section D.; ECtHR, Judgment of 24 Feb. 2017, *Polimerkonteyner, TOV v. Ukraine*, 23620/05, ECLI:CE:ECHR:2016:1124JUD002362005, m.no. 25.

obligations[377] or if a penalty is applied in addition to the tax assessment.[378] *Voje* calls this rigorous approach 'arguably erroneous'[379] and argues convincingly with reference to a dissenting opinion in *Ferrazzini*[380] that an exclusion of administrative decisions with the intention of avoiding an infringement of administrative discretion is not justified in the case of tax disputes because the objective of equal taxation does not allow for broad discretion.[381]

It is, however, not to be expected that international tax disputes are - beyond singular exceptions - about to qualify as eligible scenarios for the application of Article 6 ECHR from the ECtHR's perspective. If they were, however, the consequences mentioned above under Article 47(2) CFR regarding the right to be heard and the entitlement to a public hearing could be based on Article 6(1) ECHR without any restrictions regarding a connection of the case to EU law.

#### 4.6.4.3 *Conclusion and Consequences*

I conclude that the dispute resolution mechanism of the DRD is not fully in line with the CFR. The deficiencies are:

(1) A violation of the affected persons' right to be heard: pursuant to Article 47(2) CFR, they should be informed and - if they so demand - heard by the arbitration panel. Additionally, there are strong arguments for the right to be heard to be a general principle of EU law. Consequently, it should already be observed in the MAP stage.
(2) A disproportionate discretion of CAs to decide whether hearings take place: acknowledging the fact that hearings might not in every single case be necessary and, e.g., digital substitutes for in-person meetings can be sufficient, it stands out negatively that it is not for the arbitration tribunal to decide upon the organisation of its procedure.
(3) A disproportionate exclusion of the public: the existing rules leave little to no room to allow for the public's participation in hearings and access to the text of the arbitration tribunal's opinions.
(4) The lack of an option to challenge MAP decisions.

377. *See*, for example, ECtHR, Judgment of 23 Oct. 1997, *National & Provincial Building Society et al. v. the United Kingdom*, 21319/93, 21449/93 and 21675/93, ECLI:CE:ECHR:1997:1023JUD002131993, m.no. 94-99.
378. It is, however, to be pointed out that the ECtHR tries to differentiate between the proceedings regarding the penalty and those regarding the 'pure tax assessment' as far as possible - *see* ECtHR, Judgment of 23 Nov. 2006, *Jussila v. Finland*, 73053/01, ECLI:CE:ECHR:2006:1123JUD007305301, m.no. 45.
379. *Voje, supra* n. 322, 48 Intertax 2 (2020), at p. 170.
380. ECtHR, *Ferrazzini v. Italy* (44759/98, *supra* n. 376), Dissenting Opinion of Judge Lorenzen - joined by Judges Rozakis, Bonello, Strážnická, Bîrsan and Fischbach.
381. *Voje, supra* n. 322, 48 Intertax 2 (2020), at p. 168.

These deficiencies can, however, due to Article 47 CFR's limited scope of applicability, only be raised by affected persons in cases that have a connection to EU law. For these cases, it is necessary to examine whether the deficiencies lead to a (partial) invalidity of the DRD's provisions or whether these provisions can be applied and interpreted in light of the CFR in a way that there is no infringement of rights. This is the distinction the CJEU would be confronted with if it had to decide on the compatibility of the DRD with the CFR. As far as possible, the directive would therefore have to be interpreted *in such a way as not to affect its validity.*[382] For reasons of legal policy, I would argue in favour of an extension of these findings to all cases under the DRD to realise its goals expressed in Recital 9.

##### *4.6.4.3.1 Participation and Information of Affected Persons*

###### 4.6.4.3.1.1 In the MAP

For the MAP, there are no detailed procedural rules in general and nearly no rules for the affected persons' involvement in particular. After a complaint has been accepted, the CAs *shall*, pursuant to Article 4(1) DRD, *endeavour to resolve the question in dispute by mutual agreement within two years*. Article 4(2) DRD states that they shall, once they have reached an agreement, notify the affected person of this agreement without delay. Thus, for affected persons, the MAP can well be a black box[383] since there are no provisions guaranteeing their participation. Nevertheless, there are no provisions barring them from getting involved in the proceedings.

The open wording allows – if interpreted in light of fundamental rights, which include the right to be heard as a general principle – for the conclusion that affected persons should be informed about the progress of the MAP procedure and be involved if they demand so. If interpreted in this way, Article 4(1) DRD does not infringe on fundamental rights and remains valid.

###### 4.6.4.3.1.2 In the Arbitration Procedure

For the arbitration procedure, the involvement of affected persons is detailed in Article 13 DRD. As already pointed out, the CA's discretion to decide whether affected persons are given the opportunity to appear in front of the arbitration body pursuant to

382. CJEU, Judgment of 15 Feb. 2016, *J. N. v. Staatssecretaris van Veiligheid en Justitie*, C-601/15 PPU, ECLI:EU:C:2016:84, m.no. 48. Further on the interpretation in light of the CFR, *see* CJEU, Judgment of 13 May 2014, *Google Spain SL and Google Inc. v. Agencia Española de Protección de Datos (AEPD) and Mario Costeja González*, C-131/12, ECLI:EU:C:2014:317, m.no. 68; CJEU, Judgment of 3 Jul. 2014, *Kamino International Logistics BV and Datema Hellmann Worldwide Logistics BV v. Staatssecretaris van Financiën*, C-129/13 and C-130/13, ECLI: EU:C:2014:2041, m.no. 69; CJEU, Judgment of 11 Sep. 2014, *A v. B and Others*, C-112/13, ECLI:EU:C:2014:2195, m.no. 51.

383. As criticised for the MAP in general by *P.A. Brown*, Chapter 4: Enhancing the Mutual Agreement Procedure by Adopting Appropriate Arbitration Provisions, p. 89 (M. Lang et al. eds, IBFD 2015); *Strotkemper, supra* n. 18, at pp. 134 ff.

Article 13(2) DRD is in conflict with the guarantee of the right to be heard in Article 47(2) CFR. An interpretation in the light of the Charter must lead to the result that the CA's discretion is reduced to zero. Thus, affected persons are allowed to appear in front of the arbitration panel if they so demand.

Concerning the information of affected persons about the documents that are handed in by other actors, the directive is tacit. It allows, however, for details regarding the *rules governing the participation of the affected persons* to be set out in the Rules of Functioning (cf. Article 11(2) lit. f DRD). Consequently, an interpretation of this provision in the light of the Charter leads to the conclusion that it is mandatory to state in these Rules of Functioning that all material gathered by the arbitration panel is to be forwarded to the affected persons in order to allow for them to obtain a qualified position.[384]

#### *4.6.4.3.2 Planning of Hearings*

The same idea applies to the planning of hearings: details in this regard are set out in the Rules of Functioning as well. An important point of criticism thereby is that it is for the CAs to decide if there will be hearings and – if so – how many. To address this criticism, the Rules of Functioning should set at least one hearing as standard and leave it to an agreement in which both the affected persons and the arbitration body are involved to decide if they want to renounce the hearing or schedule further hearings.

#### *4.6.4.3.3 Inclusion of the Public*

Regarding the inclusion of the public, there is little leeway to straighten out the shortcomings of the directive in the Rules of Functioning. One could argue that it would be better if the public were admitted to participate in the procedure, but this is not the main point of criticism since the current state of the law might be compatible with Article 47(2) CFR if there are sufficient reasons to exclude the public. Instead, criticism focuses on the fact that there is no rule at all that addresses this issue, which makes an amendment of the directive seem necessary. Arguably, a differentiated rule that generally allows for the public to participate with the option for the arbitration panel to decide about an exclusion on the application of either a CA or the affected persons would be best.

#### *4.6.4.3.4 Information of the Public*

To comply with Article 47(2) CFR, judgments (i.e., the *opinions* of the arbitration body) should be published in full. It does not seem possible to interpret Article 18 DRD, which focuses on the *final decision* by the CAs, in a way that allows for *opinions* to be

384. *Perrou, supra* n. 330, 47 Intertax 8/9 (2019), at p. 724 also alludes to the option to enhance the affected persons' position via the Rules of Functioning.

published in their entirety in every case. Consequently, an amendment of the directive is necessary in this regard as well.

#### 4.6.4.3.5 *Challenging MAP Decisions*

As to what can be brought in front of an arbitration panel, the directive is clear: pursuant to Article 6(1) lit. b DRD, a question in dispute can only be made the subject of arbitration proceedings if the CAs have *failed to reach an agreement*. This provision does not leave much interpretive scope: if there is an agreement that only the affected persons do not agree with, the path towards arbitration is blocked.

If one applies the interpretation of Article 47(2) CFR in *Berlioz*, there would need to be a further lit. c in Article 6(1) DRD allowing one to challenge MAP decisions. This provision cannot be drafted by the CJEU in the course of an interpretation in the light of the CFR. As a consequence, it seems necessary to amend the directive in this regard.

### 4.6.5 Design Options under Article 10(1) DRD

Not least, frictions with European Fundamental Rights raise the question of whether an ADRC – which could also be established in the form of a *Standing Committee* – pursuant to Article 11(1) DRD could be a solution to address the shortcomings in the standard procedure.

*Piotrowski*, together with many other scholars, published a well thought out proposal for a framework that seeks to fulfil the objectives of ensuring a speedy, inexpensive and comprehensive resolution of the dispute as well as legal certainty, while at the same time guaranteeing the rule of law and taxpayer protection, ensuring transparency and acceptability and contributing to the future development of international tax law.[385] They propose the establishment of a Standing Committee with universal competence for all disputes between the participating Member States that is permanently located in the same place, supported by a secretariat and administrative staff and composed only of independent persons with expertise in international tax law who have staggered terms and do not necessarily need to be judges.[386] Irrespective of the permanent nature, they suggest including the rule on costs in Article 12 DRD and – at least initially – not granting the committee members a fixed remuneration.[387] Regarding the procedural rules, they advocate a strengthening of taxpayer rights, which mostly means that their right to provide evidence and to be heard should not be subject to the CAs' discretion, and that taxpayers should have a right to be present during the proceedings.[388] With respect to the method of arbitration, they recommend keeping the application of independent opinion arbitration because this method allows

385. *Piotrowski et al., supra* n. 308, 47 Intertax 8/9 (2019), at pp. 682 ff. Dismissing the proposal as a *dream*, however, *H. Mooij*, Chapter 14: MAP Arbitration in Tax Treaty Disputes, p. 285 (P. Pistone/J.J. de Goede eds, IBFD 2021).
386. *Piotrowski et al., supra* n. 308, 47 Intertax 8/9 (2019), at pp. 687 f.
387. *Piotrowski et al., supra* n. 308, 47 Intertax 8/9 (2019), at p. 689.
388. *Piotrowski et al., supra* n. 308, 47 Intertax 8/9 (2019), at p. 690.

for the Committee to decide each case on its merits and to contribute to the development of international tax law.[389] Apart from this, they suggest taking the procedural rules *by established players such as the Permanent Court of Arbitration or of International Chambers of Commerce* as a starting point while respecting the time frame and also the taxpayers' right to enforce it from the standard procedure.[390] To account for different types of disputes, they propose a chamber system with separate lists of independent persons who have special expertise in the relevant area and predetermining the panel composition by the secretariat, whereby arbitrators should not come from one of the involved Member States.[391] They suggest that hearings be public in general, with the option for both taxpayers and CAs to request hearings be held in private.[392] The Standing Committee's opinions should – which is not provided for under the standard procedure – be communicated to taxpayers and their reasoning should be published.[393]

I wholeheartedly agree with this proposal and its objectives and am convinced that its implementation would be a huge advance for the resolution of international tax disputes and could serve as a role model for the further development of the established dispute resolution mechanisms. It would especially address many of the existing deficiencies analysed in section 4.6.4.

## 4.7 DISPUTE RESOLUTION UNDER BILATERAL INVESTMENT TREATIES

Bilateral Investment Treaties (BITs) usually provide for a choice between different dispute resolution mechanisms for investor-state disputes,[394] mostly by either an ad hoc tribunal that is to be established under the arbitration rules of the United Nations Commission in International Trade Law (UNCITRAL)[395] or by the International Center for Settlement of Investment Disputes (ICSID) under the Convention on the Settlement of Investment Disputes between States and Nationals of Other States (ICSID Convention)[396].[397]

389. *Piotrowski et al., supra* n. 308, 47 Intertax 8/9 (2019), at p. 691.
390. *Piotrowski et al., supra* n. 308, 47 Intertax 8/9 (2019), at pp. 689 f.
391. *Piotrowski et al., supra* n. 308, 47 Intertax 8/9 (2019), at p. 690.
392. *Piotrowski et al., supra* n. 308, 47 Intertax 8/9 (2019), at p. 690.
393. *Piotrowski et al., supra* n. 308, 47 Intertax 8/9 (2019), at p. 692.
394. Alluding to the protection via an arbitration mechanism as a main objective of BITs ICSID, Decision on Objections to Jurisdiction of 24 May 1999, *Československa obchodní banka, a.s. v. Slovak Republic*, ARB/97/4, m.no. 57.
395. On the use of UNCITRAL rules *N. Horn*, Current Use of the UNCITRAL Arbitration Rules in the Context of Investment Arbitration, 24 Arbitr Int 4 (2008) DOI: 10.1093/arbitration/24.4.587.
396. Concluded in Washington on 18 Mar. 1965. The Convention and its signatories can be accessed at https://treaties.un.org/Pages/showDetails.aspx?objid=080000028012a925 (https://taxation-customs.ec.europa.eu/system/files/2019-10/2019-tax-dispute-resolution-fiscalis-project-group-report.pdf). On ICSID dispute settlement *see also Govind/Turcan, supra* n. 55, 19 DFI 5 (2017), in section 3.2.1.
397. For an overview, *see also Chaisse, supra* n. 7, 10 Contemporary Asia Arbitration Journal 1 (2017), at pp. 15 ff.

In contrast to the tax dispute resolution mechanisms introduced above, investors enjoy a wide array of procedural rights in investor-state disputes: they have the right to initiate arbitration against the common will of the states, can participate in the nomination of the arbitral tribunal as well as in the establishment of the terms of reference, are allowed to be present at the hearing and have a right to be heard that includes knowledge of the procedural files and the right to present their position in front of the panel.[398]

Tax issues can be brought forward under BITs as long as there is no specific tax carve-out clause[399] and if tax treaties are not regarded as *leges speciales*.[400] The material guarantees that might be considered towards tax measures include the guarantee of fair and equitable treatment, most-favoured nation and national treatment clauses, the guarantees in case of an unlawful expropriation and provisions granting the free transfer of capital.[401]

Even though the procedural rights in BIT arbitration are more advantageous for taxpayers, the arbitration mechanism in general does not seem fit to cope with international tax disputes because of systematic deficiencies: as a general principle, BITs are treaties between investors and host states. Consequently, the disputes do not involve the taxpayers' state of nationality or residence. Thus, BIT arbitration for tax disputes shows the same deficiency as domestic court procedures: the arbitral award only binds one out of two (or more) states and consequently cannot guarantee a harmonised solution granting the avoidance of both double taxation and double non-taxation.[402]

Consequently, BIT arbitration may well serve as a point of reference for the question of how to further develop tax treaty arbitration mechanisms, but does not as such qualify as a better mechanism to resolve tax treaty disputes.[403]

398. *P. Pistone*, Chapter 1: General Report, section 1.8.2. (M. Lang et al. eds, 2017); *Chaisse, supra* n. 7, 10 Contemporary Asia Arbitration Journal 1 (2017), at p. 25.
399. *Pistone, supra* n. 398, in section 1.3.1.; *Govind/Turcan, supra* n. 55, 19 DFI 5 (2017), in section 3.1.1. As an example of a carve-out-clause *see* Art. 7(3) of the German Model BIT, accessible at https://investmentpolicy.unctad.org/international-investment-agreements/treaty-files/2865/download (https://taxation-customs.ec.europa.eu/system/files/2019-10/2019-tax-dispute-resolution-fiscalis-project-group-report.pdf). However, even under an existing carve-out-clause tax issues might be dealt with under BITs and in investor-state-arbitration as detailed by *A.E. Gildemeister*, Chapter 12: Germany, section 12.2 (M. Lang et al. eds, 2017).
400. On this *K. Perrou*, Tax Law Disputes Before Investment Arbitration Panels: Practical Experience, ET 10, p. 452 (2016) DOI: 10.59403/g9a5mq; *Pistone, supra* n. 398, at pp. 13 ff.
401. For country-specific details, *see* the national reports in M. Lang et al. eds, The Impact of Bilateral Investment Treaties on Taxation (2017). A list of cases in which arbitral tribunals have dealt with direct taxation matters is provided by *Perrou, supra* n. 400, ET 10 (2016), at p. 452, n. 16. *See also P. Backhausen/P. Mazumdar*, International Tax Arbitration: A New Avenue for Small State International Financial Centres?, pp. 263 ff. (P. Butler et al. eds, Springer 2018); *L. de Heer/P. Kraan*, Legal Protection in International Tax Disputes – How Investment Protection Agreements Address Arbitration, 52 ET 1, pp. 6 ff. (2012).
402. Especially the last point is also stressed by *R. Ismer/S. Piotrowski*, A BIT Too Much: Or How Best to Resolve Tax Treaty Disputes?, 44 Intertax 5, p. 358 (2016) DOI: 10.54648/taxi2016028; *Strotkemper, supra* n. 18, at 632, 634.
403. In the same direction calling it '*neither the most practical nor the most convenient approach for all stakeholders*' *Gildemeister, supra* n. 399, at p. 316.

## 4.8 THE TRIBUTE INITIATIVE

One initiative worth mentioning is called Tribute. Tribute is not a separate dispute resolution mechanism but a private initiative[404] that seeks to help administrate disputes. The main feature is the offer of a *continuously expanding list of top-level international tax arbitrators, covering a range of areas of specialisation, background, nationality, and gender.*[405] Regarding the admission to the list, the initiative states:

> Selection of experts for the Tribute list is ordinarily by personal invitation from Tribute, following suggestions from present experts or reliable, well-informed outside contacts. Admission to the list is subject to a peer scrutiny process, as ultimate warrant for experts' ability, independence and neutrality.[406]

Consequently, it is neither transparent who is selected to appear on the list nor what the exact criteria for being mentioned on the list are.

Further, Tribute offers assistance regarding *the drafting of clauses, agreements, laws, regulations or procedures, the entire legal or contractual framework necessary to make any mechanisms of international tax dispute resolution operative in practice.*[407] In singular disputes, they offer to either assist with the administration of a dispute (and, for example, the organisation of [video] hearings) themselves or to arrange cooperation with (private) arbitration institutes or institutions like the Permanent Court of Arbitration.[408]

404. It is registered as a *stichting* in the Netherlands, *see* https://www.tribute-arbitration.org/wp-content/uploads/2019/09/Deed-of-incorporation-of-the-TRIBUTE-Foundation-24-September-2015.pdf (accessed 15 Jan. 2024).
405. As advertised by *Mooij, supra* n. 208, 47 Intertax 8/9 (2019), at p. 741, who is a co-founder and the chairperson of the TRIBUTE initiative. The list can be accessed at https://www.tribute-arbitration.org/international-tax-experts/tribute-list-of-experts/ (accessed 15 Jan. 2024). It only comprises the names of the international tax experts without CVs or any further information.
406. *See* https://www.tribute-arbitration.org/international-tax-experts/ (accessed 15 Jan. 2024).
407. *See* https://www.tribute-arbitration.org/governments/, section *Presentations and tailored advice* (last access 12 Feb. 2021).
408. *See* https://www.tribute-arbitration.org/governments/, section *Practical facilities* (accessed 15 Jan. 2024); *Mooij, supra* n. 208, 47 Intertax 8/9 (2019), at pp. 742 f. Rather vague also *Mooij, supra* n. 385, at pp. 285 f.

## 4.9 CONCLUSIONS FROM COMPARING THE MECHANISMS

*Table 4.1 Comparison of Dispute Resolution Mechanisms*

| | *OECD-MC* | *UN-MC* | *MLI* | *US-MC* | *SE-GER* | *AT-GER* | *AC* | *DRD* |
|---|---|---|---|---|---|---|---|---|
| MAP | | | | | | | | |
| Initiation by | TP | TP | TP | TP | TP | TP | TP | TP |
| Initiation within | 3 years | 3 years | 3 years | – | – | 3 years | 3 years | 3 years |
| Time frame for MAP | 2 years | 3 years | 2-3 years | 2 years | – | 3 years | 3 years | 2 years |
| Extension possible | | | | by agreement of CAs | | | with TP's consent | 1 year if requested by one CA |
| Arbitration | | | | | | | | |
| Initiation | By TP | By CAs | By TP | By TP | By TP | By TP | Automatically | By TP |
| Initiation within | | | | | | | | 50 days |
| Standard Method | Final-Offer | Final-Offer | Final-Offer | Final-Offer | Ind.-Op. | Ind.-Op. | Ind.-Op. | Ind.-Op. |
| TP Participation | Initiation only | None | Initiation only | Initiation only | Right to be Heard in Optional Procedure | Only as Witness | Full Right to be Heard | Discretionary Right to be Heard |
| Option of CAs to deviate from Decision | No | Yes, within 6 months | Yes, within 3 months | No | | | Yes, within 6 months | Yes, within 6 months |

The most established international dispute resolution mechanism is clearly the MAP, as provided for under the OECD/UN-MC. Despite its lack of procedural rules and the weak position of taxpayers, the MAP still serves as a successful tool for the resolution of a fair number of cases.

Arbitration mechanisms, however, are either dysfunctional – as the one under the Arbitration Convention – or fairly young. Given the lack of known cases, an assessment of their actual performance is not (yet) possible. A commonality of all arbitration mechanisms is that they are understood as a mere extension of the MAP rather than as self-standing legal remedies.[409] The arbitration mechanisms under the OECD-MC and UN-MC lack exact procedural rules and thus in practice often remain 'incomplete' if CAs do not agree on rules. The MLI, by contrast, has the benefit of more detailed procedural rules in the convention itself. These rules, however, are designed in a way that does not establish a high degree of certainty for affected persons but instead leaves as much leeway as possible for the states and their CAs. This becomes apparent, for example, with regard to the setting of deadlines: for the MAP, the MLI does not only allow for a standard extension from two to three years but also for an arbitrary extension by the CAs on a case-by-case basis. For the arbitration procedure, the MLI does not define clear deadlines but still leaves these for a further agreement in the case of final-offer arbitration – the independent opinion procedure provision does not even mention deadlines.

A prominent trend that can be analysed as underlying the latest reforms is the effort to make these mechanisms more efficient – meaning that they result in an agreement more quickly and reliably in all cases. It is vital that this aim is achieved in the near future, considering the steady increase in the number of cases, which was further fuelled by the implementation of BEPS measures. With the 2017 OECD-MC update and the MLI, a trend can be seen towards both accelerating the procedure and making it more flexible. In order to accelerate proceedings, final-offer arbitration is preferred over independent opinion arbitration as a standard method (*see also* Table 4.1). An expression of higher flexibility is the CA's option to deviate from an arbitration decision under both the MLI and the DRD.[410] Allowing for this actually runs counter to the desire for a faster procedure but seems to be a concession to the states' concern for their sovereignty.

Another approach to grant a higher degree of efficiency is taken by the European Union: under the DRD, the main instrument to ensure the progress of the procedure is a further legalisation – the establishment of clear deadlines and of effective means for taxpayers to enforce these deadlines. This is a very positive development.

However, in the pursuit of more efficiency, taxpayers' participation rights are at risk of being eroded: in final-offer arbitration, taxpayers are not even bystanders

409. *See also M. Lombardo/C. Garbarino,* Arbitration of Unresolved Issues in Mutual Agreement Cases: The New Paragraph 5, Art. 25 OECD Model Convention, a Multi-Tiered Dispute Resolution Clause p. 26, Bocconi Legal Studies Research Paper; *Strotkemper, supra* n. 18, at pp. 429 f.

410. The further spread of this option – that already existed under the AC, for example – (unfortunately) does not confirm the assumption of *Strotkemper, supra* n. 18, at pp. 418 f.

anymore. Under the DRD, taxpayers have gained a stronger position in being able to move the proceedings forward by enforcing deadlines and procedural steps. Their right to be heard has been limited, however, in that it depends on the CA's consent.

Nevertheless, the DRD represents an important step both by making it mandatory to publish an abstract of final decisions and by allowing for the establishment of permanent dispute resolution bodies. This – from my perspective – points to where the future could lead: to a further institutionalisation of dispute resolution, which is able to resolve disputes efficiently in a more judicial manner[411] and actively contributes to developing international tax law further. Also, apart from the DRD, there seems to be a perceived need for help in administration and institutionalisation that private actors such as the Tribute initiative are offering to meet. I doubt whether private actors should fill this gap and hope for an independent, transparent and rule-based institutionalisation that is borne by the states.

This is even more important considering the disputes that may occur in the future from the implementation of the OECD's Two-Pillar Solution. These disputes will go beyond the interpretation of bilateral tax treaties and call for a powerful dispute resolution mechanism that is capable of resolving multilateral disputes[412] between several states and taxpayers based on a variety of legal grounds. The OECD's proposals so far seem innovative in their institutional design but rather conservative in the sketched procedural rules in that taxpayer participation is very limited and final-offer methods seem to be preferred.[413]

411. Also calling for this *Eilers/Drüen, supra* n. 99, at 20a; *R. Ismer/S. Piotrowski,* Internationale Streitbeilegung in Steuersachen und innerstaatliches Verfassungsrecht: Auf zu gerichtsförmigen Verfahren!, 28 IStR 21, p. 845 (2019).
412. Criticising existing mechanisms in this regard *B.A. Juanpere,* The Resolution of Tax Disputes and International Tax Arbitration, 5 EJBMR 1, p. 5 (2020) DOI: 10.24018/ejbmr.2020.5.1.174.
413. For the mechanism regarding Amount A, *see* already section 2.3.6. and for ideas regarding disputes beyond Amount A OECD/G20 Base Erosion and Profit Shifting Project, *supra* n. 63, at para. 802.

# CHAPTER 5
# Suggestions for Improvement

The variety of mechanisms I examined in the last section has always been paralleled by a multitude of ideas by scholars on how to design and improve mechanisms for the resolution of international tax disputes. Among these are the early discussion of an international fiscal jurisdiction in the IFA in 1951,[414] as well as the study of *Lindencrona* and *Mattsson*[415] that dates back to 1980 and not only contains the proposal to introduce arbitration but also contemplates the establishment of an international tax court, the call of *Züger*[416] as well as of *Park* and *Tillinghast*[417] to include arbitration clauses, *Altman's* proposal for an International Tax Tribunal,[418] *Perrou's* ideas on how to enhance the participation of taxpayers in the dispute resolution mechanisms,[419] the aforementioned proposal of *Piotrowski et al.* on how to improve the dispute resolution mechanism under the DRD using the option of an ADRC[420] and *Strotkemper's* very thorough study,[421] which concludes with the proposal of both an amendment of Article 25 OECD-MC and a Multilateral Convention on the Resolution of Double Taxation Disputes under which transfer pricing issues are dealt with in an elaborated final-offer-arbitration mechanism,[422] while interpretative issues are mainly addressed in national court procedures during which a preliminary ruling procedure in front of an

414. *See W.R. Emmen Riedel*, Judicial Interpretations of Conventions on Double Taxation and the Necessity or Advisability of Establishing International Fiscal Jurisdiction: *General Report*, pp. 38 ff. (International Fiscal Association ed., Imprimerie Berichthaus 1951).
415. *G. Lindencrona/N. Mattsson*, Arbitration in Taxation (Norstedt 1982).
416. *Züger, supra* n. 214.
417. *Park/Tillinghast, supra* n. 24.
418. *Altman, supra* n. 72.
419. *Perrou, supra* n. 342.
420. *Piotrowski et al., supra* n. 308, 47 Intertax 8/9 (2019).
421. *Strotkemper, supra* n. 18.
422. *See* Art. 46 of her Draft Convention: The final-offer method (in a dual-offer variation) is used to determine actual transfer prices, while questions such as to the application of the correct method are dealt with beforehand under an independent-opinion mechanism.

International Tax Commission can be made use of,[423] an idea that has already been raised and outlined by *Mössner*[424].

In this section, I develop my own proposal for a mechanism that attempts to fit all international tax disputes. The mechanism I suggest promotes an efficient procedure that respects the rights and interests of taxpayers as well as the concerns of the public, is capable of solving multilateral disputes and supports the development of a body of international tax law.[425] I will present a specific procedural framework in the final section (Chapter 6). This should not be seen as the best or only true set of rules of procedure but rather as an inspiration in which direction the existing mechanisms could be further developed. This applies in particular to the deadlines I propose, which are mainly intended to provide a point of reference for the relationship of the procedural steps.

In developing the proposal, I first contemplate general questions of design (section 5.1). Then, I focus on particular questions of the procedural steps (sections 5.2 and 5.3). Finally, I consider the technical implementation of my suggestions (section 5.4).

## 5.1 GENERAL QUESTIONS OF DESIGN

### 5.1.1 From the Principle of Diplomatic Protection to a Mechanism Sui Generis

The current system of dispute resolution mechanisms embodied by the OECD and UN Models is rooted in the idea of diplomatic protection.[426] This concept is especially used as a justification for the limited standing of taxpayers in the design of the procedure[427] and thus deserves a closer look.

Pursuant to Article 1 of the draft Articles on Diplomatic Protection of the International Law Commission (ILC):

> diplomatic protection consists of the invocation by a State, through diplomatic action or other means of peaceful settlement, of the responsibility of another State for an injury caused by an internationally wrongful act of that State to a natural or

423. *See* Articles 18 to 37 of her Draft Convention.

424. *Mössner, supra* n. 79, 29 RIW 5 (1983), at pp. 363 f.

425. Stressing the need for the establishment of a *lingua franca*, an 'international fiscal language' *van Raad, supra* n. 17, at p. 224; *Vogel/Prokisch, supra* n. 10, 78a CDFI (1993), at p. 62.

426. *Perrou, supra* n. 342, at p. 43; *J. Strobl*, Mutual Agreement Procedure and Practice: *National Report Germany*, 66a CDFI, p. 171 (1981); *Lehner, supra* n. 233, at p. 64; *Mülhausen, supra* n. 122, at p. 84; *C. Gloria*, Das steuerliche Verständigungsverfahren und das Recht auf diplomatischen Schutz: *Zugleich ein Beitrag zur Lehre von der Auslegung der Doppelbesteuerungsabkommen*, pp. 162 ff. (Duncker & Humblot 1988); *Mössner, supra* n. 79, 29 RIW 5 (1983), at p. 362. It is interesting to note, however, that even before the introduction of these models and their MAP provisions some tax treaties provided for the mandatory and binding settlement of disputes as is detailed by *Lindencrona/Mattsson, supra* n. 415, at pp. 23 ff. and in the following section.

427. *See*, for example, *Altman, supra* n. 72, at pp. 256 f.; *Almeida, supra* n. 208, SSRN Journal (2018), at p. 3; *Bär, supra* n. 124, at p. 198.

> legal person that is a national of the former State with a view to the implementation of such responsibility.[428]

As is also pointed out in the ILC's commentary,[429] this concept goes back to the idea that a state takes up infringements of international law towards its citizens as its own case.[430] This has – as a fiction – been necessary in the early days of international law in which individuals had no place.[431] This has changed in the meantime:[432] individuals enjoy individual rights under international law – be it pursuant to human rights provisions, investment or tax treaties – but not all of these rights correspond with a remedy.[433]

Not least, the recent developments in tax dispute resolution mechanisms give rise to the question of whether these mechanisms still can be based on the idea of diplomatic protection.

First, one should keep in mind that even the established MAP procedure under the pre-2017 OECD Model goes beyond the obligations of mere diplomatic protection. For mere diplomatic protection, the ICJ has pointed out that:

> within the limits prescribed by international law, a State may exercise diplomatic protection by whatever means and to whatever extent it thinks fit, for it is its own right that the State is asserting. Should the national or legal person on whose behalf it is acting consider that their rights are not adequately protected, they have no remedy in international law. All they can do is resort to municipal law, if means are available, with a view to furthering their cause or obtaining redress. [...]
>
> The State must be viewed as the sole judge to decide whether its protection will be granted, to what extent it is granted, and when it will cease. It retains in this respect a discretionary power the exercise of which may be determined by considerations of a political or other nature, unrelated to the particular case.[434]

428. United Nations, Report of the International Law Commission p. 24, General Assembly – Official Records, http://legal.un.org/ilc/documentation/english/reports/a_61_10.pdf (accessed 15 Jan. 2024). On the background *see J. Dugard,* Diplomatic Protection, 5 (A. Peters/R. Wolfrum eds).
429. United Nations, *supra* n. 428, at p. 25. *See also Dugard, supra* n. 428, at m.no. 7.
430. The ILC cites both a sentence of the 18th-century lawyer Emmerich de Vattel (*E. de Vattel,* The Law of Nations: *Or, Principles of the Law of Nature, Applied to the Conduct and Affairs of Nations and Sovereigns, with Three Early Essays on the Origin and Nature of Law and on Luxury,* Book II, Chapter VI, para. 72, p. 299 (Liberty Fund 2008), https://oll.libertyfund.org/titles/vattel-the-law-of-nations-lf-ed (accessed 15 Jan. 2024)) and the statement that it *is an elementary principle of international law that a state is entitled to protect its subjects, when injured by acts contrary to international law committed by another state, from whom they have been unable to obtain satisfaction through the ordinary channels. By taking up the case of one of its subjects and by resorting to diplomatic action or international judicial proceedings on his behalf, a state is in reality asserting its own rights -its right to ensure, in the person of its subjects, respect for the rules of international law* by Permanent Court of International Justice, Judgment of 30 Aug. 1924, *The Mavrommatis Palestine Concessions (Greece v. Britain),* Publications of the Permanent Court of International Justice Series A (1923-1930) No. 2, p. 12.
431. United Nations, *supra* n. 428, at pp. 25 f.; *Perrou, supra* n. 342, at p. 58.
432. *See also J. Kokott et al.,* Völkerrecht und Steuerrecht – Die Rechte der Steuerpflichtigen: *Phase 1 des Projekts der International Law Association zum Internationalen Steuerrecht,* StuW 3, p. 201 (2020).
433. In detail *Dugard, supra* n. 428, at m.no. 9-10.
434. ICJ, Judgment of 5 Feb. 1970, *Barcelona Traction, Light and Power Company, Limited (Belgium v. Spain) Second Phase,* p. 44 (m.no. 78 f.).

In contrast to this full discretion of states concerning whether to exercise diplomatic protection, the MAP provision in Article 25(2) OECD-MC contains – as detailed in section 4.1.1.2.3 above – a *pactum de negotiando* and thus an obligation of CAs to negotiate (but no obligation to achieve a result)[435] and – with regard to matters of residence pursuant to Article 4(2) lit. d OECD-MC – even a *pactum de contrahendo* that entails an obligation to achieve a result.[436]

Furthermore, it is generally – in line with the *local remedies rule* in customary international law – regarded as a prerequisite for the exercise of diplomatic protection to exhaust all local remedies in the host state beforehand.[437] The exhaustion of local remedies is – as explained under section 4.1.1.2.4 above – not a premise to make use of the MAP procedure, however. This might serve as a further indication that even the pre-2017 procedure under the OECD model does not equal the diplomatic protection characteristics *stricto sensu*.[438]

The introduction of arbitration in Article 25(5) of the 2008 OECD Model, however, does not contradict the principles of diplomatic protection: with the consent of the parties, conflicts under diplomatic protection may be adjudicated by arbitration tribunals, the ICJ or mixed claims commissions.[439]

Since the 2017 update, the OECD-MC allows for taxpayers to initiate a MAP in either state. *Ismer* and *Piotrowski* conclude from this development that the procedure has *cut its roots in consular protection and has become a self-standing additional remedy* (to domestic procedures).[440] I support this argument: the concept of diplomatic protection is generally limited to the protection of nationals.[441] If taxpayers are allowed to initiate MAP procedures in either state and thus also in the state they are not tied to by nationality or residence,[442] this indicates that the procedure has moved even further away from its origin in the concept of diplomatic protection. It clearly is no mechanism (anymore) that focuses on the special ties of a person to their state.

In the light of both the already long-established deviations from general principles of diplomatic protection[443] and the newer developments, the established interpretation that the dispute resolution mechanisms in tax treaties are a form of exercising

435. In detail *Gloria, supra* n. 426, at p. 166. *See also Mooij, supra* n. 385, at p. 267.
436. On the differentiation between *pactum de negotiando* and *pactum de contrahendo H. Owada,* Pactum de contrahendo, pactum de negotiando (A. Peters/R. Wolfrum eds) and for the application to tax treaties *Gloria, supra* n. 426, at pp. 163 ff.
437. *Dugard, supra* n. 428, at m.no. 53 who refers to ICJ, Judgment of 21 Mar. 1959, *Interhandel (Switzerland v. United States of America),* I.C.J. Reports, p. 27; ICJ, Judgment of 20 Jul. 1989, *Elettronica Sicula S.p.A. (ELSI) (United States of America v. Italy),* I.C.J. Reports, p. 42.
438. Arguing for the interpretation of the MAP rules in the OECD Model as an exception to the local remedies rule *Mülhausen, supra* n. 122, at p. 125; differentiated *Gloria, supra* n. 426, at pp. 205 ff.
439. *Dugard, supra* n. 428, at m.no. 72.
440. *Ismer/Piotrowski, supra* n. 49, at m.no. 3.
441. *Dugard, supra* n. 428, at m.no. 20.
442. Analysing the concept of diplomatic protection as being inappropriate already because tax treaties focus on residence instead of nationality *Perrou, supra* n. 342, at p. 62.
443. Already highlighting for the pre 2017-Model that the theory of diplomatic protection is not suitable for the resolution of international tax disputes – mainly because it already focused on residence rather than on nationality – *Perrou, supra* n. 342, at pp. 57 ff.

diplomatic protection[444] no longer holds true. Too many of the defining elements of diplomatic protection are not or at least no longer fulfilled. Consequently, the dispute resolution mechanisms for international tax disputes already form dispute resolution mechanisms sui generis and should be further developed as such without the constraints that can be rooted in the principle of diplomatic protection – especially regarding the taxpayers' position in the procedure.

### 5.1.2 General Structure of the Procedure

The main question regarding the structure of an optimal dispute resolution mechanism is whether it is advisable to adhere to the two-stage general structure consisting of a MAP and mandatory binding dispute resolution that has developed over time and by now is established under the OECD Model, the UN Model (regarding alternative B of Article 25), the Arbitration Convention, the DRD and the MLI.

Alternatively, one could skip the negotiation phase that is in the hands of the CAs and go immediately to a mandatory dispute settlement mechanism that is organised by a third actor like an arbitration body,[445] or further develop the multi-tier-system – for example, by adding a mediation phase between the MAP and the mandatory settlement of the dispute.

#### *5.1.2.1 Retrospective on Former Multi-tier Systems*

The Draft Model Treaty of the League of Nations from 1928 already contained – in all its variations from I-A to I-C – an elaborate dispute resolution mechanism.[446] Its wording[447] was the following:

> Should a dispute arise between the Contracting States as to the interpretation or application of the provisions of the present Convention, and should such dispute not be settled either directly between the States or by the employment of any other means of reaching agreement, the dispute may be submitted, with a view to an amicable settlement, to such technical body as the Council of the League of Nations may appoint for this purpose. This body will give an advisory opinion after hearing the parties and arranging a meeting between them if necessary.
>
> The Contracting States may agree, prior to the opening of such procedure, to regard advisory opinion given by the said body as final. In the absence of such an agreement, the opinion shall not be binding upon the Contracting States unless it

444. Arguing this way *Mülhausen, supra* n. 122, at p. 149; *Gloria, supra* n. 426, at p. 207.
445. As suggested, for example, by *B. Hannes,* Qualifikationskonflikte im Internationalen Steuerrecht, pp. 280 f. (S + W Steuer- und Wirtschaftsverlag 1992). Raising this question as well *Kerlan, supra* n. 78, at p. 259.
446. League of Nations, Double Taxation and Tax Evasion, Report presented by the General Meeting of Government Experts on Double Taxation and Tax Evasion, 31 Oct. 1928, C. 562. M. 178. 1928. II. Accessible at https://archives.ungeneva.org/double-taxation-and-tax-evasion-report-presented-by-the-general-meeting-of-government-experts-on-double-taxation-and-tax-evasion (accessed 15 Jan. 2024). On the history of this clause *see Altman, supra* n. 72, at pp. 39 ff.
447. Contained in Art. 14 of Draft Convention I-A, Art. 5 of Draft Convention I-B and Art. 13 of Draft Convention I-C.

> is accepted by both, and they shall be free, after resort to such procedure or in lieu thereof, to have recourse to any arbitral or judicial procedure which they may select, including reference to the Permanent Court of International Justice as regards any matters which are within the competence of that Court under its Statute.
>
> Neither the opening of the procedure before the body referred to above nor the opinion which it delivers in any case involve the suspension of the measures complained of; the same rule shall apply in the event of proceedings being taken before the Permanent Court of International Justice, unless the Court decides otherwise under Article 41 of its Statute.

The dispute resolution mechanism seems to presuppose a MAP (or at least a negotiation phase) by referring to a settlement *directly between the states* and institutes an optional non-binding dispute resolution mechanism by a *technical body as the Council of the League of Nations may appoint for this purpose* that is to provide an opinion. This opinion could be given a binding nature – either by agreeing on it in advance or by accepting it afterwards. Alternatively, it is indicated that the states might make use of arbitration as well as of a reference to the Permanent Court of International Justice (PCIJ). No step of the dispute resolution mechanism is mandatory, however. Consequently, the provision merely serves as a roadmap of options.

The League of Nations' Fiscal Committee[448] further elaborated the dispute resolution mechanism and in 1931 proposed a very detailed multi-level approach in the draft of a *Plurilateral Convention for the Prevention of the Double Taxation of Certain Categories of Income*,[449] consisting of the following five provisions:

> *Article 17*
>
> Should a dispute arise between two or more of the contracting parties as to the interpretation or application of the provisions of the present Convention, and should such dispute not prove capable of settlement either direct between the parties or by any other method of friendly arrangement, the parties may, if they are all agreed, submit their dispute to such technical body as the Council of the League of Nations may appoint for the purpose.
>
> This body will give an opinion after hearing the parties and, if necessary, arranging a meeting between them. The opinion must be delivered within [...] months of the date on which the dispute has been referred to the said body.
>
> The High Contracting Parties may agree, prior to the opening of such procedure, to accept the opinion given by this body.
>
> *Article 18*
>
> Should the parties to the dispute decide not to ask for the opinion mentioned in the previous articles, or should they fail to agree upon this course, or, again, should they not agree to accept the opinion, the dispute shall be submitted for decision to

448. Or, much rather, *M. Barandon* as is pointed out in League of Nations, Fiscal Committee, Report to the Council on the Work of the Third Session of the Committee, 6 Jun. 1931, C.415.M.171.1931.II.A., p. 10 – accessible at https://archives.ungeneva.org/projets-de-conventions-plurilaterales-tendant-a-eviter-la-double-imposition-lettre-circulaire-transmettant-les-textes-aux-gouvernements-c-l-266-1931-26-octobre-1931 (accessed 15 Jan. 2024).
449. *Ibid.*

> the Permanent Court of International Justice unless the parties agree, under the conditions hereinafter stipulated, to have recourse to an arbitral tribunal.
>
> *Article 19*
>
> If, in the case provided for in the previous article, the parties agree to have recourse to an arbitral tribunal, they shall draw up a special agreement determining the subject of the dispute, the arbitrators and the procedure to be followed.
>
> *Article 20*
>
> If no agreement is reached between the parties as to the special agreement referred to in the previous article, or if they fail to appoint arbitrators, each party to the dispute shall, after a previous notice of [...] months, have the right to bring it direct before the Permanent Court of International Justice by means of a requisition.
>
> *Article 21*
>
> Neither the opening of the procedure before the technical body referred to in Article 17 nor the opinion which it delivers shall in any case involve the suspension of the measures complained of; the same rule shall apply in the event of proceedings before an arbitral tribunal or the Permanent Court of International Justice unless the Court decides otherwise under Article 41 of its Statute.

In comparison to the 1928 Draft Model Convention, this dispute resolution mechanism contains a mandatory element: while the procedure described in Article 17 corresponds to the one introduced in the 1928 model, Article 18 provides – by using the word *shall* – for a mandatory settlement of the dispute by the PCIJ in the case that the procedure was not made use of or failed. Alternatively, it is still possible to agree on the *recourse to an arbitral tribunal* pursuant to Article 19 – with the option for the parties, however, to resort to the PCIJ if the establishment of this tribunal fails.

#### *5.1.2.2 Focusing on a Negotiation Mechanism*

The mechanisms mentioned in the historical retrospect have one commonality: they do not mention taxpayers. Thus, it is only up to the states to initiate the resolution of a dispute. Taxpayers were mentioned, however, in clauses that established a MAP. The development of MAP clauses ran parallel to the League of Nations' considerations in the treaty practice of the states. The Income and Capital Tax Treaty between Italy and Germany from 1925[450] might serve as a first example, and stated in Article 15 that:

> Where it is proved that the actions taken by the tax authorities of the Contracting States have resulted for the taxpayer in double taxation, he may appeal against such a result to the State of which he is a resident. If the appeal is considered to be justified, the competent tax authority of that State may come to an agreement with the competent tax authority of the other State with a view to avoid double taxation in an equitable manner.[451]

450. Abkommen zwischen dem Deutschen Reiche und Italien zur Vermeidung der Doppelbesteuerung und zur Regelung anderer Fragen auf dem Gebiete der direkten Steuern of 31 Oct. 1925.
451. Translation by the IBFD, accessed via their Tax Research Platform on 2 Nov. 2020.

Thus, the contracting states had the option of initiating a MAP if taxpayers appealed in their state of residence. Comparable clauses can be found in Article 15 of the 1936 treaty between France and Sweden and Article XX of the 1939 treaty between Sweden and the United States.

With the 1943 Mexico and the 1946 London Model Conventions, the League of Nations shifted from the dispute resolution mechanism illustrated above to a MAP with the following provisions:

> *Art. XVI (Mexico) /Art. XVII (London)*
> 1. When a taxpayer shows proof that the action of the tax administration of one of the contracting States has resulted in double taxation, he shall be entitled to lodge a claim with the tax administration of the State in which he has his fiscal domicile or of which he is a national.
> 2. Should the claim be admitted, the competent tax administration of that State shall consult directly with the competent authority of the other State, with a view to reaching an agreement for an equitable avoidance of double taxation.

Article XVII of the Mexico Model Convention and Article XIX of the London Model Convention furthermore – with slight deviations from one another – provide for a state-state-MAP that is comparable to the one under Article 25(3) OECD-MC.

By drafting Article XVI/XVII, the League of Nations refrained from a multi-tier dispute resolution mechanism with an involvement of the PCIJ (or the ICJ as its successor)[452] and replaced it with a MAP. This MAP provision, however, made it mandatory for states to enter into a negotiation if the taxpayers' claim was admitted, because the word *may* that could be found in established treaties until then was replaced by the word *shall* in paragraph 2 of the clause.

As described in Chapter 4, it took until the end of the 20th century (for the Arbitration Convention) or even until the beginning of the 21st century (for the OECD/UN-MC) to enhance the MAP-centred resolution mechanisms with a mandatory settlement stage.

Having a mandatory dispute settlement as a last step is a huge advancement that I intend to retain. It not only already helps the negotiation phase by putting pressure on the disputing parties, but also guarantees an outcome. Thus, it is an integral part of an efficient dispute resolution mechanism.

#### *5.1.2.3 Focusing on a Mandatory Dispute Settlement Mechanism*

Focusing on a mandatory dispute settlement mechanism would resemble an approach that had been taken in some former tax treaties before: The Agreement between the British Government and the Government of the Irish Free State in respect of Double Income Tax from 14 April 1926, for example, stated in paragraph 7:

> Any question that may arise between the parties to this Agreement as to the interpretation of this Agreement or as to any matter arising out of or incidental to

452. Thoughts on the reasons for this shift can be found at *Altman, supra* n. 72, at pp. 54 ff.

> the Agreement shall be determined by such tribunal as may be agreed between them, and the determination of such tribunal shall, as between them, be final.[453]

Thus, there was no mention of a negotiation phase or mutual agreement procedure in this agreement.

It is worthwhile mentioning that it has also been considered to implement an international tax court to decide on matters of double taxation apart from specific tax treaties.[454]

Until today, however, the MAP is mostly the only and, in any case, the most established dispute resolution mechanism in tax treaties.[455] Skipping the negotiation phase would be tantamount to abolishing the existing MAP procedure. There are, however, many advantages to and reasons for adhering to the institution of a negotiation phase between CAs:[456] first, the CAs represent the states that originally concluded the tax treaty, the interpretation or application of which raises difficulties. Thus, it is a logical first step to allow them to sort out these difficulties. Second, the institution of the MAP has proven to be successful in many cases (*see* in detail section 4.1.3. for the OECD's mechanism).[457] Consequently, I argue in favour of keeping a negotiation phase in future dispute resolution mechanisms[458] and focus on how this negotiation phase could be improved.[459]

#### *5.1.2.4 Adding Further Layers to the Mechanism*

Adding a further layer to the dispute resolution mechanism in the form of an ADR option has, for example, been proposed by *Owens, Gildemeister* and *Turcan*.[460] They suggest adding a sixth paragraph to Article 25 alternative B of the UN-MC, which would provide for an ADR mechanism to set in if 20 months have passed after a MAP has been initiated if the CAs do not agree otherwise. This procedural step should be concluded in 120 days (if the CAs do not agree on a different time frame which is further detailed

453. Accessible at http://www.irishstatutebook.ie/eli/1926/act/35/schedule/1/enacted/en/html (accessed 15 Jan. 2024).
454. As presented (but rejected) by *A. Spitaler*, Empfiehlt sich die Errichtung eines Internationalen Steuergerichtshofes zur Entscheidung zwischenstaatlicher Steuerkonflikte?, StuW, 804 (1950). *See also Strotkemper, supra* n. 18, at pp. 547 f.
455. *See* the analysis of tax treaties by *Altman, supra* n. 72, at p. 59 n. 236. In detail on the more recent developments and assessments of the MAP *Markham, supra* n. 78, 35 Arbitr Int 2 (2019), at pp. 150 ff.
456. *See also Strotkemper, supra* n. 18, at p. 448.
457. *See also Strotkemper, supra* n. 18, at p. 207.
458. *See also Park/Tillinghast, supra* n. 24, at p. 19.
459. This approach is also taken by *Strotkemper, supra* n. 18, at pp. 614 ff.
460. *J. Owens et al.*, Proposal for a New Institutional Framework for Mandatory Dispute Resolution, 82 Tax Notes Int'l 10 (2016). *J. Gröper*, Chapter 9: Can Mediation Improve (the Efficiency of) the MAP?, p. 175 (P. Pistone/J.J. de Goede eds, IBFD 2021) also considers the option to include *mandatory non-binding mechanisms*. Against the use of mediation (at least for transfer pricing disputes), however, *Strotkemper, supra* n. 18, at pp. 824 f.

in a proposed paragraph 8).[461] The OECD's commentary also indicates the option to make use of mediation during the MAP, albeit not in a detailed way.[462]

I am sceptical as to whether it is advisable to force the use of an ADR mechanism upon the disputing parties if they do not agree in the negotiation phase. From my perspective, an ADR mechanism only offers prospects of success if the parties are generally willing to agree and recognise that they need assistance to reach an agreement. Consequently, I do not support the idea of adding a mandatory ADR layer between the negotiation phase and the mandatory settlement of the dispute because it risks prolonging the procedure without contributing to its efficiency. I would much prefer the option to make use of an ADR mechanism in the negotiation phase if the parties agree that this would be beneficial. The rules of this option should be detailed further than they are now in the OECD's commentary.[463]

#### *5.1.2.5 Conclusion*

In sum, I propose to retain the established two-step structure of the dispute resolution mechanism and to allow for a negotiation of the CAs as a first step that is followed by a mandatory resolution of the dispute if it does not lead to an agreement.[464] ADR mechanisms should optionally be made use of in the negotiation phase without the obligation that would follow from a formalisation in a procedural step for all cases.

An important feature of the mechanism should also be the option to solve multilateral tax disputes. So far, this is only possible under the Arbitration Convention and the DRD.

### 5.1.3 Institutionalising the Dispute Resolution Mechanism

Until now, the dispute resolution mechanisms are mainly in the hands of CAs: they handle taxpayers' initial requests, decide on their admissibility, and sort out whether to start and how to handle the MAP negotiation. If the MAP negotiation fails, it is for the CAs to nominate arbitrators and they can agree on the procedural rules for the arbitration phase.

The DRD did not change this fundamental distribution of procedural powers but merely installed some procedural safeguards for taxpayers via the involvement of national courts and appointing authorities. It still is up to the CAs to administer vast parts of the procedure.

Alas, this large amount of procedural powers is associated with a huge administrative burden. Placing the burden of forwarding letters on other participants and agreeing on procedural rules and dates for meetings on the CAs is very likely to slow down the procedure. It could be significantly accelerated by installing a neutral facility

461. *Owens et al., supra* n. 460, 82 Tax Notes Int'l 10 (2016), at 1004, 1011.
462. OECD, *supra* n. 37, at Commentary on Art. 25, m.no. 86.
463. For my proposal *see* section 5.2.4.
464. Also seeing a *promising model* in the established two-tier structure *Strotkemper, supra* n. 18, at p. 557.

that administers the entire dispute resolution mechanism, from the taxpayers' request to the correspondence between CAs and the initiation of the mandatory settlement.[465] This need is stressed – at least for the arbitration phase – by the actual use of the private ICDR by the US[466] and the offer of the Tribute initiative.[467] In both cases, I am sceptical as to the usefulness of private institutes and initiatives, bearing in mind, *inter alia*, the sensitivity of tax matters and the information dealt with in tax disputes.

The idea of a dispute resolution facility is not a new one: in their 1982 proposal, *Lindencrona* and *Mattsson* already suggested founding an Institute.[468] *Owens*, *Gildemeister* and *Turcan* proposed the installation of an institutional body with an International Tax Dispute Tribunal and a secretariat.[469] *Strotkemper* thinks in the same direction.[470] *Piotrowski*, *Ismer et al.* also propose to support the *Standing Committee* under the DRD with a secretariat and administrative staff.[471] However, these suggestions mainly focus on the administration and realisation of the arbitration phase.[472] In contrast, I suggest conferring to this facility the responsibility for the administration of the procedure from the outset.[473]

One main motivation for this suggestion is that a core element of my proposal is to provide an online platform for the administration of the entire procedure: via this online platform, taxpayers would file their request, and CAs would share their decisions, position papers and replies, and communicate with taxpayers and other CAs. All necessary information – whether provided by taxpayers or CAs – would be gathered on this platform. Thus, an immediate access of all participants to the procedure to all the information relevant to them would be guaranteed.

Implementing such a platform requires both a considerable number of resources for the set up and maintenance and great confidence of all participants to the procedure in the integrity of the implementing institution. Consequently, it should be implemented by an international organisation[474] that enjoys the trust of as many states and private actors around the world as possible. The two institutions that I could envision implementing such a platform are the OECD and the UN. However, the OECD is an

465. Also stressing that CAs should not administer the procedure (or at least the arbitration) *Avery Jones*, *supra* n. 182, 47 Intertax 8/9 (2019), at p. 677.
466. On this *see* section 4.4.1.
467. I highlighted this initiative in section 4.8.
468. *Lindencrona/Mattsson*, *supra* n. 415, at pp. 65 ff.
469. *Owens et al.*, *supra* n. 460, 82 Tax Notes Int'l 10 (2016); similar *C. Camino*, Chapter 31 – The Future of Arbitration: Towards an International Tax Court?, p. 731 (A. Majdanska/L. Turcan eds, Linde 2018).
470. In favour of further institutionalisation *Strotkemper*, *supra* n. 18, at pp. 424 ff. and proposing the installation of an International Tax Commission *Strotkemper*, *supra* n. 18, at p. 646.
471. *Piotrowski et al.*, *supra* n. 308, 47 Intertax 8/9 (2019), at pp. 687 f.
472. Whereby *Strotkemper*, *supra* n. 18, at p. 716 also calls for the installation of a notification body for MAPs.
473. A comparable level of institutionalisation is achieved, for example, under the WTO's dispute resolution mechanism. Pursuant to Art. 4(4) of the Dispute Settlement Understanding (DSU), concluded as Annex 2 to the WTO Agreement in 1994 and accessible at https://www.wto.org/english/tratop_e/dispu_e/dsu_e.htm (accessed 15 Jan. 2024), requests for consultations shall be notified to the Dispute Settlement Body (DSB). The notification requirement is also appreciated by *Strotkemper*, *supra* n. 18, at p. 625.
474. *See also* the considerations of *van Raad*, *supra* n. 17, at pp. 229 f. in his proposal.

organisation limited to 38 Member States, and non-Member States might hold reservations. Thus, I suggest that this platform be implemented and administered by the UN.[475] The UN – with the Committee of Experts on International Cooperation in Tax Matters – is also a recognised organisation in the field of international tax law that has expertise in the prevention and resolution of international tax disputes.[476] It especially focuses on the concerns of developing countries regarding the avoidance and resolution of tax disputes.[477] This underlines the fact that they have the concerns of all states in mind.

Apart from providing the online platform, it would be beneficial if the institution would also monitor compliance with the procedural rules, send reminders, organise meetings and initiate the next procedural steps.

Another benefit of further institutionalisation is that it would enhance the option to have multilateral disputes – an option that so far only the AC and the DRD allow for.

## 5.2 THE NEGOTIATION PHASE

### 5.2.1 Structuring the Negotiation

As shown in section 4 above, the DRD is the first mechanism that provides detailed and binding rules for the MAP, at least for the initiation and the review of the admissibility of an application.[478] For the negotiation phase of the MAP, however, the DRD also only states a time frame but does not provide for procedural rules.

No dispute resolution mechanism contains a binding set of rules for the negotiation phase – it is instead up to the CAs to determine the structure of the negotiation phase. The OECD MEMAP only provides a suggestion and shows best practices.[479]

This lack of procedural rules grants a high degree of flexibility to the acting CAs and allows them to assess each case in a way that they deem fit. However, the effectiveness of the negotiation phase depends entirely on the goodwill of the involved CAs, and there is no way to hold a CA accountable that is unwilling to advance the procedure. This bears a tremendous potential for frustration – for both CAs who find themselves confronted with an unwilling counterpart and taxpayers to whom the MAP can easily appear as a 'black box'.[480]

475. *See also Govind/Rao, supra* n. 81, 46 Intertax 4 (2018), at p. 333 who are proposing an institutional framework for arbitration under the auspices of the UN as well as *Camino, supra* n. 469, at p. 729.
476. *See* especially the designated Group on Dispute Avoidance and Resolution at https://www.un.org/development/desa/financing/what-we-do/ECOSOC/tax-committee/subcommittees/dispute-avoidance (accessed 15 Jan. 2024).
477. On this *see*, apart from the UN-MC and its commentary, also the current Handbook on Dispute Avoidance and Resolution, https://financing.desa.un.org/sites/default/files/2023-08/Dispute%20Avoidance%20and%20Resolution%20English.pdf (accessed 15 Jan. 2024).
478. *See* section 4.6.2.1.
479. *See* section 4.1.1.2.4.
480. *See also Brown, supra* n. 383, at p. 89.

Consequently, I propose the introduction of clear procedural rules with strict deadlines whose expiry brings about consequences that move the procedure forward and that can be enforced by CAs as well as by taxpayers.

### 5.2.1.1 *Initiating the Procedure*

Pursuant to all existing dispute resolution mechanisms, taxpayers are to initiate the procedure. The mechanisms differ in where and for how long the procedure may be initiated.

In all mechanisms, taxpayers are allowed to initiate the procedure with 'their' CA. Since the 2017 update, the OECD-MC allows taxpayers to file the application with *either* CA. Under the DRD, taxpayers (with the exception of private persons and smaller businesses) are even obliged to file their application with both (or in multilateral cases all) CAs. It is an important advancement from my perspective that taxpayers no longer depend on the goodwill of a CA to get the procedure going. As a further development and with further institutionalisation, one should consider creating a facility where all complaints could be filed and that forwards the complaint to the CAs involved as indicated in section 5.1.3. above.

The time frame within which the procedure can be initiated is limited under the existing mechanisms: usually, an application is possible within three years of the first notification (or rather its receipt) of the action that results in taxation that is – allegedly – not in accordance with the convention. Determining this notification can be challenging because there can be conflicts in determining what qualifies as such a notification. Thus, I suggest choosing a more precise term and relying on the first *tax assessment* which taxpayers consider to be contrary to the convention. This might lead to a longer time frame than under the established mechanisms, especially with regard to cases of a self-assessment or withholding taxes, but would increase legal certainty and thus – hopefully – help to avoid conflicts as to what exactly was the first notification.

It should, however, remain possible for taxpayers to initiate a procedure before they receive a tax assessment if they have a good reason to believe that a taxation not in accordance with a tax treaty is imminent.[481]

### 5.2.1.2 *Review of Admissibility*

To be pursued by the states, the taxpayers' application needs to be admissible: the application needs to be filed in time by the right person and provide sufficient information to substantiate the claim for a taxation not in accordance with the convention.

A leading example of the procedural rules for this phase is provided by the DRD: all authorities involved are to check whether sufficient information is provided to them. If they deem this not to be the case, they have the opportunity to ask for further

481. For the criteria under the OECD-MC that I intend to adopt *see* section 4.1.1.2.1.2.

information. They are also to check whether they can provide unilateral relief for the request. A decision on the admissibility must be taken within six months of receiving the application (or of further information if this was demanded). If there is no decision in time, the application is regarded as admissible. Negative decisions can be challenged by taxpayers.

I propose to build on these rules. In combination with the implementation of an online platform and an administrative facility, the procedure might contain the following rules: Taxpayers file their complaint via a form on the online platform that asks for specific information, including:

(1) their name, address, contact details and taxpayer identification number with the option to name a legal representative and insert their contact details to grant them access to the online platform as well;
(2) the measure the taxpayer considers to be in conflict with a tax treaty and – if there already has been a tax assessment – the date and reference of the tax assessment;
(3) the tax administrations involved – with the option to name the local offices that issued or are about to issue the measures the taxpayer intends to challenge;
(4) a short description of the conflict in keywords – the form could thereby include check boxes for frequent sources of disputes like transfer pricing or matters of residence;
(5) whether they have made use of domestic remedies.

This form allows for the attachment of files, like an application letter in which taxpayers are given the chance to reason their application in detail, a copy of the challenged tax assessment and documentation (especially in transfer pricing cases).

The online platform automatically confirms the receipt of the application. The administrative facility checks the application for obvious inconsistencies and asks for their correction. Thereafter, it involves the concerned CAs by linking them to the case on the online platform. This triggers the automatic sending of an e-mail to the concerned CAs and at the same time creates a folder for a new case in their profile of the platform that contains the taxpayer's application and all attachments. The date on which the administrative facility involves the CAs is considered the starting date of the procedure for the determination of further deadlines.

In the next step, it is the CAs' task to decide upon the admissibility of the application. Within three months, the CAs can ask for further information to assess the validity of the claim. All communication takes place via the online platform to guarantee that all participants to the procedure are on the same information level.

Within three months of the taxpayer providing the final pieces of information to the CAs via the platform or within six months after the starting date – with the later date being decisive, each CA has to issue a decision on the admissibility of the application. If there is no decision of a CA in time, a positive decision is assumed.

Negative decisions can be challenged by taxpayers, making use of domestic remedies. This serves to respect the national sovereignty of the states involved. However, I suggest a time frame during which these domestic remedies have to be decided as well: if there is no decision taken in six months, a panel that is installed by the administrative facility following the same rules that apply to the panel for the mandatory resolution of a dispute is to decide on the admissibility of the application. The panel shall also decide in case of divergent decisions on the admissibility from different CAs or states. After a positive panel decision, a negotiation phase shall only begin (as under the DRD) if all states are interested in it. Otherwise, the negotiation phase shall be skipped, and the procedure shall begin with the mandatory resolution phase.

### 5.2.1.3 *Procedural Rules for the Negotiation*

For the negotiation phase, there are no strict and binding rules established yet. The most elaborate set of rules can be found in the OECD MEMAP and is a mere proposal on how to conduct the MAP. I suggest taking this set of rules that is derived from best practices as a basis and to enhance it with stricter deadlines.

First, the established practice to exchange position papers should be transformed into a procedural rule. Thus, all CAs should provide an initial position paper within six months after the admission of the taxpayers' application. After receiving the other CA's position paper(s), all participants should be granted three months for a written reply. One month after receiving the last reply, an oral exchange should be scheduled – via a videoconference, a conference call or an in-person meeting. In the course of this oral exchange, the CAs should be allowed to agree on the further structure of the negotiation phase, i.e., on the means of communication and the dates.

The administrative facility is to supervise the negotiation. One week before a deadline, the platform automatically sends a reminder if no paper has been uploaded. The platform provides for a scheduling tool similar to the established service Doodle[482] as well as for an integrated videoconferencing option.[483] The parties are free to enter negotiations immediately if they deem an exchange of position papers to be unnecessary.

If the parties find themselves in a deadlock (and at any other point in the negotiation phase when they deem it beneficial), they have the option to agree on the use of mediation.[484] The administrative facility therefore can help in finding a mediator.

482. *See* https://www.doodle.com.
483. On details for technical suggestions, *see* section 5.4.2. Also promoting the use of videoconferencing technology *C. Dimitropoulou et al.*, Applying Modern, Disruptive Technologies to Improve the Effectiveness of Tax Treaty Dispute Resolution: Part 2, 46 Intertax 12, p. 961 (2018) DOI: 10.54648/taxi2018103.
484. In detail on mediation, *see* section 5.2.4.

Alternatively, the parties can also agree to disagree if they find themselves in a deadlock. Then, the negotiation phase ends with a notice to the taxpayer who can thereafter initiate the mandatory resolution phase.[485]

If one of the deadlines for the exchange of papers or the agreement of a date is missed, the administrative facility asks the participant who missed the deadline whether they intend to further conduct the negotiation proceedings. If they do, they can apply for an extension of time by up to one month. This extension may only be granted if the other participants agree. If this consent is denied or they show no reaction, the administrative facility sends a notice to the taxpayer that the negotiation phase has ended without an agreement.

If two years[486] have passed since the application has been admitted, the administrative facility also sends a request to the CAs asking whether they assume an agreement to be possible in the near future. The CAs then can ask the taxpayer for their consent with an extension of the negotiation phase by an exactly specified period of time.[487] If the taxpayer does not consent or the CAs do not assume an agreement to be possible, the administrative facility notifies the taxpayer that the negotiation phase is over. The CAs shall provide reasons as to why they could not agree on a solution to inform both the taxpayer and a possible later panel.

If the CAs manage to agree on a solution of the dispute, they shall communicate the intended agreement to the affected person via the online platform and ask for their consent. If this consent is granted, the agreement can formally be concluded by an exchange of letters. If there is no consent within one month after the solution is communicated to the affected person, this is to be interpreted as a refusal of consent.[488]

### 5.2.2 Participation of Taxpayers

Under none of the established mechanisms is the taxpayer granted a right to be heard.[489] They are only given the opportunity to detail facts or give insights if the CAs deem it beneficial. Apart from this, the MAP is mostly shrouded in secrecy.[490] The OECD MEMAP spells this out very clearly in Best Practice N°14:[491]

> Whilst giving due respect to the confidentiality of government-to-government communications and without allowing taxpayers to become involved in the actual MAP negotiations, competent authorities are encouraged to consider obtaining

485. Also in favour of granting the option to move on to the mandatory resolution phase if the negotiation phase remains unsuccessful *Strotkemper, supra* n. 18, at 343-345, 626.
486. Also – with strong arguments – for a two-year time limit for the MAP instead of three years *Strotkemper, supra* n. 18, at p. 341.
487. Also in favour of restrictive extension options *Strotkemper, supra* n. 18, at p. 345; *Markham, supra* n. 78, 35 Arbitr Int 2 (2019), at pp. 161 ff.
488. This procedural feature is also provided for (with a deadline of 45 days) in Art. 25(9) lit. k US-MC; supporting this approach *Strotkemper, supra* n. 18, at p. 627.
489. *See also Backhausen/Mazumdar, supra* n. 401, at p. 258.
490. *See also van Hout, supra* n. 74, at p. xxxv.
491. OECD, *supra* n. 94, at p. 25.

input from the taxpayer on factual and legal issues that may arise in the course of the MAP.

Why is it that taxpayers are not allowed to take part in MAP negotiations and do not yet receive the papers the CAs exchange? Is *confidentiality of government-to-government communications* an overriding principle that always outweighs the taxpayer's right to be heard?

It is not intuitive that there needs to be confidentiality in relation to affected taxpayers at all: tax authorities are usually obliged by the national laws binding them to guarantee equal taxation and thus to abide by the letter of the law.[492] Consequently, it is not evident that negotiations on the interpretation and application of these laws should be subject to secrecy.

The main reasons to treat information in the procedure confidential are tax secrecy[493] and the protection of trade secrets. As also acknowledged in the OECD MEMAP:

> a competent authority should recognize that the disclosure of sensitive or confidential information such as a trade secret could harm a taxpayer's competitive position, and should ensure that all measures are taken to protect such information.[494]

The main aim of these secrets is, however, to protect the taxpayer involved. In relation to the taxpayer involved, there is no reason to keep information confidential that regards themselves.

Another argument is that, under the rule of law, a high level of transparency of the taxpayers – as it has not least been further achieved with the implementation of BEPS measures – should be linked to a high level of transparency of the state and tax authorities themselves.[495]

Furthermore, allowing for taxpayer participation can help to avoid the suspicion of package deals being concluded that is often articulated.[496]

Thus, I am convinced that there is no basis to deny taxpayers participation in the negotiation phase but argue that they should be granted a right to be heard[497] that implies the right to receive all exchanged papers,[498] the right to be present at meetings and the right to make statements to the positions of other actors both in writing and

492. Pointing this out as well *Mellinghoff* discussing *K. Becker*, Internationale Zusammenarbeit – Konsultation und Verständigung, p. 198 (M. Achatz ed., Verlag Dr. Otto Schmidt 2013). Also critical regarding the low level of taxpayer participation in the MAP *Eilers/Drüen, supra* n. 99, at m.no. 11.

493. On the international recognition of tax secrecy *L.E. Schoueri/M.C. Barbosa*, Transparency: From Tax Secrecy to the Simplicity and Reliability of the Tax System, B.T.R. 5, pp. 672 f. (2013).

494. OECD, *supra* n. 94, at p. 16.

495. So *R. Seer*, Thematic Report – Purpose and Problems of Tax Transparency: The Legal Perspective, p. 20 (F. Başaran Yavaşlar/J. Hey eds, IBFD 2019).

496. *See* section 4.1.1.2.4. as well as *Altman, supra* n. 72, at p. 249.

497. Supporting this position, arguing with the *audita altera parte* principle, *Pistone/Goede, supra* n. 268, at pp. 485 f.

498. Described as *habeas data* principle by *Kokott et al., supra* n. 432, StuW 3 (2020), at p. 207.

orally.[499] If tax secrecy of persons other than the affected taxpayer demands for information not to be disclosed to taxpayers, the relevant information should be blacked out or anonymised. It seems questionable, however, whether this will be the case very often. Even regarding third persons, taxpayers might already have access to a range of information from persons who they entertain business relations with.[500]

If there is information that taxpayers should for compelling reasons not be granted access to, this could be managed via individual access rights on the online platform.

### 5.2.3 Reasoning and Publishing Agreements

Until now, MAP agreements from taxpayer-initiated MAPs (other than agreements resulting from state-state MAPs pursuant to Article 25(3) OECD-MC) need to be neither reasoned nor published.[501] A minor exception is that, according to the DRD, the *general reasons* for a failure of the MAP have to be provided to the taxpayer. For MAP agreements, however, the DRD also demands neither reasons nor a publication. The OECD MEMAP suggests that reasons be given[502] which – reportedly[503] – is mostly not done in practice.[504]

The main argument for this practice is that MAP agreements are often based more on compromises for individual cases that might rather result from a hands-on approach of the involved authorities than from an agreement on the exact interpretation of a treaty provision.[505] I do not intend to criticise the practice of finding compromises but think that this practice does not necessarily need to lead to the consequence that no reasons are communicated to taxpayers. In fact, I support the communication of the exact reasons that led to the result: if the agreement is based on the certain interpretation of a treaty provision, this should be communicated; if it is based on a compromise, it might still be communicated that there is an *agreement to disagree regarding the interpretation of the treaty while concluding a compromise on the allocation of the tax base* in a certain relation.

The same idea applies to the publication of agreements. Those opposed to publication argue that it could be misunderstood as having precedential value[506] and that it might conflict with the tax secrecy of the affected taxpayer.[507] These arguments are not compelling: while it is true that agreements in individual cases have no precedential value for other cases, they might still be of interest for the general public

499. Sharing this aim *Perrou, supra* n. 342, at pp. 183 f. *See also Kokott et al., supra* n. 432, StuW 3 (2020), at pp. 207 f.
500. Stressing this point *Seer, supra* n. 495, at p. 34.
501. Even though the suggestion of a publication is everything but new – *see* already calling it an *urgent matter O. Bühler,* Prinzipien des Internationalen Steuerrechts: *Ein systematischer Versuch,* pp. 43 f. (IBFD 1964).
502. Best Practice N°17, OECD, *supra* n. 94, at p. 30.
503. *Flüchter, supra* n. 90, at m.no. 171.
504. *See* already section 4.1.1.2.7.
505. Cf. *Flüchter, supra* n. 90, at m.no. 171.
506. *Gloria, supra* n. 426, at p. 184; *Flüchter/Liebchen, supra* n. 122, at m.no. 172.
507. *Becker, supra* n. 105, at m.no. 34; *Flüchter/Liebchen, supra* n. 122, at m.no. 172.

and other authorities in comparable situations. To avoid misconceptions, they could be published with a disclaimer stating that the agreement does not have binding precedential value. Respecting taxpayers' right to secrecy can also be accomplished by only allowing for the full publication of an agreement with their consent and otherwise publishing an anonymised[508] or - if even anonymised facts allow a conclusion about the person and their tax or trade secrets - redacted version.

The publication of agreements would help to build trust in the functioning of the mechanism and allow for the assessment of academia, other tax authorities and stakeholders.[509]

### 5.2.4 Mediation as an Option in the Negotiation Phase

If all participants to the procedure agree,[510] they may make use of mediation in the negotiation phase.[511] Mediation is thereby understood in the wide sense attributed to it in *Black's Law Dictionary* as a *method of non-binding dispute resolution involving a neutral third party who tries to help the disputing parties reach a mutually agreeable solution.*[512] This can also imply that the mediator is - if this is in the participants' interest - not only facilitating the negotiations but also making recommendations for the participants to consider.[513]

Mediation should not be made use of with the intention to delay the procedure[514] and to avoid the beginning of the mandatory resolution phase. Consequently: (1) its initiation should depend on the taxpayers' consent and (2) it needs to fit in the negotiation time frame of two years (or more if an extension is agreed upon) and be based on an efficient time frame itself as sketched out before in section 5.2.1.3.[515]

To facilitate the start of the mediation procedure, the administrative facility should suggest a mediator. Mediators should on the one hand be impartial and

508. *Strotkemper* also suggests the anonymised publication of agreements in her draft Art. 25(5), *see Strotkemper, supra* n. 18, at p. 969.
509. Also in favour of a publication of agreements (with considerations in the context of mediation) *Pistone/Goede, supra* n. 268, at p. 509. *See also Albert, supra* n. 99, at pp. 44 f.
510. *See* on this requirement already the end of section 5.1.2.
511. Contemplating the best time to make use of mediation *Pistone/Goede, supra* n. 268, at pp. 499 f.
512. *Garner, supra* n. 120, at the term *mediation*. On other definitions *see D. van Hout,* Is Mediation the Panacea to the Profusion of Tax Disputes?, 10 WTJ 1, pp. 44 ff. (2018).
513. In contemplating options for non-binding dispute resolution, the UN's Committee of Experts on International Cooperation in Tax Matters also supports such a broad understanding, pointing out that it might cover what is generally understood under *conciliation* as well, *see* the Report of its Twelfth Session, *supra* n. 79, at Annex 3, p. 33. *See also Gröper, supra* n. 460, at p. 170. Differentiating between *facilitative, evaluative* and *transformative* mediation *P.A. Brown,* Chapter 10: Mediation: The Swiss Army Knife in the Competent Authority's Toolbox, pp. 187 f. (P. Pistone/J.J. de Goede eds, IBFD 2021), who, at pp. 191 ff., also highlights in which scenarios the different methods might apply. For a summary *see also Pistone/Goede, supra* n. 268, at p. 514.
514. Seeing this danger as well *Gröper, supra* n. 460, at p. 176.
515. Regarding the second point *see also K. Perrou,* Chapter 11: Using Mediation for the Resolution of Cross-Border Tax Disputes, p. 208 (P. Pistone/J.J. de Goede eds, IBFD 2021); *Pistone/Goede, supra* n. 268, at pp. 517 f.

independent and on the other hand have sufficient expertise and knowledge to grasp the material questions in dispute.[516] Thus – even though it must be acknowledged that deciding a case and serving as a mediator are different tasks[517] – there is at least an overlap in potential mediators and potential panel members for the mandatory resolution of disputes. Therefore, the administrative facility should be able to choose a person out of the pool of potential panel members[518] who indicated that they are willing and capable of serving as a mediator as well. This person should be neither a national nor a resident of the states in dispute to avoid conflicts of interest. The participants should, within one month, decide whether they accept the suggested person or – if this is not the case – agree on another mediator. With the mediator, they should first determine the exact mandate (e.g., if the role is limited to facilitating the participants to express their positions and to interact with each other or if the mediator is asked to form and express an opinion for the participants to consider), structure and time frame of the procedure. As to both the confidentiality requirements and the remuneration of the mediator, I suggest referring to the regulations on panel members.[519]

Furthermore, if mediation does not lead to a mutual agreement, the mediator shall be obliged to file a report that sums up the dispute and the key questions from their perspective. This could still facilitate the procedure in the mandatory resolution phase.[520]

## 5.3 THE MANDATORY RESOLUTION

### 5.3.1 What to Decide?

Until now, most dispute resolution mechanisms do not allow for a full review of the case in the mandatory resolution phase but only for the solution of questions that no agreement could be reached on in the negotiation phase.[521] This is a crucial design

516. For further considerations as to the qualification of mediators *see Pistone/Goede, supra* n. 268, at p. 506.
517. As pointed out by *P.A. Brown*, Chapter 12: A Negotiator, Not a Judge: Choosing the Right Mediator to Aid in Resolving Cross Border Tax Disputes, p. 211 (P. Pistone/J.J. de Goede eds, IBFD 2021), who, at p. 224 suggests to appoint *former competent authorities and senior treaty analysts who were successful resolving disputes when they were in the government* as mediators.
518. On these *see* section 5.3.2.
519. On this *see* sections 5.3.2 and 5.3.3.6.
520. Pointing out that mediation can *be useful also as preparation for a proper and efficient arbitration process Mooij, supra* n. 385, at pp. 254 f.; *Pistone/Goede, supra* n. 268, at p. 498; *H.J. Oortwijn*, Dispute Resolution in Cross-Border Tax Matters, 56 ET 4, p. 166 (2016) DOI: 10.59403/1f7z34m.
521. *See*, for the OECD-MC, *Desax/Veit, supra* n. 172, 23 Arb. Int'l 3 (2007), at pp. 413 f. and section 4.1.2. Under the Arbitration Convention, a review of the entire case seems possible, *see* section 4.5.3. The Dispute Resolution Directive does not differentiate between *unresolved issues* and the *case* but operates with the term of the *question in dispute* (as defined in Art. 1 second sentence DRD). Mandatory dispute resolution is possible pursuant to Art. 6(1) lit. b if the CAs *failed to reach an agreement on how to resolve the question in dispute*. I tend to interpret this provision in the way that the mandatory resolution only covers unresolved questions and that

feature of the mandatory resolution phase because it stresses its character as a mere enhancement of the MAP instead of a fully fledged self-standing legal remedy.[522] A further expression of this character trait is that MAP agreements cannot be challenged under any of the established mechanisms.

It is pivotal to determine whether these limitations should be kept or whether taxpayers should be allowed to submit the entire case to mandatory resolution,[523] no matter whether there are remaining unresolved issues or the CAs managed to agree on a solution for all issues in case. Allowing for a submission of the entire case to mandatory resolution would further develop the mandatory resolution phase into a self-standing legal remedy.

In favour of a limitation to unresolved issues and against the option of challenging agreements made in the MAP phase, one might argue that the implementation of a MAP usually depends on the taxpayers' consent – if they are not satisfied, they might disagree with it and thus avoid the implementation. While this is technically correct, the option to disagree is not a very constructive one given the lack of alternatives for solutions that bind at least two states at the same time: the only real alternative is to strive for separate unilateral solutions via domestic remedies. Whether these lead to uniform results is a game of chance: taxpayers might well end up with contradictory decisions (which can also be in their favour and lead to double non-taxation).[524]

One further argument against introducing an option to challenge (partial or entire) agreements in the mandatory resolution phase might also be that it results in effort and costs for the states involved. This could, however, be addressed with a more elaborate rule for the bearing of costs: for example, taxpayers could be obliged to pay for the costs incurred due to the mandatory resolution phase if the CAs' agreement is upheld in this stage. While it is true that – especially in the current setting of mechanisms – challenging MAP agreements would bind resources at the CAs that are limited, this calls for a further institutionalisation due to which the effort for CAs in the mandatory resolution phase could be limited. Finally, challenging already concluded agreements takes time and prolongs the procedure. This is not a decisive counterargument, however: the most time-sensitive actors in the procedures are the taxpayers, and it would be up to them to balance their interests in reviewing the agreement against those of a faster implementation.

For the further development of a body of international tax law and to foster legal certainty, it would be beneficial if MAP agreements could be challenged because it would result in a further exchange of legal arguments. Furthermore, this option is likely

---

multiple *questions in dispute* can be dealt with in one case. The same result is reached by *Flüchter, supra* n. 90, at m.no. 293 who bases his interpretation on the provisions regarding the Rules of Functioning that in Art. 11(2) lit. b DRD allow for the CAs to determine the *legal and factual questions to be resolved*.

522. As pointed out by *Ismer/Piotrowski, supra* n. 49, at m.no. 112.

523. Also criticising the lack of an option to challenge MAP decisions *Strotkemper, supra* n. 18, at p. 347.

524. *Strotkemper, supra* n. 18, at p. 203; *S. Merz/D. Sajogo*, Aktuelle Entwicklungen bei internationalen Verständigungs- und Schiedsverfahren, 11 PIStB (Praxis internationale Steuerberatung) 2, p. 46 (2010).

to incentivise the participating CAs both to involve taxpayers more in the negotiation phase to get to know and to consider their position and to reason their decision in greater detail to convince taxpayers of its correctness.

Thus, the benefits clearly outweigh the disadvantages from my perspective, which leads me to advocate in favour of allowing agreements made between the CAs in the negotiation phase to be challenged in the mandatory resolution phase and consequently to further develop this procedural step to a real remedy.

### 5.3.2 Who Is to Decide?

Under nearly all established mechanisms (with minor exceptions like the mandate of the ICJ in the Swedish-German[525] or the CJEU in the Austrian-German[526] tax treaty), ad hoc panels are to be established to decide in the mandatory resolution phase. One promising option for further institutionalisation has been created with the DRD: the opportunity to establish a Standing Committee (cf. Article 10(1) second sentence DRD).[527]

Regarding the qualifications of the persons who are to decide during the mandatory resolution phase, there is a wide consensus across all established dispute resolution mechanisms: they should be highly qualified experts of international tax law and their impartiality and independence must be beyond doubt.[528]

The OECD spells this out rather vaguely in paragraph 3(1) of their Sample Mutual Agreement.[529] The UN's commentary is not any clearer but points out that doubts as to whether it is possible to find experienced arbitrators and whether their neutrality and independence could be guaranteed were one component that led the UN to only offer arbitration as an alternative in their model.[530]

Both the Arbitration Convention and the DRD operate with lists that contain the names of possible *independent persons* nominated by Member States as well as an indication of whether the respective persons are eligible to serve as a chair.[531] The DRD in particular sets comparably strict standards for impartiality and independence that can be concluded from the reasons that a Member State's CA can base an objection to the appointment of particular panel members to an Advisory Commission on; those are listed in Article 8(4) DRD. CAs may object to an appointment if the appointed person:

525. On this *see* section 4.4.2.
526. On this *see* section 4.4.3.
527. *See* especially the inspiring proposal of *Piotrowski et al.* I discussed in section 4.6.5. as well as section 4.6.2.3.2.
528. For an overview *see also Mooij, supra* n. 385, at pp. 281 ff.; *Markham, supra* n. 78, 35 Arbitr Int 2 (2019), at pp. 162 ff. *See also* the abstract considerations of *Park/Tillinghast, supra* n. 24, at pp. 33 ff.
529. *See* section 4.1.2.4 above.
530. *See* para. 4 and 5 of the commentary to Art. 25 UN-MC 2017 (pp. 556 f.).
531. For the Arbitration Convention *see* section 4.5.3.1. and for the Dispute Resolution Directive section 4.6.2.3.1.

(1) was working for or belonging to one of the tax administrations involved within the last three years;
(2) shows a proximity to the affected person, either through a material holding or a holding conferring the right to vote or through an activity as an employee or consultant in the last five years;
(3) gives other reasons to assume a lack of sufficient guarantee of impartiality; or
(4) was working in a tax advisory profession in the last three years, whether as an employee in a consulting firm or in another professional capacity - even without any reference to a party or affected person to the proceedings.

One should note, however, that persons who fulfil any of these criteria might still be appointed as independent persons if no CA objects. The taxpayer has no right to object to the nomination of a panel member.

The perfect mixture of knowledge and experience in international tax law on the one hand and impartiality on the other hand seems hard to find. The DRD places its hope mainly in judges, as can be concluded from Article 8(6) DRD, which sets the rule that the chairperson shall be a judge unless the CA's representatives and independent persons agree otherwise. While judges surely guarantee a high degree of impartiality,[532] they might not necessarily be specialised or experienced in international tax law.[533] A specialisation and vast experience in international tax law can, however, be found with practitioners like lawyers and tax advisors, in-house counsels of MNEs and tax officials in CAs. The involvement of specialised academics is also promising.

The doubt as to the impartiality of practitioners has several causes: (1) a doubt arising from a past or current involvement in cases concerning the affected person, (2) a doubt arising from the prospect of a possible future involvement in cases concerning the affected person and (3) the assumption of an underlying bias that results from the affiliation to a particular professional group (e.g., for advisors to be generally pro-taxpayer and officials to be generally pro-fiscus).

Above this, all prospective panel members have a potential bias due to their nationality or home jurisdiction: the fact that they are more involved in matters of national tax law and the intersection of national with international tax law might decide their opinion on matters of international tax law and make them less willing to try their best to interpret treaty provisions autonomously.[534] Additionally, a potential bias may arise from an - at least perceived - obligation towards the state who

532. Retired judges of supreme courts are reportedly already favoured as arbitrators, *see A. Herlinghaus*, Gedanken zum abkommensrechtlichen Schiedsverfahren nach Art. 25 Abs. 5 OECD-MA, 19 IStR 4, p. 125 (2010).

533. An interesting overview of the expertise of national judges in matters of international tax law is given in the national reports in M. Lang et al. eds, Tax Treaty Arbitration (IBFD 2020). *See also Mooij, supra* n. 385, at p. 282; *van Raad, supra* n. 17, at pp. 218 f.

534. Describing a state's tendency to prefer the application of its own law under Art. 3(2) OECD-MC instead of an autonomous interpretation of the treaty as 'striving home' phenomenon (*Heimwärtsstreben*) *D. Beck*, Qualifikationskonflikte im Internationalen Steuerrecht, p. 335 (Springer 2016); *Strotkemper, supra* n. 18, at p. 453; *Hannes, supra* n. 445, at pp. 199 f.

appointed a panel member if (as provided for under most arbitration mechanisms) it is up to the states in conflict to appoint individual ad hoc panel members.[535]

All these causes should be addressed when composing a panel. To account for the potential home jurisdiction bias, I propose that no panel member should be a national or resident of one of the states involved in the dispute.[536] This automatically excludes representatives of the CAs involved as panel members – a consequence I consider positive for other reasons as well: since the CAs were responsible for the MAP negotiations, it is very likely that they will stick to the position they have taken before.[537]

To avoid potential bias that might result from the affiliation to a particular professional group, I suggest introducing a quota for the composition of panels. Thus, a rule might be that out of three panel members[538] there shall only be one tax advisor or counsel and only one tax official. The position of a chairperson could be reserved for judges or academics.

In addition to these abstract criteria, there should be the option of an objection to suspected partiality because of an affiliation with one of the involved states or taxpayers that may be raised by both the participating states and taxpayers. Furthermore, a cooling-off period should be stated, prohibiting engagements for an involved state or taxpayer for both the panel member and the panel member's firm or company, e.g., for three years following the panel's decision.[539] A breach of this rule should trigger a notification obligation and allow for the involved states and taxpayers to void the panel's decision or the agreement following it and to enter a new mandatory resolution phase at the expense of the person who has broken the obligation.

Further institutionalisation bears the chance of developing a significant amount of expertise in the resolution of international tax disputes if fewer panel members are mandated more frequently. To begin with, I suggest following the proposal that the Fiscalis Project Group 093 developed for the ADRC under Article 10(1) DRD:[540] to start with part-time panel members who reserve time slots on a regular basis and are remunerated depending on their actual workload[541] and to move to permanently mandated full-time panel members if there is a sufficient demand.

For the negotiation phase, I already suggested building a facility that administrates this phase and a supporting online platform. This facility, preferably one under

535. This is described as a *moral hazard* by *Strotkemper, supra* n. 18, at pp. 876 f.
536. The WTO's DSU contains a comparable provision for the formation of panels in Art. 8(3). The ICSID Convention addresses the issue by stating in Art. 39 that *the majority of the arbitrators shall be nationals of states other than the contracting state party to the dispute and the contracting state whose national is a party to the dispute*. Seeking for a compromise *Strotkemper, supra* n. 18, at pp. 857 ff.
537. This assumption is anecdotally proven by *Lodin, supra* n. 241, 42 Intertax 3 (2014), at pp. 173 f., who served as a panel member under the Arbitration Convention's dispute resolution mechanism.
538. Contemplating the right number of panel members *Strotkemper, supra* n. 18, at pp. 736 f.
539. Suggesting longer cooling-off periods as well *Piotrowski et al., supra* n. 308, 47 Intertax 8/9 (2019), at p. 688.
540. On this *see* section 4.6.2.3.2.
541. *See also Strotkemper, supra* n. 18, at p. 760.

the auspices of the UN, should also administer the mandatory resolution phase, build panels and assign cases to these panels.[542]

Thus, panels for individual cases are set up by the administrative facility using a random algorithm[543] that sets in after determining key exclusion factors like the panel members' home jurisdiction and that takes the quota regarding the panel members' professional background into account. It should also be possible to group potential panel members regarding their focus of interest and expertise (such as transfer pricing or matters of residence). Once the algorithm has created a panel, the panel members are introduced to the case and given the chance to recuse themselves if they see a conflict of interest stemming from past, current or future activities.

But how should persons be appointed to possible panel members?[544] For the election of the possible panel members and subsequent appointment issues, I suggest establishing an assembly of states' representatives (subsequently referred to as assembly of representatives): each state that participates in the dispute resolution mechanism therefore appoints one representative.

Possible panel members can either apply themselves or be nominated by states and their CAs, as well as by taxpayers or other actors such as NGOs. The applications shall be standardised[545] and published on the dispute resolution facility's webpage to eliminate any suspicion of opacity right from the start.[546] The applicants need to fulfil certain hard qualifications like a relevant expertise in the area of international tax law and a sufficient proficiency in the standard language of procedures (which is presumably English). There shall not be a national pre-selection,[547] but the states will have a right to a reasoned objection if they deem a candidate unfit.

The administrative facility organises public hearings that are led by the two highest-ranking members of both the UN Committee of Experts on International Cooperation in Tax Matters and the OECD Centre for Tax Policy and Administration. At

542. Also expressing a preference to appoint panel members using an appointing authority *Park/Tillinghast, supra* n. 24, at p. 31.

543. A comparable mechanism is used for the WTO's Appellate Body, for which the members shall serve *in rotation* (Art. 17(1) third sentence DSU) what is detailed in Rule 6(2) of the Working Procedures for Appellate Review (accessible at https://www.wto.org/english/tratop_e/dispu_e/ab_e.htm, accessed 15 Jan. 2024) with the sentence: *The Members constituting a division shall be selected on the basis of rotation, while taking into account the principles of random selection, unpredictability and opportunity for all Members to serve regardless of their national origin. Strotkemper, supra* n. 18, at pp. 756 ff. draws inspiration from this rule in her proposal.

544. A good overview of the election of judges in international courts is given by *R. Mackenzie/P. Sands*, Judicial Selection for International Courts: Towards Common Principles and Practices, pp. 220 ff. (K. Malleson/P.H. Russell eds, University of Toronto Press 2006). *See also Strotkemper, supra* n. 18, at pp. 740 ff.

545. This can be achieved, *inter alia*, with a model CV as established in the appendix to Resolution 1082 (1996) of the Parliamentary Assembly of the Council of Europe for candidates for the ECtHR (accessible at https://pace.coe.int/en/files/16493, accessed 15 Jan. 2024).

546. This is already practised, for example, for nominations of judges for the International Criminal Court, as detailed by *Mackenzie/Sands, supra* n. 544, at p. 228.

547. This is the case in most established election procedures for international courts and it is criticised as being untransparent and leaving room for the utilisation of informal networks, *see Mackenzie/Sands, supra* n. 544, at p. 221; *Strotkemper, supra* n. 18, at p. 748; more general *K. Oellers-Frahm*, International Courts and Tribunals, Judges and Arbitrators, 10 (A. Peters/R. Wolfrum eds).

least one member per institution shall be female to avoid any appearance of gender bias in the hearings. The hearings are broadcast via the facility's webpage. The states' representatives are given the opportunity to ask questions in these hearings.

Not before one day after the last hearing, the assembly of representatives votes on who is to be appointed.[548] Therefore, the applicants are grouped by their affiliation to states. Multiple affiliations are possible – either because a candidate applied for more than one state or was nominated by more than one state or other actors from multiple states. In the respective state group, the applicants are ranked in alphabetical order.[549] One panel member can be voted on per state.[550] If a person is voted for by two or more states, the person has to decide which state's mandate to accept. For the other state(s), the person with the second most votes is appointed.

In this constellation, it is a challenging task to achieve equal gender representation, an aim that should be taken seriously in view of both the UN's Sustainable Development Goal No. 5[551] and the very sparse representation of women to date.[552] To achieve equal gender representation, I suggest that every state has two votes per possible position (i.e., per state's 'seat'). Within these votes, one can only be used for female applicants, while the other can be used for all genders. Both votes can be directed at one person (who must logically be female).[553] This should incentivise both women to apply themselves and states and other actors to nominate qualified women.

The person who receives the most votes is elected. In the event of a tie vote, the female candidate wins. If there are two or no women, there shall be a final ballot between the two candidates. If this leads to a tie again, the decision shall be taken by lot.

In view of the elaborate election procedure and to ensure the active engagement and focus of panel members, the mandate should last for a considerable timespan (e.g., five years)[554] with the option of a one-time extension if the term has ended. Thereafter,

548. *See also* the proposal by *Govind/Rao, supra* n. 81, 46 Intertax 4 (2018), at p. 333.
549. This has also been proposed for the election procedure of candidates for the ECtHR by the Parliamentary Assembly of the Council of Europe, *see* Recommendation 1429 (1999) para. 6.5. (accessible at https://assembly.coe.int/nw/xml/XRef/Xref-XML2HTML-en.asp?fileid=16755&lang=en, accessed 15 Jan. 2024) and is practised in the election of the ICJ's judges (Art. 7(1) ICJ Statute).
550. This proposal is made under the assumption that a large number of countries – ideally all 193 Member States of the UN – are participating in the mechanism. If the mechanism is supported by fewer members at first, one might consider increasing the number of panel members per state (e.g., to two).
551. For details *see* https://sdgs.un.org/goals/goal5 (accessed 15 Jan. 2024).
552. A clue as to the relations of gender representation in dispute resolution panels is provided on the basis of the list of possible panel members under the Arbitration Convention (accessible at https://www.consilium.europa.eu/en/documents-publications/treaties-agreements/agreement/?id=1990093, accessed 6 Feb. 2021): Out of 120 possible panel members, there are 25 women listed, which amounts to a quota of 20 %.
553. Alternatively – if there are as indicated in n. 550 more panel members per state – it can be considered to determine that one of the panel members per state needs to be a woman. This could be achieved with a comparable two-vote system, without the option of concentrating two votes on one person.
554. While the persons forming the WTO's Appellate Body serve four-year terms with the option of a one-time reappointment (Art. 17(2) DSU), the judges of international courts usually serve longer terms (nine years with the option of a re-election at the ICJ pursuant to Art. 13(1) of the

a re-application shall be possible, but the election procedure shall be the same as described above to allow for new candidates to have equal chances. Panel members can also be removed with a two-thirds majority vote of the assembly of representatives after a reasoned application for their removal that can be initiated by both CAs and taxpayers. If new states join the mechanism, the assembly of representatives gets together and elects a potential panel member who is affiliated to the new states.

To allow panel members to gain access to all necessary information, I suggest stating that they shall be deemed as persons under Article 26(2) first sentence OECD/UN-MC and that they are obliged to respect the confidentiality requirements[555] of this provision.

### 5.3.3 How to Decide?

#### *5.3.3.1 The Choice of Method*

Among the established dispute resolution mechanisms, there is mainly a choice of two methods for the mandatory resolution of disputes: the independent opinion approach and the final-offer approach. While the independent opinion approach resembles the method courts use to decide cases by reflecting upon the parties' submissions and finding their own reasoned position, under the final-offer approach, the parties each present a solution proposal, and all the panel does is to choose one over the other. Thus, the question seems to be what the mandatory resolution phase intends to achieve: is it in search of *justice* (meaning the legally correct application of a treaty) or is it in search of a *solution* of the dispute in the fastest possible way?[556]

There are benefits attributed to the final-offer approach: economists suggest that at least rather risk-averse parties will take more moderate positions[557] (if there is no high level of uncertainty[558]) – a suggestion that is not undisputed.[559] Furthermore, the

---

ICJ's Statute; also nine years at the International Criminal Court – generally without the option of a re-election – pursuant to Art. 36(9)(a) of its Statute; nine years with the option of a re-election at the International Tribunal for the Law of the Sea pursuant to Art. 5(1) of its Statute; six years with the option of a re-election at the CJEU pursuant to Art. 253(1) TFEU; nine years without the option of a re-election at the ECtHR pursuant to Art. 23(1) ECHR).

555. On these *D. Ring*, Article 26: Exchange of Information section 2.2.5. (R. Vann et al. eds, IBFD 6 Dec. 2018); *R. Seer*, Internationales Steuerverfahrensrecht: *Kommentierung der Art. 26, 27 OECD-MA*, Art. 26 m.no. 35, 41 (NWB 2020).
556. A similar differentiation is also made by *F. Vanistendael*, Democracy, Revolution and Taxation, 71 BIT 8, p. 448 (2017), who points out that under the final-offer approach the overall outcome, rather than a detailed analysis, is important. *See also Ault, supra* n. 140, 7 Florida Tax Review 3 (2005), at p. 149.
557. *C.M. Stevens*, Is Compulsory Arbitration Compatible with Bargaining?, 5 Industrial Relations 2, pp. 45 ff. (1966) DOI: 10.1111/j.1468-232x.1966.tb00450.x. Following this assumption *Strotkemper, supra* n. 18, at pp. 379 f.; *N. Kuntschik/A. Bödefeld*, Schiedsverfahren nach den DBA mit Großbritannien, der Schweiz und Liechtenstein, 21 IStR 4, p. 138 (2012); *J. Monsenego*, Designing Arbitration Provisions in Tax Treaties: Reflections Based on the US Experience, 42 Intertax 3, p. 166 (2014) DOI: 10.54648/taxi2014017.
558. So restrictive *H.S. Farber*, An Analysis of Final-Offer Arbitration, 24 The Journal of Conflict Resolution 4 (1980) DOI: 10.1177/002200278002400407.

application of the final-offer method might allow for a faster procedure.[560] Additionally, the limited range of options for the deciding panel is regarded as beneficial for the sovereignty of the states in conflict since the mandatory resolution stage is much more a continuation of the MAP than an independent procedural stage, and the panel has no chance to create precedent because it usually[561] is not given the opportunity to provide reasons.[562]

Possibly the earliest known example of the final-offer method's application is the trial of Socrates in which the jury had – after having found Socrates guilty – to vote on a penalty; they could not decide on a penalty of their own but had to choose between the one proposed by the prosecution (death) and the one proposed by Socrates himself (he proposed a fine of 30 mina after mocking the jury by suggesting being declared a civic hero and being given free meals in the *prytaneion* for the rest of his life as a fine [thus not being a perfect sample to prove the assumption of a more reasonable party's behaviour under the final-offer approach]).[563] In the 20th century, the final-offer method became increasingly popular for the settlement of labour disputes in the United States – especially for the determination of the wage in disputed contracts for major league baseball players, which earned it the name *baseball arbitration*.[564]

It was also the United States that brought the final-offer method to the stage of international tax dispute resolution: in the 2006 protocol to the treaty with Germany, both states agreed on the use of final-offer arbitration.[565] From there on, the final-offer method has embarked on a victory tour: it was mentioned in the context of an alternative *streamlined procedure* in the 2008 OECD Sample Mutual Agreement,[566] as the standard method from the 2011 UN Sample Mutual Agreement onwards[567] and as

559. *See*, for example, *S.J. Brams/S. Merrill*, Equilibrium Strategies for Final-Offer Arbitration: There is No Median Convergence, 29 Management Science 8 (1983), http://www.jstor.org/stable/2631036; *O. Ashenfelter et al.*, An Experimental Comparison of Dispute Rates in Alternative Arbitration Systems, 60 Econometrica 6 (1992), http://www.jstor.org/stable/2951527; *D.L. Dickinson*, A Comparison of Conventional, Final-Offer, and 'Combined' Arbitration for Dispute Resolution, 57 Industrial and Labor Relations Review 2 (2004) DOI: 10.2307/4126621. Especially for tax treaty arbitration *I. Grlica*, Chapter 14 – Baseball Arbitration: *Comparison of the Rules under the U.S.-Canada Tax Treaty with the Rules under the Multilateral Instrument*, p. 322 (A. Majdanska/L. Turcan eds, Linde 2018).
560. Assuming time and cost benefits *Kuntschik/Bödefeld, supra* n. 557, 21 IStR 4 (2012), at p. 138.
561. Only under the UN's Sample Mutual Agreement is the panel's decision to be reasoned using the final-offer method.
562. *J. Pauwelyn*, Baseball Arbitration to Resolve International Law Disputes: Hit or Miss?, 22 FTR 1, pp. 56 f. (2018) DOI: 10.5744/ftr.2018.1015; *Grlica, supra* n. 559, at p. 321.
563. *See also Ashenfelter et al., supra* n. 559, 60 Econometrica 6 (1992), at p. 1408 who refer to the description of *I.F. Stone*, The Trial of Socrates, pp. 186 ff. (Anchor Books 1989).
564. For details *see J. Monhait*, Baseball Arbitration: An ADR Success, 4 Harvard Journal of Sports & Entertainment Law 1 (2013); *Pauwelyn, supra* n. 562, 22 FTR 1 (2018), at pp. 48 ff.
565. *See* section 22 lit. h second sentence of the Protocol of 1 Jun. 2006 to the Convention between the Federal Republic of Germany and the United States of America for the Avoidance of Double Taxation and the Prevention of Fiscal Evasion with Respect to Taxes on income and Capital and to certain other Taxes.
566. *See* section 4.1.2.5.
567. *See* section 4.2.

the standard method in both the 2017 OECD Sample Mutual Agreement[568] and the MLI.[569]

It is regarded as a main advantage of the final-offer approach that it creates uncertainty as to which proposal the panel is going to select, and thus encourages the parties to choose a more moderate position or even to propose a compromise.[570] I would argue, however, that this effect can be achieved by the establishment of a mandatory resolution phase: the mere existence of a mandatory resolution phase creates uncertainty and should incentivise CAs to find a solution in the MAP.[571] This is even more so if they know that the procedure will be taken out of their hands in the mandatory resolution phase.[572] If the argument for the implementation of final-offer arbitration is that this way a compromise can be achieved more efficiently, I would like to contradict: the implementation of final-offer arbitration (possibly combined with the option for the CAs to deviate from a solution afterwards) does not incentivise the CAs to achieve a compromise in the MAP in the most efficient way, since it could also be an incentive to argue more extreme positions in this stage, knowing that they can still take a more moderate position in the final-offer mandatory resolution phase. Implementing an independent opinion mandatory resolution phase without the option of deviating from the panel's solution, however, incentivises the CAs to already agree on a compromise solution in the MAP because they know that the procedure will be taken out of their hands if they are not able to agree at this stage.[573]

There is a wide consensus that the final-offer method is only suitable for 'numeric' disputes.[574] Thus, under the MLI, for example, an attempt is made to squeeze

568. In detail section 4.1.2.5.1.
569. *See* section 4.3.
570. So *Pauwelyn, supra* n. 562, 22 FTR 1 (2018), at pp. 57 f.; *L. Flávio Neto,* Baseball Arbitration: The Trendiest Alternative Dispute Resolution Mechanism in International Taxation, 2 Intl. Tax Stud. 8, 3 (2019) DOI: 10.59403/p7bpe2.
571. *See* OECD/IMF, *supra* n. 72, at p. 37 stating: *It should be noted that the mere existence of including an arbitration provision in the text of a tax treaty incentivises competent authorities to reach an agreement during the MAP phase.* Also seeing a main function for the establishment of a mandatory resolution phase in it being a deterrent *K. Kubik/L. Turcan,* Chapter 3: Austria, section 3.3.1. (M. Lang et al. eds, IBFD 2020); *P. Pistone,* Chapter 1: General Report, section 1.3. (M. Lang et al. eds, IBFD 2020); *K. Flüchter,* Ein Mindeststandard für Verständigungsverfahren, peer reviews und die Aussicht auf mehr Schiedsklauseln, 24 IStR 24, p. 947 (2015); *Diete, supra* n. 113, at p. 16; *H.J. Ault/J. Sasseville,* 2008 OECD Model: The New Arbitration Provision, 63 BIT 5, p. 215 (2009) DOI: 10.59403/py7khf; *M. van Herksen,* Chapter 3: International Developments, p. 41 (A. Bakker/M.M. Levey eds, IBFD 2011); *Ruiter, supra* n. 239, 48 ET 9 (2008), at p. 499 cites one of her predecessors saying '*we love arbitration but we never use it*'. Illustrative is also the case described by *A. Christians,* Take MAP with a Grain of Salt: Sifto and the Legal Nature of Competent Authority Agreements, 86 Tax Notes Int'l, p. 83 (2017). Differentiated, however, *Mooij, supra* n. 385, at p. 263.
572. *See also Park/Tillinghast, supra* n. 24, at pp. 9 f.
573. Analysing this effect for the special clause between Austria and Germany *M. Lang,* Der EuGH als Interpret von Doppelbesteuerungsabkommen, p. 380 (J. Lüdicke et al. eds, Haufe-Gruppe 2013) and for the WTO's dispute resolution mechanism *Strotkemper, supra* n. 18, at p. 621.
574. *Pauwelyn, supra* n. 562, 22 FTR 1 (2018), at pp. 64 ff.; *Strotkemper, supra* n. 18, at p. 385; *Grlica, supra* n. 559, at p. 321; *R. Walz,* Final-Offer-Arbitration – oder: Drittentscheidung anhand verbindlicher Angebote, 1 SchiedsVZ 3, p. 122 (2003). Stating that the final-offer method is not suitable to solve disputes on interpretative issues *E. Farah,* Mandatory Arbitration of International Tax Disputes: A Solution in Search of a Problem, 9 FTR 8, 748 (2009) DOI:

all kinds of disputes into numeric ones in order to make the final-offer method applicable to all disputes. Paragraph 242 of the MLI's Explanatory Statement therefore states:

> For each adjustment or similar issue in the case, the proposed resolution will include only the disposition of specific monetary amounts (for example, of income or expense) or the maximum rate of tax charged pursuant to the Covered Tax Agreement. In some cases, however, unresolved issues will include questions regarding whether the conditions for applying a provision of a Covered Tax Agreement have been met. Where the unresolved issues in a case include such a 'threshold question', such as whether a person is a resident of a Contracting Jurisdiction or whether an enterprise of one of the Contracting Jurisdictions has a permanent establishment in the other Contracting Jurisdiction, the competent authorities may submit their proposed answers to the threshold question (i.e. yes or no). If there are other unresolved issues the disposition of which is contingent on the answer reached with respect to the threshold question, it is expected that the competent authorities would also submit alternative proposed resolutions of those remaining issues.

I seriously doubt whether this approach is more efficient than using the independent opinion approach and allowing each state (and affected person) to provide one well-reasoned position paper that details their legal assessment and provides for a coherent and comprehensible solution proposal.[575] Thus, the panel would not run the risk of getting lost in the branches of a complex decision tree but could focus on weighing arguments up against each other.

Especially the approach taken by the MLI feeds the suspicion that efficiency considerations are not the main reason for the rise of the final-offer approach. On the contrary, this development seems to be driven by the states' concern about giving up sovereignty.[576] The fact that the role of taxpayers is very limited under all mechanisms that make use of the final-offer method also contributes to this impression. This development is most unfortunate because it deprives the dispute resolution mechanisms of the opportunity to make a real contribution to the interpretation and development of international tax law. In the context of a well-organised (and in the best case institutionalised) procedural structure, it is possible to achieve an efficient and rule-based mandatory resolution phase using the independent opinion method, which

10.5744/ftr.2009.1008; *Ault, supra* n. 140, 7 Florida Tax Review 3 (2005), at p. 149; *W.W. Park*, Income Tax Treaty Arbitration, 10 Geo. Mason L. Rev. 4, pp. 824 f. (2002); *Strotkemper, supra* n. 18, at p. 461.

575. *See also A. Mammen et al.*, Instrumente der Verständigung im internationalen Steuerrecht: *Bestandsaufnahme, Anwendungsfragen, Konfliktpotentiale und Reformbedarf*, 28 IStR 10, p. 375 (2019).

576. Also seeing sovereignty considerations as a main factor for states to choose the final-offer method *Strotkemper, supra* n. 18, at p. 394; *Grlica, supra* n. 559, at p. 320; *H.D. Rosenbloom*, Chapter 7 – Mandatory Arbitration of Disputes Pursuant to Tax Treaties: The Experience of the United States, p. 165 (M. Lang et al. eds, IBFD 2015); *M. Markham*, The Comparative Dimension Regarding Approaches to Decision-Making in International Tax Arbitration, pp. 131 f. (J.H. Farrar et al. eds, Springer 2019). *See also J. Gröper*, The Mutual Agreement Procedure in International Taxation: *The Need for Procedural and Administrative Rules*, p. 108 (utzverlag 2020).

benefits not only the cases in dispute but also the further development of international tax law as a whole.

Consequently, I strongly advocate the use of the independent opinion method in all cases. While the final-offer method might be (solely) suitable in transfer pricing issues and accounts for the fact that there often is no single right decision but a range of justifiable results, it would still be beneficial in many cases if the decisions were reasoned and rule-based.[577] I would only consider making use of the final-offer method as an option that requires the consent of all affected persons and CAs.

### 5.3.3.2 *The Procedural Rules*

#### 5.3.3.2.1 *Initiation*

The first question in shaping the procedural rules for the mandatory resolution phase is whether this phase should start automatically after an unsuccessful negotiation phase or whether it must be initiated by either a CA or the taxpayer. All of these options can be found among established mechanisms: an automatic start is provided for under the Arbitration Convention,[578] while the UN-MC only allows for CAs to initiate the procedure[579] and most other mechanisms leave it to taxpayers to initiate the mandatory resolution phase.[580] At least under the Arbitration Convention, the automatic start has not proven to be successful since it can be concluded from the statistics that there are many cases pending in which the deadline for the MAP has passed some time ago, but no arbitration phase has been started yet.[581]

Apart from this anecdotal evidence, I see benefits in an initiation requirement: it gives those who initiate the mandatory resolution phase the opportunity to provide the dispute resolution panel with a comprehensive statement and their main arguments. Following my proposal to also allow for agreements concluded by the CAs in the negotiation phase to be challenged in the mandatory resolution phase,[582] an initiation letter is also necessary to determine the scope of the mandatory resolution phase. Consequently, it is necessary to at least state that taxpayers are to initiate the mandatory resolution phase. Furthermore, the proposal of *Owens, Gildemeister* and *Turcan* also allows CAs to initiate the mandatory resolution phase.[583] This could be explained by the fact that their proposal is based on the UN-MC. However, I consider it beneficial to allow CAs to initiate the mandatory resolution phase as well since it has

577. Differentiated on the publication of decisions regarding transfer pricing disputes *Strotkemper, supra* n. 18, at p. 408.
578. *See* section 4.5.3.
579. *See* section 4.2.
580. *See* for the OECD-MC section 4.1.2.1 and for the DRD section 4.6.2.3.1.
581. *See* in detail section 4.5.6. *See also* the extensive criticism by *Strotkemper, supra* n. 18, at pp. 409 ff.
582. *See* section 5.3.1.
583. *Owens et al., supra* n. 460, 82 Tax Notes Int'l 10 (2016), at p. 1003.

the potential to advance the procedure. This should not limit the taxpayers' opportunity to determine the scope of the mandatory resolution phase or to provide a statement and arguments to the panel, though.

The DRD furthermore introduced a time limit for the initiation of the mandatory resolution phase: the initiation is possible within 50 days of the taxpayer receiving a notification of the MAP's failure.[584] I welcome this development because it both speeds up the procedure and creates legal certainty.

Consequently, I propose that the mandatory resolution phase can be initiated by taxpayers as well as by CAs within one month of either the administrative facility's notification that the negotiation phase is over (on this *see* section 5.2.1.3.) or the notification of an agreement being concluded. If the mandatory resolution phase is initiated by a CA, the taxpayers should still have the right to provide their own initiation letter and especially to decide whether they want to include matters already agreed upon by the CAs in the mandatory resolution. Therefore, they can submit their letter within one month of the reference points mentioned before or within two weeks after a CA's initiation letter.

The initiation letter can but does not necessarily need to contain extensive reasoning. It needs to contain the formal notice that the initiation of the mandatory resolution phase is requested and to list its scope. The reasoning can be provided with a second letter within two months after the reference dates.

If there has not been a final assessment in one state, the mandatory resolution phase can still be initiated but will be suspended immediately. All participants to the procedure are to be notified if the assessment is issued. The reasoning can be provided within two months of the notification.

##### *5.3.3.2.2 Panel Setup*

Under section 5.3.2, I proposed a further institutionalisation of the dispute resolution panels and suggested setting up panels of three members (including one chairperson) using a random algorithm that takes into account several quotas to address the panel member's potential bias. This algorithm should be set in motion after the administrative facility has received an initiation letter. Since this requires no special effort and the administrative facility already knows the details of all affected states and taxpayers, the initial setup should be possible within two weeks of the receipt of the initiation letter. The algorithm's result should then be communicated to the assigned panel members, who have the opportunity to decide within two weeks whether they accept the assignment or recuse themselves if they see a conflict of interest. If they recuse themselves, the algorithm is used again to find a replacement. Once the setup of the panel is completed, it is communicated to the CAs and the taxpayers. They have the opportunity to object to the appointment of a panel member if they see a reason to doubt the panel member's impartiality. Therefore, they should be allowed to file a reasoned objection within one month of being notified of the panel's setup (or at a later

584. *See* section 4.6.2.3.1.

date if the reason arises later). The panel is to decide upon an objection without the member whose impartiality is doubted within two weeks.[585]

#### 5.3.3.2.3 *Statements*

As already foreseen under the established mechanisms using the independent opinion approach,[586] there should first be a written exchange to give the panel a comprehensive insight into the facts of the case and the arguments in dispute.

The written exchange starts with the initiation letter of either a CA or a taxpayer and the reasons provided in either the same or a later letter. All other actors should be given the chance to respond to the initiation's reasons within one month of receiving the reasons.

#### 5.3.3.2.4 *Panel Meeting*

Other than under the established mechanisms where the CAs remain in charge of the procedure and determine if, where and when meetings of the panel take place, I propose to grant the panel autonomy to decide on these questions. Therefore, it is necessary for the panel to get together at an early stage to determine the general structure of the mandatory resolution phase. They should be free to agree on the form of their internal meetings – be it via videoconference, telephone calls or in-person meetings.

#### 5.3.3.2.5 *Hearing*

It is thus also up to the panel to schedule a hearing. They can decide whether to have the hearing immediately after all actors have had the chance to provide a written statement or whether to grant the actors further opportunities to exchange positions in writing if they deem it necessary and beneficial. In any case, the hearing should be scheduled within one month of the last written submission being received.

Date, form and (if applicable) place of the hearing should be agreed with all actors involved. I propose to have a videoconference as the default option since it is a very cost- and time-efficient way of meeting that still allows for all actors to get a personal impression of and to interact with each other. In-person meetings should take place if all participants agree.

It should be at the panel's discretion to determine whether they deem a further hearing necessary or consider the case ready for a decision.

---

585. This concept is inspired by German procedural law (cf. sections 42 ff. Civil Procedure Code [*Zivilprozessordnung – ZPO*] and sections 24 ff. Criminal Procedure Code [*Strafprozessordnung – StPO*]).

586. For the OECD-MC's optional procedure *see* section 4.1.2.5.2; under both the AC and the DRD it is provided that the panel shall be given all necessary information, *see* sections 4.5.3.2 and 4.6.2.3.3.

#### 5.3.3.2.6 *Panel Decision*

Within three months of the last hearing, the panel is to submit its decision. The decision is made by a simple majority. The decision has to consist of a verdict, a statement of facts and legal reasons. A dissenting panel member is to be given the chance to attach a separate opinion to the decision.[587] This should not discourage the search for a consensus, but it seems especially beneficial to allow for a differentiated analysis of the panel's considerations since this will hopefully spur academic debate on controversial issues.[588]

### 5.3.3.3 *Participation and Rights of Taxpayers*

As until now only provided under the Arbitration Convention,[589] I advocate a full and unlimited right for taxpayers to be heard.[590] I am convinced that not only it is beneficial and important to ensure their fundamental rights protection but also it serves the procedure because taxpayers can be extremely helpful in determining the facts of the case[591] and can contribute legal arguments to the decision-making process.

The taxpayers' right to be heard includes the opportunity to provide written and (in the hearing) oral statements, to be present at all hearings and to access the procedure's files. The latter can - as already in the negotiation phase - easily be implemented if the procedure makes further use of the online platform I suggested establishing in section 5.1.3.

One element common to most established mechanisms is that the implementation of the final decision depends on the taxpayers' consent.[592] This is often considered a counterbalance to their low degree of participation rights in the procedure.[593] Thus, it appears questionable whether the implementation of the decision should still depend on the taxpayers' consent if they are granted a higher degree of participation rights as proposed in this section. There is a strong argument for maintaining this procedural step: to avoid conflicting decisions, taxpayers usually need to waive the exercise of

587. This is practised as well, for example, under the WTO's dispute settlement mechanism (in detail *J. Flett,* Separate Opinion: Dispute Settlement System of the World Trade Organization (WTO), 2-13 (A. Peters/R. Wolfrum eds)), at the ICJ (Art. 57 of its Statute) and at the ECtHR (Art. 45(2) ECHR).
588. Providing a differentiated analysis of the functions of separate opinions at the ICJ *R. Hofmann,* Separate Opinion: International Court of Justice (ICJ), 46-50 (A. Peters/R. Wolfrum eds). *See also* in favour of reasoned awards and the option of dissenting opinions *Park/Tillinghast, supra* n. 24, at p. 40.
589. *See* section 4.5.3.3.
590. This is also proposed by the ICC in their Arbitration Proposal in Art. 25A(7). The proposal is attached to the OECD MEMAP as Annex 5. Differentiated *Camino, supra* n. 469, at p. 730.
591. Pointing this out as well *Strotkemper, supra* n. 18, at p. 403. Sceptical towards an unlimited right to be heard, however, and rather trusting in the arbitrator's decision on whether they need more information *Avery Jones, supra* n. 182, 47 Intertax 8/9 (2019), at p. 676.
592. *See* sections 4.1.1.2.6 (OECD-MC), 4.6.2.2 and 4.6.2.3.3 (DRD).
593. *See,* for example, *Strotkemper, supra* n. 18, at p. 432. Criticising this 'safety valve' as a threat for the finality of the arbitration process, however, *Snodgrass, supra* n. 155, 19 DFI 5 (2017), in section 4.1.

national remedies for a final decision to become valid. I am in favour of retaining this requirement and thus deem the taxpayers' right to decide whether to accept the final decision necessary because they are to consider whether to waive the procedural rights to which they are entitled under national law.

#### *5.3.3.4 Determining Questions of National and European Law*

The panel consists of members who have been appointed due to their knowledge and experience in international tax law.[594] International tax law, however, sometimes refers to the national law of the contracting states.[595] At this point, the panel members' expertise ends – especially if my suggestion to appoint panel members who are neither nationals nor residents of the states in dispute[596] is followed. This results in a stark asymmetry of expertise between the panel and the states' CAs (as well as the taxpayer). Their interpretation of national law should not be decisive, however. Additionally, it seems questionable to entrust an international body with the binding interpretation of national law.[597]

Consequently, there needs to be a mechanism that ensures the correct and impartial interpretation of a state's national law. The most promising approach[598] seems to be the involvement of the highest national courts for matters of tax law. They could provide an advisory opinion on decisive questions of national law that are referred to them by the panel. Alternatively, one could consider involving independent national tax experts, such as academics.

While courts have greater authority, it is also more difficult to bind them to strict deadlines by threatening and enforcing consequences. Therefore, I suggest setting the referral to national courts as the standard procedure and stating a time frame of six months for their response. As an alternative to the referral to national courts from the beginning as well as after the time frame has elapsed without a national court's response, national tax experts might be mandated as expert witnesses. The decision on

594. On this *see* section 5.3.2.
595. *See* section 2.2.
596. In section 5.3.2.
597. On this *Strotkemper, supra* n. 18, at p. 460. *See also* the considerations of *Park/Tillinghast, supra* n. 24, at pp. 46 f.
598. *Mössner, Züger* and *Strotkemper* suggest the implementation of a preliminary ruling procedure – comparable to the one established under Art. 267 TFEU – for matters of international tax law that may be used out of national court procedures, *see Mössner, supra* n. 79, 29 RIW 5 (1983), at pp. 363 f.; *Züger, supra* n. 214, at pp. 147 ff.; *Strotkemper, supra* n. 18, at pp. 660 ff. A similar proposal is that made by *van Raad*, to establish international panels of tax treaty experts that issue opinions when asked by courts and CAs, *see van Raad, supra* n. 17, at pp. 225 ff. I, however, prefer to have an international procedure as a standard for three reasons: (1) developing an international procedure with strict deadlines could lead to a much more efficient procedure compared to often lengthy national court procedures; (2) the international procedure should focus on an autonomous interpretation of tax treaties – while national courts might often seek to return to their national law (on this *see also* n. 534) – and (3) lead to a binding decision for all states involved.

Additionally, *Strotkemper, supra* n. 18, at pp. 727 f. suggests to support international panels with ad hoc members of the disputing states.

whether to involve national tax experts instead of national courts should be subject to the parties' consent. In particular, the representatives of the state whose law is to be interpreted should be able to decide whether a non-state actor is allowed to determine the panel's interpretation of national law. Possible panel members from the jurisdictions in dispute should also be able to serve as national experts, especially those who are eligible to serve as chairpersons because they deserve a higher level of trust in their independence.

Finally, it is to address how questions of European Union law should be dealt with.[599] In *Achmea*, the CJEU has stated that final decisions of arbitral tribunals that are not part of the EU's judicial system on matters of EU law are not compatible with the autonomy of EU law.[600] Thus, it is necessary for the mandatory dispute resolution mechanism to be in line with the autonomy of European Union law to allow for an involvement of the CJEU to respect its prerogative to ultimately interpret EU law.[601] A reference to the panel itself under Article 267 TFEU does not seem possible because it most likely will not be regarded as a 'court or tribunal *of a Member State*' by the CJEU if non-EU Member States are signatories to the convention as well.[602] Consequently, the reference mechanism needs to be two-fold: first, the panel needs to refer the question to a Member State's court, which thereafter can refer it to the CJEU under Article 267 TFEU. The reference court may also, recurring to the doctrines of *acte clair* or *acte éclairé*,[603] decide not to refer a question to the CJEU but to answer it itself. The panel may decide which participant's reference court shall be made use of – not only with regard to the relationship of the question in dispute to the national law of one of the states but also with regard to the prospect of a swift and cooperative reaction.

#### 5.3.3.5 Publicity of Hearings and Publication of Decisions

Currently, hearings generally take place *in camera* – mostly even to the exclusion of taxpayers. The publication of decisions is only an option under independent opinion mechanisms and depends on the consent of the involved states and taxpayers.[604] Furthermore, under the DRD, the panel's decision is never published and not even disclosed to taxpayers – indeed, it is only the *final decision* by the CAs that is subject to publication and in every case needs to be published in an abstract form.[605] Outside the area of international tax law, the publication of redacted arbitration awards is the rule rather than the exception: the International Council for Commercial Arbitration (ICCA), for example, publishes yearbooks with arbitral awards from the United

599. On possible intersections of treaty and European law *see* already section 4.6.4.1.1.1.
600. CJEU, *Slovak Republic v. Achmea BV* (C-248/16, *supra* n. 307), m.no. 60.
601. *See also Monsenego, supra* n. 310, 47 Intertax 8/9 (2019), at p. 731.
602. For the panels under the DRD, however, *see* section 4.6.3.
603. On these doctrines *see M. Broberg*, Preliminary Ruling: European Court of Justice (ECJ), 68-69 (A. Peters/R. Wolfrum eds).
604. *See* sections 4.1.2.7 (OECD-MC), 4.5.3.4 (AC) and 4.6.2.4 (DRD). Very critical also *M.J. McIntyre*, Comments on the OECD Proposal for Secret and Mandatory Arbitration of International Tax Disputes pp. 8 ff., Wayne State University Law School Research Paper.
605. *See* sections 4.6.2.4 and 4.6.4.1.1.2.3.

Nations Commission on International Trade Law (UNCITRAL), the International Centre for Settlement of Investment Disputes (ICSID),[606] the International Chamber of Commerce (ICC),[607] the North American Free Trade Agreement (NAFTA), the Permanent Court of Arbitration,[608] the World Intellectual Property Organization (WIPO) and national arbitration bodies.[609] The WTO also publishes decisions of both the Dispute Settlement Body and the Appellate Body.[610]

#### *5.3.3.5.1 Publicity of Hearings*

While hearings of international courts and tribunals are open to the public in principle,[611] the lack of publicity used to be a general feature of ad hoc arbitration.[612] It stems from the historical roots of arbitration as a private dispute resolution mechanism in which the panel derives its authority from the disputing parties who are in control of the process.[613] In international tax disputes, the non-public nature of the procedure is usually justified by the taxpayers' interest in the protection of tax secrecy.[614]

Investor-state arbitration systems, however, are not (or rather no longer) as strictly opaque as the established tax treaty arbitration mechanisms:[615] Rule 32(2) of the ICSID Rules – that, pursuant to Article 44 of the ICSID Convention, apply to disputes that are referred to the ICSID – states:

> Unless either party objects, the Tribunal, after consultation with the Secretary-General, may allow other persons, besides the parties, their agents, counsel and advocates, witnesses and experts during their testimony, and officers of the

606. On this also *H. Kahlert*, Vertraulichkeit im Schiedsverfahren, p. 363 (Mohr Siebeck 2015). Cases are also published on ICSID's webpage at https://icsid.worldbank.org/cases/case-database (accessed 15 Jan. 2024).
607. Case information is also published at https://iccwbo.org/dispute-resolution/dispute-resolution-services/arbitration/arbitrators/ (accessed 15 Jan. 2024).
608. *See also* the court's webpage at https://pca-cpa.org/en/cases/ (accessed 15 Jan. 2024).
609. As pointed out by *J.F. Avery Jones*, Chapter 15: Arbitration and Publication of Decisions, section 15.4.2. (M. Lang et al. eds, IBFD 2015).
610. *See* https://www.wto.org/english/tratop_e/dispu_e/dispu_status_e.htm (accessed 15 Jan. 2024).
611. To varying degrees: at the ICJ and the ITLOS, the hearings are generally public unless the court decides otherwise or the parties (who need to agree on this – *see T. Neumann/B. Simma*, Transparency in International Adjudication, p. 449 (A. Bianchi/A. Peters eds, Cambridge University Press 2013)) demand so. The procedural rules of international criminal and human rights courts leave less room for the parties to decide upon the publicity of the hearings (in detail *Neumann/Simma, supra* n. 611, at pp. 449 ff.). In contrast, hearings of the WTO's panels and the Appellate Body are generally not public but can be opened on request of the parties (for details and restrictions *see P. Delimatsis*, Institutional Transparency in the WTO, pp. 131 ff. (A. Bianchi/A. Peters eds, Cambridge University Press 2013)).
612. For commercial arbitration *see N. Eslami*, Die Nichtöffentlichkeit des Schiedsverfahrens, p. 201 (Mohr Siebeck 2016).
613. *S. Heppner*, Procedural Transparency in Investor-State Arbitration (Dissertation, Trinity College Dublin, 2019), p. 1.
614. *See*, for example, regarding her own proposal *Strotkemper, supra* n. 18, at p. 942.
615. On the recent history in this regard *see K. Hober*, Investment Treaty Arbitration: A Brief Overview, 42 Intertax 3, pp. 192 f. (2014) DOI: 10.54648/taxi2014022.

> Tribunal, to attend or observe all or part of the hearings, subject to appropriate logistical arrangements. The Tribunal shall for such cases establish procedures for the protection of proprietary or privileged information.

Consequently, it is generally at the panels' discretion to decide whether to allow the public to attend or observe hearings, but the parties have an unconditional right to object.[616]

The UNCITRAL system goes one step further and states as a general rule that hearings *shall be public* in Article 6(1) of the UNCITRAL Rules on Transparency. This general rule can be limited with regard to concerns of confidentiality, as indicated in Article 6(2) and detailed in Article 7(7) of the UNCITRAL Rules on Transparency. However, these rules have only been in place since 1 April 2014 and are not (yet) applied widely.[617] To achieve the application of these transparency rules for treaties concluded before 1 April 2014 and even for cases that are not initiated under the UNCITRAL Arbitration Rules, the United Nations Convention on Transparency in Treaty-Based Investor-State Arbitration (Mauritius Convention) is an accompanying measure.[618]

These more recent developments account for the public interest involved in investor-state arbitration[619] as well as for the fact that open justice is a general principle of law,[620] recognised by nations around the world.

Public interests are involved in tax treaty disputes, too: as already highlighted in section 3.3., the public has an eminent interest in the uniform application of tax laws. To make sure and to witness the fact that the mandatory resolution phase is a procedure that really is about the application of the law and not about horse deals between the CAs and the affected person, publicity is necessary. Until now, this public interest has been completely disregarded. Moving away from the status quo, I propose to search for a solution that balances the public interests and the confidentiality concerns of states and taxpayers.

As a baseline, I suggest – as is the case with procedural rules of international courts and the UNCITRAL Rules on Transparency – that all hearings be public in principle. Exceptions should only be made by the panel after a reasoned application of states or taxpayers if they raise specific confidentiality concerns. This includes the concern that the publication of specific information would violate tax, trade, business, industrial or professional secrets or would be contrary to public policy as well as the private interests of witnesses or other persons involved in the procedure. The panel should then balance the importance of the reason raised against the public's interest. The discussion on whether to close the hearing to the public should take place in a

616. *See also Heppner, supra* n. 613, pp. 23-24.
617. As – among other restrictions – detailed by *Heppner, supra* n. 613, pp. 27-33.
618. The Mauritius Convention's signatories and the status of ratification are accessible at https://treaties.un.org/Pages/ViewDetails.aspx?src=IND&mtdsg_no=XXII-3&chapter=22&clang=_en (accessed 15 Jan. 2024).
619. As stated in the preambular clauses of the Resolution adopted by the UN's General Assembly on 16 Dec. 2013 on the report of the Sixth Committee (A/68/462).
620. As impressively shown by *Heppner, supra* n. 613, pp. 81-95.

non-public setting; the decision as to whether the hearing is closed to the public should be pronounced publicly, however.

Technically, the public should be able to follow the hearings via a livestream on the administrative facility's platform.[621] This option is not only logical because hearings are by default taking place in the form of a videoconference.[622] It should also be granted for hearings in the form of in-person meetings because: (1) this avoids logistical constraints like the size of meeting rooms[623] and (2) allows, accounting for the international character of the procedure, persons from around the world to follow the procedure.[624] For private hearings or private parts of hearings, it seems questionable how to handle public access. One option would be to offer a delayed stream that allows for 'on-the-fly redactions'.[625] This is practised, for example, by the ICSID.[626] I am sceptical, though, as to who is then to decide what to redact. Thus, I propose streaming all public parts live and offering a recording of the entire hearing later on, which avoids mention of confidential information to the degree the panel deems it necessary. A remaining question is for how long recordings of hearings should be available to the public. I am in favour of granting unlimited access because these recordings provide valuable insights and can be very helpful both in informing the general public and in allowing for the professional public to assess arguments in context. Again, the ICSID provides a good example of how this practice can enhance the understanding of a case.[627] However, I do not consider this question to be crucial enough to deserve a mention in the convention itself – it rather is an administrative issue that should be discussed and decided upon by the assembly of representatives.

Finally, the question of whether or not to allow for publicity is one concerning the very nature of the mandatory resolution stage since *publicity is the authentic hall-mark of judicial as distinct from administrative procedure*:[628] thus, also in this context, it is relevant whether the mandatory resolution stage is a mere extension of the mutual agreement procedure or a self-standing and rule-based remedy.

#### *5.3.3.5.2 Publication of Decisions*

I would attribute the hesitant attitude regarding the publication of decisions to two causes: (1) the fear of precedents and (2) the (supposed) protection of secrets. Of these

621. Instructive on the range of options *A. Paschke*, Digitale Gerichtsöffentlichkeit, pp. 261 ff. (Duncker & Humblot 2018).
622. As suggested in section 5.3.3.2.5.
623. Such constraints are a reason to limit public access under Art. 6(3) second sentence of the UNCITRAL Rules on Transparency.
624. This benefit is also highlighted and detailed by *Neumann/Simma, supra* n. 611, at p. 453.
625. As described by *Neumann/Simma, supra* n. 611, at p. 454.
626. The case of *Vattenfall v. Germany*, for example, was streamed with a four-hour delay.
627. The ICSID provides recordings on its YouTube channel (https://www.youtube.com/channel/UCaH9aUQlhYs-XrUX-TocSHg, accessed 15 Jan. 2024). For example, the hearings of the case *Vattenfall v. Germany* can be accessed at https://www.youtube.com/watch?v=-WC31lMGqwU&list=PLTPAfLBOjfQLKBlDfhmY_nWsThNBpaa2w (accessed 15 Jan. 2024) and allow for very valuable insights.
628. Privy Council, Judgment of 16 Dec. 1935, *McPherson v. McPherson*, Appeal Cases, p. 200.

two, the fear of precedents is predominant: most mechanisms explicitly state that there shall be no precedent.[629]

The fear of precedents does not seem well founded: there is no formal (binding) precedent of arbitration decisions because there is no doctrine of stare decisis in international (tax) law,[630] and there is no written rule establishing a formal precedent.[631] Furthermore, in nearly all established mechanisms,[632] there are ad hoc arbitration panels. Thus, it is not very likely that precedent in the form of *jurisprudence constante* will be employed.[633] Under the established mechanisms, it might consequently rather be resorted to *persuasive precedent*. This, however, does not appear to be problematic: it is hard to argue that an arbitration panel should not be able to rely on the arguments of a well-reasoned decision of another panel in the same way that it can rely on commentaries, journal articles or the decisions of national courts.[634]

Under the institutionalised mechanism I propose in this chapter, there might additionally be panels' search for consistency, which would create a form of *jurisprudence constante* – a development I would consider positive for the development of a body of international tax law. This would most likely not be a uniform jurisprudence of one fixed panel since it is not too likely that panels will often act in the same composition as they will be set up randomly from case to case. One can assume, however, that panels will study the relevant decisions of previous panels very thoroughly and consider whether they agree with them. To clarify that they are always free in their decision and not bound by any doctrine of precedent, I suggest a provision in the instrument establishing the mechanism.[635]

---

629. *See* sections 4.1.2.7, 4.1.2.5.1 and 4.1.2.5.2 (OECD-MC) as well as 4.6.2.4 (DRD).
630. *G. Acquaviva/F. Pocar,* Stare decisis, 2 (A. Peters/R. Wolfrum eds); *G. Guillaume,* The Use of Precedent by International Judges and Arbitrators, 2 JIDS 1, p. 7 (2011) DOI: 10.1093/jnlids/idq025; *S.W. Schill,* The Multilateralization of International Investment Law, p. 282 (Cambridge University Press 2009); Court of Appeal, Judgment of 13 Jan. 1977, *Trendtex Trading Corporation v. Central Bank of Nigeria,* Law Reports, Queen's Bench Division, p. 554 (per Lord Denning M.R. and Shaw L.J.). Illustrative regarding International Investment Law *F. Grisel,* The Sources of Foreign Investment Law, pp. 223 ff. (Z. Douglas et al. eds, Oxford University Press 2014) who, however, at p. 330 describes 'the creation of *de facto stare decisis*'. *Heppner, supra* n. 613, p. 220 takes this thought one step further and analyses the existence of a 'flexible doctrine of *stare decisis* in the investment treaty arbitration system'.
631. In general on the concept of judicial precedent *M. Gammie,* Judicial Precedent in the English Legal System, 73 BIT 8, pp. 417 f. (2019) DOI: 10.59403/2rb75zd and on 'arbitral precedent' *G. Kaufmann-Kohler,* Arbitral Precedent: Dream, Necessity or Excuse? *The 2006 Freshfields Lecture,* 23 Arb. Int'l 3, pp. 357 ff. (2007) DOI: 10.1093/arbitration/23.3.357; on the role of precedent in the US tax judiciary *L.P. Marvel,* Tax Litigation in the Federal Courts of the United States: The Role of Precedent in a Changing Legal Environment, 73 BIT 8, pp. 432 ff. (2019) DOI: 10.59403/jhxt4x.
632. For exceptions, *see* sections 4.4.2 and 4.4.3.
633. *Guillaume, supra* n. 630, 2 JIDS 1 (2011), at pp. 14 ff.; *Strotkemper, supra* n. 18, at p. 377.
634. *See also Avery Jones, supra* n. 609, at p. 374; *Mooij, supra* n. 385, at p. 284.
635. This – hopefully – would also prevent situations like the one of the WTO's Appellate Body: the US, under both the Obama and the Trump administration, provoked the dysfunctionality of this body by boycotting the nomination of new panel members, *inter alia,* because it did not agree with what it perceived as the application of a stare decisis doctrine in the relation of the Appellate Body and the lower panel. *See* on this and the legal background *Z. Flowers,* The Role of Precedent and Stare Decisis in the World Trade Organization's Dispute Settlement Body, 47 Int. J. of Legal Inf. 2, p. 91 (2019) DOI: 10.1017/jli.2019.21; *A. Scully-Hill/H. Mahncke,* The

To address the confidentiality concerns of taxpayers, I suggest anonymising the decision.[636] As pointed out by *Avery Jones*, this might not be sufficient in cases that, for example, mention trade secrets in their facts.[637] Thus, the redacted decision should be made accessible to taxpayers before publication, allowing them to object to the publication of individual items of information by invoking trade, business, industrial or professional secrets or public order – as is the practice under the DRD[638] – within one month. If they object, the panel shall decide on whether to further redact the decision. In general, the entire decision (verdict, facts and reasons) shall be published. In order not to create a conflict with the rule in Article 26 OECD/UN-MC, I suggest stating in the convention establishing the mechanism that the panel's decisions shall be deemed *judicial decisions* in the meaning of Article 26(2) third sentence OECD/UN-MC.[639]

The publication of decisions is not only beneficial in promoting consistency or advertising the use of dispute resolution mechanisms[640] but will also serve as an important impulse for academic debate and thus help to advance the body of international tax law in many more respects beyond the legal argument of the panel in the individual case.[641] Additionally, cases that point out regulatory deficiencies are important stimuli for legislative action (or, in the case of treaties, treaty [re-] negotiations) and can also in this regard further the development of international tax law.

#### *5.3.3.5.3 Amicus Curiae Briefs*

An amicus curiae is *someone who is not a party to a lawsuit but who petitions the court or is requested by the court to file a brief in the action because that person has a strong interest in the subject matter.*[642] Amicus curiae briefs are thus statements issued by actors who are not directly involved in the dispute. The range of possible actors is wide: it spans academics and NGOs, other states, business associations and corporations.[643] The institution of amicus curiae briefs is widespread among international courts and tribunals[644] as well as in investor-state arbitration[645].[646] Benefits to the institution are

---

Emergence of the Doctrine of Stare Decisis in the World Trade Organization Dispute Settlement System, 36 Legal Issues of Economic Integration 2, p. 134 (2009) DOI: 10.54648/leie2009010; *F. David*, The Role of Precedent in the WTO – New Horizons?, Maastricht Faculty of Law Working Paper, https://papers.ssrn.com/sol3/papers.cfm?abstract_id=1666169 (accessed 15 Jan. 2024).

636. This is also suggested by *Mooij, supra* n. 385, at pp. 284 f.; *Camino, supra* n. 469, at p. 731; *Park/Tillinghast, supra* n. 24, at p. 41.
637. *Avery Jones, supra* n. 609, in section 15.3.1.
638. *See* section 4.6.2.4.
639. On this *see also Ring, supra* n. 555, in section 2.2.4.; *Seer, supra* n. 555, at Art. 26 m.no. 42; *M. Engelschalk*, Art. 26 OECD-MA m.no. 85 (K. Vogel/M. Lehner eds, C.H. Beck 2015).
640. As pointed out by *Avery Jones, supra* n. 609, in section 15.1.
641. *See also Strotkemper, supra* n. 18, at 407, 462-464; *van Raad, supra* n. 17, at pp. 228 f.
642. As defined in *Garner, supra* n. 120, at the term 'amicus curiae'.
643. *P.J. Sands/R. Mackenzie*, International Courts and Tribunals, Amicus Curiae, para. 5 (A. Peters/R. Wolfrum eds).
644. At the ICJ, they have a basis in Art. 34(2) of the Statute in combination with Art. 69 of the ICJ Rules; the ICJ's practice is restrictive, however, as described by *A. Wiik*, Amicus Curiae before

that it can extend the deciding body's access to relevant information and bring new arguments to the table,[647] that it grants the opportunity to voice matters of public interest that might otherwise not have been considered[648] and that it can contribute to a higher degree of transparency.[649] These benefits come with the price that the procedural structure needs to fit the institution in what might cause a delay in the procedure – especially if the participants as well as the deciding body are given the chance to consider the briefs and to react to them, particularly if they disagree.[650] Additionally, the danger exists that one participant to the dispute might gain an unfair advantage because seemingly objective arguments are presented by an amicus with the (hidden) agenda to support the party.

With respect to the clear benefits – especially the chance that the panel's view is widened beyond the participating actors' interests – I am in favour of allowing for amicus curiae briefs with a provision that keeps possible procedural delays within narrow limits, gives participants the chance to consider and to comment on the briefs and seeks for transparency regarding the *amici's* agenda.[651]

The provisions in paragraphs 43 through 46 of Annex 29-A to the Comprehensive Economic and Trade Agreement (CETA) between Canada and the European Union form a good starting point:

> 44. Unless the Parties agree otherwise within five days of the date of the establishment of the arbitration panel, the arbitration panel may receive

---

International Courts and Tribunals, pp. 180 ff. (Nomos Verlagsgesellschaft mbH & Co. KG 2016). For the ITLOS, the wording of Art. 84 of the ITLOS Rules is largely congruent with the ICJ's provisions – for differences and on the application *see Wiik, supra* n. 644, at pp. 191 ff. Under the WTO's dispute settlement mechanism, (also unsolicited) amicus curiae briefs are considered by both the panels and the Appellate Body. For the panels, this is practised since the Appellate Body's decision in *US-Shrimp* of 6 Nov. 1998 – WT/DS58/AB/R, para. 99-110 (accessible at https://docs.wto.org/dol2fe/Pages/SS/directdoc.aspx?filename=Q:/WT/DS/58ABR.pdf, accessed 15 Jan. 2024) that was based on Art. 13 DSU; in detail *Wiik, supra* n. 644, at pp. 200 ff. For itself, the Appellate Body found in the decision on *US-Lead and Bismuth II* of 7 Jun. 2000 – WT/DS138/AB/R, para. 39 (accessible at https://docs.wto.org/dol2fe/Pages/SS/directdoc.aspx?filename=Q:/WT/DS/138ABR.pdf, accessed 15 Jan. 2024) that there was no rule allowing or prohibiting the acceptance of unsolicited amicus curiae briefs and thus stated that it could accept briefs because of its power to adopt procedural rules that are not in conflict with other rules; in detail *S. Charnovitz*, Transparency and Participation in the World Trade Organization, 56 Rutgers Law Review 4, p. 940 (2004); *Wiik, supra* n. 644, at pp. 207 ff.

645. Rule 37(2) of the ICSID Arbitration Rules allows in a detailed provision for unsolicited amicus curiae briefs to be accepted, subject to the tribunal's discretion after consulting the parties. Even more detailed – especially with regard to the information the *amici* need to disclose – is the rule laid out in Art. 4 of the UNCITRAL Rules on Transparency. Additionally, some investment treaties include provisions on whether or not amicus curiae briefs might be accepted, *see Wiik, supra* n. 644, at pp. 211 ff.
646. The option of amicus curiae briefs is also considered and supported by *van Raad, supra* n. 17, at p. 228, while *Strotkemper, supra* n. 18, at pp. 912 f. does not favour their use in her proposal because she fears a *politicisation* of the procedure.
647. *Wiik, supra* n. 644, at p. 45.
648. *Wiik, supra* n. 644, at pp. 50 f.
649. *Wiik, supra* n. 644, at p. 64.
650. *Wiik, supra* n. 644, at p. 65.
651. Generally also in favour of allowing for amicus curiae briefs by other states in international tax disputes *Strotkemper, supra* n. 18, at pp. 771 f.

unsolicited written submissions, provided that they are made within 10 days of the date of the establishment of the arbitration panel, and in no case longer than 15 typed pages, including any annexes, and that they are directly relevant to the issue under consideration by the arbitration panel.

45. The submission shall contain a description of the person making the submission, whether natural or legal, including the nature of that person's activities and the source of that person's financing, and specify the nature of the interest that that person has in the arbitration proceeding. It shall be drafted in the languages chosen by the Parties in accordance with paragraphs 48 and 49.
46. The arbitration panel shall list in its ruling all the submissions it has received that conform to these Rules. The arbitration panel shall not be obliged to address in its ruling the arguments made in such submissions. The arbitration panel shall submit to the Parties for their comments any submission it obtains.

These provisions contain strict time limits as well as a maximum page number for submissions, disclosure obligations for amici curiae and the obligation that the parties need to be able to comment on submissions. Other than under the CETA provisions, I would not allow for parties to decide on whether or not to accept amicus curiae briefs. This is rather reminiscent of the ad hoc arbitration character and the parties' discretion on how to design the procedural rules in a degree that I intend to avoid in an institutionalised mandatory resolution phase.

The remaining question is how possible amici curiae know what they can comment on. Under the CETA arbitration rules, the parties' submissions are publicly available (paragraph 38 of Annex 29-A, if relevant in a redacted version that does not disclose confidential information pursuant to paragraph 39).

This degree of transparency might pose too high an administrative burden in international tax disputes if the submissions need to be redacted in order not to disclose confidential information. This is, as detailed in the previous section, a complex coordination process in which I would prefer the panel to have the last say. As a compromise, I suggest requiring that the participant who initiates the procedure phrases the issues in dispute in an abstract form. Based on this wording (that might be amended by the panel), the administrative facility shall publish an abstract description of the case and the relevant questions on its webpage. Possible amici curiae are then free to upload submissions on the webpage within one month of the publication of the case description. These submissions shall be made publicly available if they meet the formal requirements (especially regarding disclosure obligations). This way, all participants to the procedure can comment on amicus curiae briefs in the hearing, and a high degree of transparency is granted that also allows for the public and the press to assess the arguments as well as possible affiliations of the *amici*.

#### *5.3.3.6 Costs*

For the mechanism to be attractive, it is crucial that it is cost-efficient and affordable for all participating states and taxpayers. Costs should not deter them from making use of it.[652] A cautionary example in this regard is provided by investor-state arbitration mechanisms, which are known to cause enormous costs for the participants.[653]

There are three main sources of costs in disputes under the mechanism I suggest:

(1) the participants' own costs, especially if they pay advisors to assist them;
(2) the remuneration and reimbursement of panel members; and
(3) general administrative costs, e.g., for the administrative facility's infrastructure and staff.

Additionally, costs might occur from hearing witnesses or determining matters of national law with the assistance of national courts or experts.

The established rules usually address the first two points in the way that every participant bears their own costs as well as costs that are attributable to them, while the costs for arbitrators (or the chairperson) are shared equally among states.[654] This resembles the so-called *American Approach* to the distribution of costs.[655] Under the DRD, it is also possible to encumber affected persons with procedural costs if they withdraw their complaint or if it was rejected.[656]

The remuneration of panel members is coined by the practice under the Arbitration Convention: its Code of Conduct in paragraph 7.3. lit. f suggests a remuneration of EUR 1,000 per panel member per meeting day with a 10% surcharge for the chairperson. The DRD continues with a remuneration of EUR 1,000 per meeting day without the 10% surcharge for chairpersons in Article 12(1) lit. b. The OECD Sample Mutual Agreement does not state an explicit rule regarding the remuneration but only mentions in its commentary that CAs have in practice relied on either the regulation under the Arbitration Convention's code of conduct or the ICSID schedule of fees.[657] The ICSID schedule of fees is considerably more generous than the European regulations, as it states:

> In addition to receiving reimbursement for any direct expenses reasonably incurred, conciliators, arbitrators, commissioners and ad hoc Committee members are entitled to receive a fee of USD 3,000 per day of meetings or other work performed in connection with the proceedings, as well as subsistence allowances and reimbursement of travel expenses [...].[658]

652. Especially on costs as a deterrent for developing countries *see M. Lennard*, Transfer Pricing Arbitration as an Option for Developing Countries, 42 Intertax 3, p. 181 (2014) DOI: 10.54648/taxi2014021.
653. This, admittedly, mainly results from the parties' costs for representation, which usually amount to several million USD for each party. However, tribunal costs in average exceed USD 800,000 what also is a dimension that can act as a deterrent. For figures *see* http://arbitrationblog.kluwerarbitration.com/2016/02/29/how-much-does-an-icsid-arbitration-cost-a-snapshot-of-the-last-five-years/ (accessed 15 Jan. 2024).
654. *See* sections 4.1.2.8. (OECD-MC) and 4.5.3.5 (AC).
655. In contrast to the *English Approach* under which *the costs follow the event*, as explained by *K. Duggal/G. Niehoff*, The Conflicting Landscape Relating to Costs in Investor-State Arbitration, 5 Indian J. Arb. L. 2, p. 169 (2017).
656. *See* section 4.6.2.5.
657. OECD, *supra* n. 37, at Commentary on Art. 25, para. 39 to the Sample Mutual Agreement.
658. *See* https://icsid.worldbank.org/services/content/schedule-fees (accessed 15 Jan. 2024).

This generous rule in practice often is, when applied to tax disputes, confined by limiting the number of compensable days and travel expenses.[659]

For the compensation of the panel members under the mechanism I propose, I suggest following the European approach and thus remunerating the panel members with USD 1,000 and the chairperson with USD 1,100 per actual meeting or hearing day, which at the same time also compensates them for their preparation. Additionally, *inter alia*, to avoid wrong incentives, I suggest capping the remuneration – for example, at a total amount of USD 10,000 per panel member (and USD 11,000 for the chairperson). Travel expenses in most scenarios should not occur if the videoconferencing option is used. For in-person meetings, the travel costs should be limited to economy class.

A higher remuneration is not necessary from my perspective because: (1) panel members should not be incentivised to draw out the procedure, (2) panel members only are acting part-time and as such do not depend on the compensation for their living expenses, and (3) being able to take part in developing international tax law further includes an 'intangible value'. To support the last argument, one might have a look at other activities in the search to take part in the development of international tax law such as speaking at conferences or publishing articles in international tax journals. These activities are rarely, if at all, compensated with enormous amounts of money. Apart from some (e.g., advisors) who might indirectly benefit financially from these activities, many take part in the debates without financial incentives.

While the compensation of panel members can easily be attributed to a case and thus be charged to the participants, it is questionable how the general administrative costs of the institution should be financed. Whereas a part might be covered by charging advance payments when a case is initiated, the institution needs secure funding to build and maintain the necessary (especially digital) infrastructure and to employ sufficient staff. Thus, I suggest that the institution be granted its own budget, funded by the participating states.[660] The financial contributions of the states should be based on their ability to pay as well as on the likelihood that they will make use of the mechanism. As an indicator, I suggest using the states' volume of foreign trade. The volume of foreign trade should correlate with the cross-border economic activity of taxpayers that – in combination with a strong tax treaty network – is likely to cause tax disputes.

The current reason for not charging taxpayers for the arbitration procedure is well explained in the OECD's commentary on their sample mutual agreement:

> Since the arbitration process is an extension of the mutual agreement procedure that is intended to deal with cases that cannot be solved under that procedure, it would seem inappropriate to ask the person who makes the request to pay in order

659. The Arbitration Board Operating Guidelines for the treaty between Canada and the United States, for example, in para. 10 limit the travel expenses to economy class costs and the compensation to three days of preparation, two meeting days and travel days (https://www.irs.gov/pub/irs-utl/2010_-_arbitration_-_board_operating_guidelines_nov_8-10_final.pdf, accessed 15 Jan. 2024). The fee is thus capped at USD 15,000 for meetings and preparation plus travel days.
660. For comparable considerations concerning her own proposal *see Strotkemper, supra* n. 18, at pp. 789 f.

> to make such request or to reimburse the expenses incurred by the competent authorities in the course of the arbitration proceedings. Unlike taxpayers' requests for rulings or other types of advance agreements, where a charge is sometimes made, providing a solution to disputes between the Contracting States is the responsibility of these States for which they in general should bear the costs.[661]

Consequently, one must ask whether these considerations still hold true under the mechanism I suggest, in which the mandatory resolution phase is more than just *an extension of the mutual agreement procedure* and where taxpayers have the opportunity to challenge MAP agreements. A viable way of addressing this shift is a differentiation: if the affected persons only ask for matters not yet agreed upon to be resolved, they should not be obliged to bear procedural costs beyond those of their own legal advice and representation. If they challenge MAP agreements between states, however, they should be obliged to pay a share of the procedural costs. For this, there are several options: one is to continue with the approach of distributing costs between states and treating affected persons like another party that has to pay an equal share of the costs, irrespective of the procedural outcome. It would be preferable, however, to take the procedural outcome into account because this would set beneficial incentives for affected persons as well as for states. If affected persons were to pay the (and only the) procedural costs that are attributable to the panel confirming an agreement concluded between states before, this would on the one hand incentivise states to conclude agreements at all and in a manner that is likely to be held to be in line with treaty provisions. On the other hand, it would discourage affected persons from challenging agreements out of mere protest but to only challenge agreements that they are convinced are not in line with treaty provisions. Furthermore, I support the DRD's approach to grant the panel the opportunity to encumber affected persons with procedural costs if they withdraw their complaint.

Because mediation can only be made use of if all participants agree and takes place in the negotiation phase, the mediator's fees shall be borne in equal share by the participating states.

### 5.3.4 Implementation of the Decision

Under most established mechanisms, arbitration decisions are to be implemented via mutual agreements: Article 25(5) third sentence OECD-MC/Alt. B UN-MC states this with the addition that the decision shall be binding if the taxpayer accepts the mutual agreement. The decisions of panels under both the AC and the DRD are also to be implemented via mutual agreements if the CAs do not agree on another solution in the respective time frame (Article 12(1)(2) AC, Article 15(2) second sentence DRD). This approach requires the CAs to actively implement the decision.

Another approach is taken by Article 25(9) lit. k of the US Model: thus, the decision itself *shall constitute a resolution by mutual agreement*. This approach has the

661. OECD, *supra* n. 37, at Commentary on Art. 25, para. 7 to the Sample Mutual Agreement.

clear advantage of avoiding delays and providing certainty.[662] I suggest adopting it and regarding panel decisions as mutual agreements between the states in dispute if affected persons agree with them.[663]

## 5.4 TECHNICAL IMPLEMENTATION

### 5.4.1 Legal Grounds

The International Tax Dispute Resolution Mechanism should be based on a multilateral convention.[664] I prefer this approach over the amendment of existing tax treaties not only because it is less cumbersome (even compared to a mechanism like the MLI)[665] but also because the mechanism I propose establishes a new multilateral institutional framework and procedural rules. To guarantee that it is also applicable to disputes arising from future tax treaties, it should be established in a singular and special convention so that this convention forms *lex specialis* for the resolution of international tax disputes.

The convention should have a broad scope to cover all possible disputes arising from tax treaties - not only including those regarding the taxation of income and capital. It is important to have an efficient multilateral dispute resolution mechanism at hand, particularly for possible future multilateral treaties. Furthermore, a broad scope ensures a general - and hopefully high - standard in the protection of taxpayers' rights. Finally, it is also more efficient to concentrate all disputes in international tax law in one institution with the infrastructure to facilitate and the expertise and capacity to discuss and decide disputes on all matters of international tax law.

### 5.4.2 Establishing an Institutionalised Online Dispute Resolution Platform

The backbone of the dispute resolution mechanism will be its IT infrastructure, with an online dispute resolution platform that allows taxpayers to file applications, provides a case management system in which all files are stored and can be accessed (if necessary with differentiated access rights) by the participants and enables communication between participants up to meetings and hearings that are hosted via an integrated videoconferencing tool.[666]

A rough inspiration for how such a platform could be designed can, for example, be drawn from the European Commission's online dispute resolution platform for the

662. *See also Strotkemper, supra* n. 18, at p. 406. Criticising the OECD's approach as cumbersome and lacking an autonomous procedure-ending effect *M. Lehner*, Streitbeilegung im Internationalen Steuerrecht, p. 673 (P. Kirchhof/H. Nieskens eds, Verlag Dr. Otto Schmidt 2008). Contemplating a multilateral approach as well (but preferring the use of bilateral clauses) *Park/Tillinghast, supra* n. 24, at pp. 25 f.
663. *Strotkemper, supra* n. 18, at p. 948 also supports this approach.
664. *See also Hannes, supra* n. 445, at p. 281; *Strotkemper, supra* n. 18, at pp. 458 f.
665. *See*, however *Strotkemper, supra* n. 18, at p. 616, who proposes an MLI-like mechanism to implement her suggested amendment of Art. 25 OECD-MC.
666. *See also* the suggestions for a web portal to handle MAP disputes under the established mechanisms by *Dimitropoulou et al., supra* n. 483, 46 Intertax 12 (2018), at pp. 961 ff.

settlement of consumer claims with ADR mechanisms.[667] This platform requires users to create an account and assists them in filing claims via a form. The procedure is laid out in a comprehensible way, and the platform indicates when actions are required. Furthermore, the platform offers an integrated translation tool.

The dispute resolution platform should also allow users to schedule meetings, inform them via e-mail or other notifications if there are new actions by other participants and automatically remind them of approaching deadlines.[668] An idea worth considering is also to include specific resources to help in disputes such as an own database for comparables in transfer pricing disputes.

In designing the platform, a strong focus should be placed on data protection and information security, not least to avoid sensitive information falling into the wrong hands. Confidentiality, integrity and availability of information need to be protected.[669] This includes basic elements such as secure access methods (e.g., multi-factor authentication), the encryption of stored data and the hosting of the platform in the organisation's own infrastructure[670] or other mechanisms to avoid the access of third parties.[671] Other elements should be considered as well: offering a translation tool on the platform can help prevent users from copying sensitive information into free online translation services.[672] Hosting an own videoconferencing tool avoids the transfer of data to third parties – one could, for example, make use of the open-source software Jitsi.[673] Communicating via an encrypted platform not only guarantees that all communication is in one place but also is more secure than the exchange of unencrypted e-mails.

An advantage of an online dispute resolution platform would also be that it would vastly help in understanding the efficiency of the dispute resolution mechanism, not least because statistics could be compiled automatically.[674]

667. *See* https://ec.europa.eu/consumers/odr/main/?event=main.home2.show (accessed 15 Jan. 2024). Guidance on the platform's functions is given at https://ec.europa.eu/consumers/odr/userguide/pdf/Y29uc3VtZXI/userguide-consumer-en.pdf (accessed 15 Jan. 2024).

668. This is also proposed by *C. Dimitropoulou et al.*, Applying Modern, Disruptive Technologies to Improve the Effectiveness of Tax Treaty Dispute Resolution: Part 1, 46 Intertax 11, p. 871 (2018) DOI: 10.54648/taxi2018093 in their Figure 5.

669. This is the so-called CIA triad that sums up the three core principles of information security; *see*, for example, *A. Agarwal/A. Agarwal*, The Security Risks Associated with Cloud Computing, 1 International Journal of Computer Applications in Engineering Sciences CNS Special Issue, pp. 257 f. (2011). Differentiated and in detail *S. Samonas/D. Coss*, The CIA Strikes Back: Redefining Confidentiality, Integrity and Availability in Security, 10 JISSec 3, pp. 21 ff. (2014).

670. In a so-called private cloud *see also Dimitropoulou et al., supra* n. 668, 46 Intertax 11 (2018), at p. 867.

671. Such as the employment of a blockchain as detailed by *Dimitropoulou et al., supra* n. 483, 46 Intertax 12 (2018), at pp. 968 ff.

672. On the privacy issues with regard to the use of these services *see P. Kamocki/J. O'Regan*, Privacy Issues in Online Machine Translation Services – European Perspective, p. 4459 (N. Calzolari et al. eds, European Language Resources Association (ELRA) 2016).

673. https://jitsi.org/about/ (accessed 15 Jan. 2024).

674. Highlighting this benefit as well *Dimitropoulou et al., supra* n. 483, 46 Intertax 12 (2018), at p. 965. As of now, they are compiled manually in many jurisdictions as reported by *Dimitropoulou et al., supra* n. 668, 46 Intertax 11 (2018), at p. 859.

### 5.4.3 Establishing an Administrative Facility

To administer the dispute resolution mechanism and its online platform, the establishment of a facility seems advisable. This facility should guarantee efficient procedures in all possible stages by maintaining the online platform and corresponding with participants to the procedure. For this, a moderate number of permanent staff should be employed. With all procedures taking place online per default, the facility does not need to provide large meeting rooms. As factors to consider in determining the best location for the facility, I suggest: (1) experience with e-administration in the country, (2) good prospects in finding staff with a high proficiency in English and (3) a jurisdiction with highly democratic standards and especially a support of the rule of law, to ensure that the procedural rights and guarantees I propose in the mechanism are practised under the state's national law and ideally seem natural to the staff.

A matching of states with experience and a high standard in e-government,[675] a high proficiency in English among the population[676] and a high respect for the rule of law[677] leads to a list of possible states that include Australia, Denmark, Estonia, Finland, the Netherlands, New Zealand, Norway, Sweden, the Republic of Korea, Singapore and the United Kingdom. When focusing on states that already play an important role in the world of both international taxation and international justice, the Netherlands stands out as it is home to the International Bureau of Fiscal Documentation (IBFD), the International Fiscal Association (IFA) and both the International Court of Justice and the Permanent Court of Arbitration.[678] However, the establishment of the administrative facility could be a good chance to involve countries other than those who already play an important role in international taxation and international justice. Regarding their high e-government standard and IT infrastructure, Estonia, the Republic of Korea and Singapore stand out in particular. Finally, it is up to the signatories to the convention implementing the mechanism to agree on a location for the administrative facility.

675. The United Nations' ranking is indicative United Nations, E-Government Survey 2020 p. 6, https://publicadministration.un.org/egovkb/en-us/Reports/UN-E-Government-Survey-2020 (accessed 15 Jan. 2024). In this ranking, Denmark, the Republic of Korea, Estonia, Finland, Australia, Sweden, the United Kingdom, New Zealand, the United States, the Netherlands, Singapore, Iceland, Norway and Japan are rated to have a 'very high' e-government standard.
676. Proficiency in English is, for example, rated by Education First, EF English Proficiency Index, https://www.ef.com/wwen/epi/ (accessed 15 Jan. 2024).
677. Rankings in this regard are drawn up, for example, by the World Justice Project, Rule of Law Index 2020, https://worldjusticeproject.org/sites/default/files/documents/WJP-ROLI-2020-Online_0.pdf (accessed 15 Jan. 2024).
678. *See also Strotkemper, supra* n. 18, at p. 643, who contemplates whether and to what extent the Permanent Court of Arbitration might be involved in resolving international tax disputes.

CHAPTER 6

# Draft Convention for the Resolution of International Tax Disputes

**Contents**

## *Chapter I*

## General Provisions

### *Article 1 – Scope*

This Convention shall apply to all disputes arising from the application or interpretation of agreements or conventions between two or more states that concern the distribution of the exercise or the allocation of taxing rights (tax treaties)[679] between the signatories.

### *Article 2 – Definitions*

(1) Participants to the procedure means both the competent authorities of the states involved and affected persons.
(2) Competent authorities means authorities designated as such by the signatories.
(3) Affected persons means individuals and bodies corporate, regardless of their legal form, whose taxation is directly affected in a dispute.
(4) Referring courts means courts designated as such by the signatories.

### *Article 3 – Language of the Procedure*

All procedures shall be conducted in English.[680]

### *Article 4 – Administrative Facility*

[1]There shall be an administrative facility based in [Tallinn, Estonia].[681] [2]The administrative facility maintains the online dispute resolution platform, assists in the administration of disputes and supports the assembly of representatives and its chairperson. [3]The staffing is decided upon by the assembly of representatives.

679. Limitations in scope are possible – for example, for tax treaties regarding income and capital. I advise against such limitations and advocate a broad wording, however, to make the mechanism future-proof and open for further developments, including those implementing the OECD's Unified Approach.
680. One might consider allowing other languages if the participants of a dispute agree on it. This, however, might result in conflicts with the language proficiency of the administrative facility's staff on the one hand and panel members later on the other hand. Especially to avoid any restrictions in the determination of panel members, I thus prefer to conduct every procedure in English.
681. On considerations regarding the location *see* section 5.4.3.

*Article 5 – Assembly of Representatives*

(1) [1]Each participating state shall appoint one representative. [2]All representatives together form the assembly of representatives. [3]The assembly of representatives is chaired by one of the representatives on the basis of equal rotation for the duration of one year. [4]The chairperson organises, invites to and chairs meetings and votes; in these tasks, the chairperson is assisted by the administrative facility.

(2) [1]The assembly of representatives convenes at least once a year for a regular meeting. [2]Meetings shall further be held if the chairperson deems it necessary or at least a quarter of the representatives request it.

(3) [1]The assembly of representatives monitors and takes fundamental decisions on the governance of the dispute resolution mechanism. [2]The assembly shall take decisions by a majority of representatives present. [3]The decisions are valid if all representatives have been invited to take part in the meeting or vote and at least half the representatives are present. [4]Both meetings and votes can take place online; the opportunity of an online participation is always to be granted.[682]

*Article 6 – Election of Possible Panel Members*

(1) [1]Possible panel members are elected by the assembly of representatives. [2]One possible panel member per signatory shall be elected. [3]For the election, the candidates with an affiliation to a signatory are ranked in an alphabetical order. [4]Every representative has two votes per signatory; one of these votes can be used for female candidates only, the other one can be used for all genders; both votes can be directed at one person. [5]The person who receives the most votes per signatory-affiliation is elected; in the event of a tie vote, the female candidate wins; if there are two or no women, there shall be a final ballot between the two candidates; if this leads to a tie again, the decision shall be taken by lot. [6]If one person receives the most votes for more than one signatory, the person has to decide which signatory's mandate to accept; for each other signatory, the person with the second most votes is appointed.

(2) [1]Possible panel members shall have both a sufficient expertise in the area of international tax law and a sufficient proficiency in the language of the procedure pursuant to Article 3. [2]Candidates can either apply themselves or be nominated by signatories, their competent authorities or the general public. [3]The applications shall be standardised and published on the administrative facility's webpage. [4]The applications shall contain information
   (a) regarding which signatory or signatories the candidate is applying for,
   (b) regarding the candidate's qualifications,
   (c) regarding the candidate's area of special expertise in international tax law,

682. This option ensures that all representatives can take part in meetings and votes even if their states' budgetary restrictions do not allow for travel.

(d) whether the candidate is willing and/or qualified to serve as a mediator, and
(e) as to who, if anyone, nominated the candidate.

[5]The candidates may attach a CV as well as a list of publications. [6]They shall be given the chance to upload a video of up to five minutes in which they state their motivation for applying. [7]Signatories may file a reasoned objection regarding candidates who apply for them; this reasoned objection shall be included in and published with the candidate's application. [8]The administrative facility organises public hearings that are led by the two highest ranking members of both the UN Committee of Experts on International Cooperation in Tax Matters and the OECD Centre for Tax Policy and Administration; at least one member per institution shall be female. [9]The hearings are broadcast via the administrative facility's webpage. [10]The representatives are given the opportunity to ask questions at these hearings. [11]The election shall take place no earlier than one day after the last hearing.

(3) [1]Possible panel members are mandated for five years. [2]Their mandate can be extended once for five years with a majority vote of the assembly of representatives. [3]Thereafter, as well as if their mandate is not extended, they may reapply. [4]Possible panel members can be removed with a two-thirds majority vote of the assembly of representatives after a reasoned application of a signatory or an affected person. [5]Reapplications of removed panel members are not permitted.

## *Chapter II*

## Negotiation Phase

### *Article 7 – Initiation*

(1) [1]Where a person considers that the actions of one or more of the signatories result or will result in taxation not in accordance with the provisions of one or more tax treaties concluded between the signatories, they may file an application on the administrative facility's webpage, irrespective of the remedies provided by and the time limits prescribed in the domestic law of the signatories within three years from the receipt of the first tax assessment giving rise to such concerns. [2]The application is to be filed by the affected person or a legal representative and shall include information regarding
(a) the name, address, contact details and taxpayer identification numbers of the affected person; in case of legal representation, their contact details shall be mentioned as well,
(b) the states and tax administrations involved; if possible, by naming the local offices that have issued or are about to issue the measure that gives rise to the affected person's concern,
(c) the measure the affected person considers to be in conflict with a tax treaty and – if there already has been a tax assessment, audit report or

other measure – the date and reference of the measure; the relevant documents shall be attached,

(d) whether the affected person has made use of domestic or other international remedies and – if so – their status, and

(e) a description of the dispute and the affected person's position.

[3]The application may include an application letter with detailed reasoning and further documentation.

(2) [1]The administrative facility automatically confirms the receipt of the application and checks it for obvious inconsistencies. [2]In the case of inconsistencies, affected persons are requested to complete or correct their application. [3]Once the application is complete and correct, the administrative facility links the competent authorities of the involved states to the case and sends them a notification. [4]The date of this notification shall be regarded as the starting date of the negotiation phase.

(3) [1]All communication between the participants shall take place via the online platform. [2]All participants and their legal representatives can access the case files on the online platform. [3]The right of affected persons to access the case files may be limited with regard to specific documents if this is imperative to protect secrets of persons not involved in the dispute; if this is the case, the respective competent authority shall provide the affected person with a redacted document.

*Article 8 – Review of Admissibility*

(1) [1]The competent authorities involved shall review the admissibility of the application, especially regarding the timeframe stated in Article 7 paragraph 1 first sentence, and shall review whether sufficient information is provided. [2]Within three months of the negotiation phase's starting date, they may require the affected person to provide further information if they deem it necessary to assess the validity of the claim. [3]Within three months of the affected person providing the final pieces of information via the online platform or within six months of the starting date, each competent authority shall issue a decision on the admissibility of the application; the later of these dates is decisive. [4]If a competent authority fails to issue a decision in time, a positive decision shall be assumed.

(2) [1]Negative decisions of competent authorities may be challenged by affected persons with the respective domestic remedies. [2]In the case of divergent competent authority decisions or when all competent authorities have issued negative decisions, but a domestic remedy is not decided upon within six months, affected persons may apply for a panel decision on the admissibility of their application. [3]For the panel procedure, the rules in Chapter III apply. [4]In the case of a positive panel decision, the negotiation phase is initiated if all competent authorities confirm their interest in a negotiation within one month of the panel decision's receipt; otherwise, the procedure commences with the mandatory resolution phase.

*Article 9 – Exchange of Position Papers*

(1) [1]Within six months of the affected person's application being admitted, each competent authority shall provide an initial position paper. [2]Within three months of receiving a competent authority's initial position paper, each participant may issue a reply.

(2) The participants may agree to enter an oral negotiation immediately after the admission of the application if they consider this approach to be beneficial.

*Article 10 – Negotiation*

(1) [1]One month after the last reply has been issued, an oral exchange is to be scheduled by the administrative facility in consultation with the participants. [2]The exchange shall take place by means of a videoconference unless the participants agree on other means of communication, such as a conference call or an in-person meeting. [3]In the oral exchange, the participants shall agree on the further structure of the negotiation phase and endeavour to agree on a solution of the dispute.

(2) [1]If the competent authorities agree on a solution, this solution shall be implemented by means of a mutual agreement, subject to the consent and waiver of domestic remedies by the affected person. [2]If the affected person does not consent within one month of the solution being communicated, this shall be deemed a refusal of consent. [3]The solution shall indicate the reasons that led to the result. [4]The reasoned mutual agreement shall be published in an anonymised form unless the affected person agrees to a full publication; the mutual agreement has no precedential value.

(3) [1]If the competent authorities do not arrive at a solution within two years of the starting date of the negotiation phase, they shall provide a reasoned statement explaining why they were not able to agree on a solution. [2]The negotiation phase may, subject to the affected person's consent, be extended for a specific timeframe if the competent authorities assume an agreement to be possible in this timeframe. [3]At any time during the negotiation phase, the competent authorities may agree to disagree; if this is the case, the negotiation phase is over. [4]The negotiation phase also ends if a competent authority misses the deadline in Article 9 paragraph 1 first sentence, does not respond to the scheduling pursuant to paragraph 1 first sentence of this Article or misses other deadlines agreed upon; an extension of time for up to one month may be granted upon application with the consent of the other participants.

(4) The negotiation phase officially ends when the administrative facility notifies that it is – for whatever reason, including an agreement being concluded – over.

*Article 11 – Mediation*

(1) [1]If all participants to the procedure agree, they may endeavour to settle the dispute by means of mediation. [2]The administrative facility shall, upon the

notice that the participants agree to make use of mediation, suggest a mediator from the ranks of possible panel members who has indicated to be willing to serve as a mediator, and is neither a national nor a resident of one of the states in dispute. [3]Within one month of the suggestion, the participants shall either accept the suggestion or agree on another mediator.

(2) [1]The mediation shall commence with an agreement between the participants and the mediator that determines the mediator's mandate, as well as a structure and a timeframe for the procedure. [2]The mediation procedure shall be concluded in the timeframe of the negotiation phase. [3]Irrespective of the mediation's outcome, the mediator shall file a report that sums up the issues in dispute and the progress achieved in the mediation phase.

(3) Regarding the confidentiality requirements and the remuneration of mediators, the provisions for panel members in the mandatory resolution phase shall apply accordingly.

## *Chapter III*

## Mandatory Resolution Phase

### *Article 12 – Initiation*

(1) [1]Within one month of the administrative facility's notification that the negotiation phase is over pursuant to Article 10 paragraph 4, each participant may initiate the mandatory resolution phase. [2]In their initiation letter, the participant shall define the desired scope of the mandatory resolution phase; this may include aspects as to which the competent authorities reached an agreement pursuant to Article 10 paragraph 2 without the affected person's consent. [3]Within the timeframe stated in the first sentence of this paragraph or within two weeks after another participant has filed an initiation letter, the later date being decisive, other participants may indicate if they wish the mandatory resolution phase to have a wider scope.

(2) [1]The initiation letter shall include a short description of the questions in dispute. [2]It may but does not need to contain reasons. [3]Reasons shall be provided within two months of the respective reference date for the initiation letter in paragraph 1.

(3) [1]The mandatory resolution phase shall be initiated regardless of whether there have been final assessments in all states involved. [2]If there has not yet been a final assessment in one or more states involved, the mandatory resolution phase shall be suspended until there are final assessments in all states. [3]All participants shall be notified by the respective competent authority of a final assessment in its jurisdiction. [4]Reasons pursuant to paragraph 2 shall be provided within two months of this notification.

(4) [1]The administrative facility publishes a notice of the case with a description of the questions in dispute on its webpage. [2]The notice shall mention the states involved and the relevant tax treaties. [3]The publication of the affected

person's identity is subject to their consent; if this is not given, their identity shall be anonymised.

(5) [1]The case file of the negotiation phase pursuant to Article 7 paragraph 3 is continued in the mandatory resolution phase. [2]The participant's access rights remain the same.

*Article 13 – Amicus Curiae Briefs*

(1) [1]Actors other than the participants to the procedure may submit statements via the administrative facility's webpage within one month of the case description being published. [2]The statements shall not exceed 9,000 words (including annexes). [3]Additionally, the submissions shall
   (a) describe the authors, including, where relevant, their membership and legal status, their general objectives, the nature of their activities and any parent organisation (including any organisation that directly or indirectly controls the authors),
   (b) disclose any connection, direct or indirect, which the author has with any participant to the procedure,
   (c) provide information on any government, person or organisation that has provided to the author any financial or other assistance in preparing the submission and/or made contributions that exceeded a share of 20 per cent of their annual budget in the last two years, and
   (d) describe the nature of the interest that the authors have in the case.[683]

(2) [1]The administrative facility shall assess whether the submission meets the formal requirements stated in paragraph 1. [2]If this is the case, the submission shall be forwarded to both the panel and the participants and be published on the administrative facility's webpage. [3]If the administrative facility denies the acceptance of a submission, the submission's authors may appeal this decision in front of the panel.

(3) The panel is under no obligation to consider statements submitted under paragraph 1 in finding a decision.

*Article 14 – Composition of a Panel*

(1) Panels consist of three members, including one chairperson.

(2) [1]Panels are set up by the administrative facility using a random algorithm as soon as an initiation letter has been filed and the timeframe to file initiation letters or to extend the scope of the mandatory resolution phase pursuant to Article 12 paragraph 1 has elapsed. [2]All possible panel members who have an affiliation to one of the states or persons involved in the dispute are excluded. [3]Panels shall be composed of no more than one tax advisor or counsel and no more than one official; they shall be chaired by either a judge or an academic. [4]The algorithm shall prefer possible panel members whose area of expertise matches the matters in dispute.

683. This list is inspired by Art. 4(2) of the UNCITRAL Rules on Transparency.

(3) [1]Panel members may recuse themselves within two weeks of their appointment if they have a conflict of interest stemming from past, current or future activities. [2]After a recusal, the random algorithm shall select another panel member with respect to the requirements stated in paragraph 2. [3]After completion, the panel setup is to be communicated to the participants. [4]Within one month of the notification - or within one month of a reason arising, each participant may file a reasoned objection if they have reason to doubt a panel member's impartiality. [5]Within two weeks, the panel shall decide upon the objection without the member whose impartiality is in doubt.

(4) [1]Panel members are obliged to notify to the participants of any engagements by themselves as well as by their firm or company for the involved states or affected persons within three years of the panel's decision. [2]Each participant may, within three months of the notification, void the panel's decision and initiate a new mandatory resolution phase. [3]The costs for this procedure shall be borne by the panel member.

*Article 15 – Access to Information and Confidentiality*

Panel members shall be deemed qualified persons under Article 26 paragraph 2 OECD/UN Model Convention or comparable provisions and are obliged to respect the confidentiality requirements stated in the relevant provision.

*Article 16 – Exchange of Statements*

All participants who do not file a reasoned initiation pursuant to Article 12 paragraph 2 may respond to the reasons of the other participants within one month of their receipt.

*Article 17 – Hearings*

[1]The panel may decide whether to extend the exchange of statements or whether to schedule a hearing after the receipt of the last statement pursuant to Article 16. [2]A hearing shall be scheduled within one month of the receipt of the last written submission in coordination with the participants. [3]Unless the panel and the participants agree otherwise, the hearing shall be conducted by means of a videoconference. [4]Further hearings may be scheduled if the panel deems this necessary.

*Article 18 – Publicity*

(1) [1]Hearings shall be public. [2]They shall be made available to the public via a livestream on the administrative facility's webpage.

(2) [1]The panel may exclude the public upon the reasoned application of a participant to the procedure from a hearing or from a part thereof if
   (a) a threat to the security or the public order of one of the participating states is to be feared,
   (b) an endangerment of the life, limb or liberty of a witness or another person is to be feared,

(c) an important business, trade, industry or tax secret is mentioned, the public discussion of which would violate overriding interests meriting protection, or
(d) a private secret is discussed, the unauthorised disclosure of which by a witness or expert carries a penalty.[684]

[2]The discussion as to whether the hearing or parts of the hearing shall be private takes place in a private setting. [3]The panel's decision on whether or not to exclude the public is pronounced publicly. [4]Private hearings shall be recorded and, if possible, be published in a redacted version no later than one week after they take place.

(3) [1]Panel decisions are published on the administrative facility's webpage in an anonymised version. [2]Before publication, they are made available to the participating states and affected persons. [3]Within one month, they may invoke concerns regarding the public order or the publication of trade, business, industrial, professional or tax secrets. [4]The panel shall consider these concerns and redact the decision before publication to the degree it deems necessary. [5]Panel decisions shall be deemed *judicial decisions* pursuant to Article 26 paragraph 2 third sentence of the OECD and UN Model Conventions and comparable provisions.

*Article 19 – Determining Questions of National and European Law*

(1) [1]If the panel considers that a decision on a question of national law is necessary to enable it to decide a case, it shall request the respective highest national court for tax matters to provide an advisory opinion. [2]If the respective court fails to give an advisory opinion within six months and the competent authority of the respective state agrees or if all participants agree in the first place, a national tax expert may be heard on the question of national law. [3]Possible panel members from the respective jurisdiction – especially those who might serve as chairpersons – qualify as national experts.

(2) If the panel considers that a decision on a question of European law is necessary to enable it to decide a case, it shall request a referring court of the states involved in the procedure to refer the question to the Court of Justice of the European Union.

*Article 20 – Panel Decisions*

[1]Within three months of the last hearing, the panel shall submit a decision. [2]The decision is taken by a majority vote. [3]It shall consist of a verdict, a statement of facts and legal reasons. [4]A dissenting panel member shall be given the opportunity to formulate a dissenting opinion.

684. This list is inspired by Section 172 of the German Courts Constitution Act [*Gerichtsverfassungsgesetz – GVG*] that is accessible at http://www.gesetze-im-internet.de/englisch_gvg/englisch_gvg.html#p0825 (accessed 15 Jan. 2024).

*Article 21 – Binding Force and Precedential Value of Decisions*

(1) [1]Decisions are final and binding on the disputing parties with respect to the particular case if the affected person declares their acceptance and waives all remedies under the national law of the states in dispute within one month of the decision being communicated by the panel. [2]If the affected person does not accept the decision within the time limit, it shall be regarded as not accepted and shall not be implemented. [3]Accepted decisions shall be regarded as mutual agreements concluded by the states in dispute and can be enforced by the affected person under the national laws of the states as such.

(2) [1]Decisions and their *ratio decidendi* have no binding precedential value. [2]Panels may consider a previous decision if they find its reasoning to be persuasive, but they are always free to deviate.

*Article 22 – Costs*

(1) [1]Each participant bears their own costs. [2]The procedural costs, in particular the panel members' remuneration and the compensation of witnesses and experts, are borne by the states in equal share. [3]For general administrative costs, advance payments of the states may, subject to a resolution of the assembly of representatives, be charged by the administrative facility. [4]Affected persons shall bear the share of procedural costs that is attributable to them challenging an agreement between states that is upheld by the panel; the exact amount shall be determined by the panel, if necessary by way of estimation. [5]Affected persons shall, subject to a panel decision, bear the procedural costs if they withdraw their application.

(2) [1]Panel members shall be remunerated with USD 1,000 per person per meeting or hearing day; this includes compensation for preparation time. [2]The remuneration shall be limited to ten days per case. [3]The chairperson shall receive a ten per cent surcharge. [4]Panel members are to be reimbursed for unavoidable travel expenses; this is limited to economy class travel. [5]The amount in the first sentence can be amended with a simple majority vote of the assembly of representatives.[685]

## *Chapter IV*

## Final Provision

*Article 23 – Amendments to this Convention*

[1]This Convention may be amended by the assembly of representatives. [2]An amendment requires a two-third majority vote.

685. This is a deviation from Art. 23 to allow for easier amendments, e.g., for inflation adjustments.

# References


*Markus Achatz* (ed.), Internationales Steuerrecht: *37. Jahrestagung der Deutschen Steuerjuristischen Gesellschaft e.V. Linz, 10. und 11. September 2012* (Verlag Dr. Otto Schmidt 2013).

*Guido Acquaviva & Fausto Pocar,* Stare decisis (A. Peters/R. Wolfrum eds).

*Ashish Agarwal & Aparna Agarwal,* The Security Risks Associated with Cloud Computing, 1 International Journal of Computer Applications in Engineering Sciences CNS Special Issue, pp. 257-259 (2011).

*Markus Albert,* DBA-Verständigungsverfahren: *Probleme und Verbesserungsvorschläge* (IFSt 2009).

*Gilda Almeida,* Should Taxpayers Have Access to the International Tax Arbitration Procedure?, SSRN Electronic Journal (2018), https://papers.ssrn.com/sol3/papers.cfm?abstract_id=3266492 (accessed 15 January 2024).

*Philip Alston & Nikki Reisch* (eds), Tax, Inequality, and Human Rights (Oxford University Press 2019).

*Zvi Daniel Altman,* Dispute Resolution under Tax Treaties (IBFD 2006).

*Orley Ashenfelter, Janet Currie, Henry S. Farber & Matthew Spiegel,* An Experimental Comparison of Dispute Rates in Alternative Arbitration Systems, 60 Econometrica 6, p. 1407 (1992), http://www.jstor.org/stable/2951527.

*Hugh J. Ault,* Improving the Resolution of International Tax Disputes, 7 Florida Tax Review 3, pp. 137-151 (2005).

*Hugh J. Ault & Jacques Sasseville,* 2008 OECD Model: The New Arbitration Provision, 63 Bulletin for International Taxation 5, pp. 208-215 (2009).

*Anthony Aust,* Pacta Sunt Servanda (A. Peters/R. Wolfrum eds).

*John F. Avery Jones,* Chapter 15: Arbitration and Publication of Decisions, pp. 369-376 (M. Lang et al. eds, IBFD 2015).

*John F. Avery Jones,* Guest Editorial: *Types of Arbitration Procedure,* 47 Intertax 8/9, pp. 647-677 (2019).

*Reuven S. Avi-Yonah,* The Rise and Fall of Arm's Length: A Study in the Evolution of U.S. International Taxation, 15 Virginia Tax Review 1, pp. 89-160 (1995).

*Patricia Backhausen & Payel Mazumdar,* International Tax Arbitration: A New Avenue for Small State International Financial Centres?, pp. 251-278 (P. Butler et al. eds, Springer 2018).

*Andrés Báez Moreno,* GAARs and Treaties: From the Guiding Principle to the Principal Purpose Test. What Have We Gained from BEPS Action 6?, 45 Intertax 6/7, pp. 432-446 (2017).

*Eduardo Baistrocchi* (ed.), A Global Analysis of Tax Treaty Disputes: *OECD Countries* (Cambridge University Press 2017).

*Anuschka Bakker & Marc M. Levey* (eds), Transfer Pricing and Dispute Resolution: *Aligning Strategy and Execution* (IBFD 2011).

*Ulrike Bär,* Verständigungen über Verrechnungspreise verbundener Unternehmen im deutschen Steuerrecht (Duncker & Humblot 2009).

*Funda Başaran Yavaşlar & Johanna Hey* (eds), Tax Transparency: *2018 EATLP Annual Congress Zürich, 7-9 June 2018* (IBFD 2019).

*Diana Beck,* Qualifikationskonflikte im Internationalen Steuerrecht (Springer 2016).

*Enno Becker,* Die Selbständigkeit der Begriffsbildung im Steuerrecht und ihr Einfluß auf die Auslegung der internationalen Doppelbesteuerungsverträge vom Standpunkt der deutschen Entwicklung aus betrachtet, II Cahiers de Droit Fiscal International, 1-23 (1939).

*Johannes Becker, Gerit Kimpel, Andreas Oestreicher & Ekkehart Reimer,* Das Verfahrensrecht der Verrechnungspreise: *Grundlagen, Erfahrungen und Perspektiven* (Springer Gabler 2017).

*Katharina Becker,* Seminar J: Verfahren zur Lösung von DBA-Konflikten, 16 Internationales Steuerrecht 16, pp. 592-595 (2007).

*Katharina Becker,* Internationale Zusammenarbeit – Konsultation und Verständigung, pp. 167-190 (M. Achatz ed., Verlag Dr. Otto Schmidt 2013).

*Ulrich Becker, Armin Hatje, Johann Schoo & Jürgen Schwarze* (eds), EU-Kommentar (Nomos 2019).

*Christoph Bergedahl,* Anti-Abuse Measures in Tax Treaties Following the OECD Multilateral Instrument – Part 1, 72 Bulletin for International Taxation 1, pp. 11-30 (2018).

*Andrea Bianchi & Anne Peters* (eds), Transparency in International Law (Cambridge University Press 2013).

*Ramazan Biçer,* The Effectiveness of Mutual Agreement Procedures as a Means for Settling International Transfer Pricing Disputes, 21 International Transfer Pricing Journal 2, pp. 76-84 (2014).

*Karl-Heinz Böckstiegel, Hans-Ernst Folz, Jörg Manfred Mössner & Karl Zemanek* (eds), Law of Nations. Law of International Organizations. World's Economic Law: *Liber Amicorum honouring Ignaz Seidl-Hohenveldern* (Carl Heymanns Verlag KG 1988).

*Axel Bödefeld & Elmar Krüsmann,* Abkommensberechtigung für Betriebsstätten in Verständigungsverfahren nach dem OECD-MA, 27 Internationales Steuerrecht 2, pp. 45-52 (2018).

*Axel Bödefeld & Nina Kuntschik,* Der Überarbeitete Verhaltenskodex zur Anwendung des EU-Schiedsübereinkommens, 19 Internationales Steuerrecht 13, pp. 474-478 (2010).

*Steven J. Brams & Samuel Merrill,* Equilibrium Strategies for Final-Offer Arbitration: There is No Median Convergence, 29 Management Science 8, pp. 927-941 (1983), http://www.jstor.org/stable/2631036.

*Nathalie Bravo,* Mandatory Binding Arbitration in the BEPS Multilateral Instrument, 47 Intertax 8/9, pp. 693-714 (2019).

*Michael P. Bricker,* Arbitration Procedures in Tax Treaties, 26 Intertax 3, pp. 97-108 (1998).

*Morten Broberg,* Preliminary Ruling: European Court of Justice (ECJ) (A. Peters/R. Wolfrum eds).

*Luc de Broe,* International Tax Planning and Prevention of Abuse (IBFD 2007).

*Luc de Broe & Joris Luts,* BEPS Action 6: Tax Treaty Abuse, 43 Intertax 2, pp. 122-146 (2015).

*Patricia A. Brown,* Chapter 4: Enhancing the Mutual Agreement Procedure by Adopting Appropriate Arbitration Provisions (M. Lang et al. eds, IBFD 2015).

*Patricia A. Brown,* Chapter 10: Mediation: The Swiss Army Knife in the Competent Authority's Toolbox (P. Pistone/J.J. de Goede eds, IBFD 2021).

*Patricia A. Brown,* Chapter 12: A Negotiator, Not a Judge: Choosing the Right Mediator to Aid in Resolving Cross Border Tax Disputes (P. Pistone/J.J. de Goede eds, IBFD 2021).

*Ottmar Bühler,* Prinzipien des Internationalen Steuerrechts: *Ein systematischer Versuch* (IBFD 1964).

*Eva Burgstaller & Katharina Haslinger* (eds), Conflicts of Qualification in Tax Treaty Law (Linde 2007).

*Svitlana Buriak,* Chapter 2: The Application of the Principal Purpose Test under Tax Treaties (M. Lang et al. eds, IBFD 2019).

*Gabriele Burmester & Dieter Endres* (eds), Außensteuerrecht, Doppelbesteuerungsabkommen und EU-Recht im Spannungsverhältnis: *Festschrift für Helmut Debatin zum 70. Geburtstag* (C.H. Beck 1997).

*Kirsten Burmester,* Chapter 37: United States, pp. 821-836 (M. Lang et al. eds, IBFD 2020).

*Mukesh Butani,* Chapter 16: Action 14: Making Dispute Resolution Mechanisms More Effective - An Asian Perspective (S. Sim/M.-J. Soo eds, IBFD 2017).

*Petra Butler, Eva Lein & Rhonson Salim* (eds), Integration and International Dispute Resolution in Small States (Springer 2018).

*Qiang Cai,* A Package Deal Is Not a Bad Deal: Reassessing the Method of Package Negotiation Under the Mutual Agreement Procedure, 46 Intertax 10, pp. 744-752 (2018).

*Christian Calliess & Matthias Ruffert* (eds), EUV, AEUV: *Das Verfassungsrecht der Europäischen Union mit Europäischer Grundrechtecharta* (C.H. Beck 2016).

*Nicoletta Calzolari, Khalid Choukri, Thierry Declerck, Sara Goggi, Marko Grobelnik, Bente Maegaard, Joseph Mariani, Helene Mazo, Asuncion Moreno, Jan Odijk &*

*Stelios Piperidis* (eds), Proceedings of the Tenth International Conference on Language Resources and Evaluation (LREC'16) (European Language Resources Association (ELRA) 2016), https://www.aclweb.org/anthology/L16-1000.

*Cristina Camino,* Chapter 31 – The Future of Arbitration: Towards an International Tax Court?, pp. 711-735 (A. Majdanska/L. Turcan eds, Linde 2018).

*Daniele de Carolis,* The EU Dispute Resolution Directive (2017/1852) and Fair Trial Protection under Article 47 of the EU Charter of Fundamental Rights, 58 European Taxation 11, pp. 495-504 (2018).

*Julien Chaisse,* Making Tax Dispute Resolution Mechanisms More Effective – The Base Erosion and Profit Shifting Project and Beyond, 10 Contemporary Asia Arbitration Journal 1, pp. 1-50 (2017).

*Steve Charnovitz,* Transparency and Participation in the World Trade Organization, 56 Rutgers Law Review 4, pp. 927-960 (2004).

*Allison Christians,* Take MAP with a Grain of Salt: Sifto and the Legal Nature of Competent Authority Agreements, 86 Tax Notes International, pp. 81-83 (2017).

*Martin J. Chwalek & Lukas Bühl,* Obligatorisches Verfahren zur Beilegung von Doppelbesteuerungsstreitigkeiten in der EU ab 2019, Internationale Wirtschaftsbriefe 6, pp. 214-216 (2018).

*Nevia Čiin-Šain, Tina Ehrke-Rabel & Joachim Englisch,* Joint Audits: Applicable Law and Taxpayer Rights, 10 World Tax Journal 4, pp. 585-631 (2018).

*Adrian Cloer & Nicola Niemeyer,* EuGH mit Entscheidungsbefugnis durch DBA-Schiedsklausel – Vorbildcharakter für die Streitbeilegung innerhalb der EU?, Finanzrundschau, pp. 674-684 (2018).

*Richard Collier & John Vella,* Five Core Problems in the Attribution of Profits to Permanent Establishments, 11 World Tax Journal 2, pp. 159-187 (2019).

*Giuseppe Antonino Corciulo,* Arbitration under the Dispute Resolution Directive: *Does the Directive Solve the Problems Encountered with the EU Arbitration Convention?,* pp. 447-467 (A. Majdanska/L. Turcan eds, Linde 2018).

*Georg Crezelius,* Steuerrechtliche Verfahrensfragen bei grenzüberschreitenden Sachverhalten, 11 Internationales Steuerrecht 13, pp. 433-441 (2002).

*Diana Criclivaia,* Joint Audits – Ten Years of Experience: *A Literature Review,* 12 World Tax Journal 3, pp. 663-707 (2020).

*Jürgen Damrau & Karlheinz Muscheler* (eds), Erbrecht und Vermögensnachfolge: *System, Struktur, Vertrag* (Verlag C.H. Beck 2012).

*Robert Danon, Daniel Gutmann, Guglielmo Maisto & Adolfo Martin Jimenez,* The OECD/G20 Global Minimum Tax and Dispute Resolution: A Workable Solution Based on Article 25(3) of the OECD Model, the Principle of Reciprocity and the Globe Model Rules, 14 World Tax Journal 3, pp. 489-515 (2022).

*Manfred A. Dauses & Markus Ludwigs* (eds), Handbuch des EU-Wirtschaftsrechts (C.H. Beck).

*Felix David,* The Role of Precedent in the WTO – New Horizons?, Maastricht Faculty of Law Working Paper, https://papers.ssrn.com/sol3/papers.cfm?abstract_id=1666169 (accessed 15 January 2024).

*Filip Debelva & Joris Luts,* Directive on Tax Dispute Resolution Mechanisms in the EU, 89 Tax Notes International 1, pp. 71-83 (2018).

*Panagiotis Delimatsis,* Institutional Transparency in the WTO, pp. 112-141 (A. Bianchi/A. Peters eds, Cambridge University Press 2013).

*Marcus Desax & Marc Veit,* Arbitration of Tax Treaty Disputes: The OECD Proposal, 23 Arbitration International 3, pp. 405-430 (2007).

*Virginia Di Francesco & Nicolas Liakas* (eds), 1977 Tax Treaties and Competent Authority (Matthew Bender 1978).

*David L. Dickinson,* A Comparison of Conventional, Final-Offer, and 'Combined' Arbitration for Dispute Resolution, 57 Industrial and Labor Relations Review 2, pp. 288-301 (2004).

*Matthias Diete,* Das obligatorische Schiedsverfahren in der deutschen DBA-Praxis: *Erweiterung des zwischenstaatlichen Rechtsschutzes bei Doppelbesteuerungskonflikten* (Peter Lang 2014).

*Christina Dimitropoulou, Sriram Govind & Laura Turcan,* Applying Modern, Disruptive Technologies to Improve the Effectiveness of Tax Treaty Dispute Resolution: Part 1, 46 Intertax 11, pp. 856-872 (2018).

*Christina Dimitropoulou, Sriram Govind & Laura Turcan,* Applying Modern, Disruptive Technologies to Improve the Effectiveness of Tax Treaty Dispute Resolution: Part 2, 46 Intertax 12, pp. 960-970 (2018).

*Jelka Dombrowsky,* Die Einwirkungen des Unionsrechts auf Doppelbesteuerungsabkommen (Duncker & Humblot 2020).

*Zachary Douglas, Joost Pauwelyn & Jorge E. Viñuales* (eds), The Foundations of International Investment Law: *Bringing Theory into Practice* (Oxford University Press 2014).

*Ana Paula Dourado,* Editorial: *Post-BEPS International Tax Arbitration,* 47 Intertax 8/9, pp. 671-673 (2019).

*Klaus-Dieter Drüen,* Verständigungs- und Schiedsverfahren, pp. 505-514 (W. Wassermeyer ed., C.H. Beck 2015).

*Klaus-Dieter Drüen, Rudolf Mellinghoff & Johanna Hey* (eds), 100 Jahre Steuerrechtsprechung in Deutschland 1918-2018: *Festschrift für den Bundesfinanzhof* (Verlag Dr. Otto Schmidt 2018).

Duff & Phelphs (ed.), Guide to International Transfer Pricing: *Law, Tax Planning and Compliance Strategies* (Kluwer Law International 2017).

*John Dugard,* Diplomatic Protection (A. Peters/R. Wolfrum eds).

*Kabir Duggal & Gerrit Niehoff,* The Conflicting Landscape Relating to Costs in Investor-State Arbitration, 5 Indian Journal of Arbitration Law 2, pp. 164-176 (2017).

*Daniel Dürrschmidt,* 'Europäisches Steuerrecht' nach Lissabon, 63 Neue Juristische Wochenschrift 29, pp. 2086-2090 (2010).

Education First, EF English Proficiency Index, https://www.ef.com/wwen/epi/ (accessed 15 January 2024).

*Maarten J. Ellis,* Issues in the Implementation of the Arbitration of Disputes Arising under Income Tax Treaties – Response to David Tillinghast, 56 Bulletin for International Taxation 3, pp. 100-101 (2002).

*W.R. Emmen Riedel,* Judicial Interpretations of Conventions on Double Taxation and the Necessity or Advisability of Establishing International Fiscal Jurisdiction: *General Report,* pp. 31-46 (International Fiscal Association ed., Imprimerie Berichthaus 1951).

*Nassim Eslami,* Die Nichtöffentlichkeit des Schiedsverfahrens (Mohr Siebeck 2016).

*Ehab Farah,* Mandatory Arbitration of International Tax Disputes: A Solution in Search of a Problem, 9 Florida Tax Review 8, 703-753 (2009).

*Henry S. Farber,* An Analysis of Final-Offer Arbitration, 24 The Journal of Conflict Resolution 4, pp. 683-705 (1980).

*John H. Farrar, Vai Io Lo & Bee Chen Goh* (eds), Scholarship, Practice and Education in Comparative Law: *A Festschrift in Honour of Mary Hiscock* (Springer 2019).

*Günther Felix* (ed.), Von der Auslegung und Anwendung der Steuergesetze: *Erschienen aus Anlaß des 60. Geburtstages von Armin Spitaler* (Pöschel 1958).

Fiscalis Project Group (FPG) 093, Working Paper on the Implementation of Article 10 of Directive (EU) 2017/1852 on Tax Dispute Resolution Mechanisms in the European Union, https://taxation-customs.ec.europa.eu/system/files/2019-10/2019-tax-dispute-resolution-fiscalis-project-group-report.pdf (accessed 15 January 2024).

*Luís Flávio Neto,* Baseball Arbitration: The Trendiest Alternative Dispute Resolution Mechanism in International Taxation, 2 International Tax Studies 8 (2019).

*Clifton J. Fleming, Jr.,* Searching for the Uncertain Rationale Underlying the US Treasury's Anti-treaty Shopping Policy, 40 Intertax 4, pp. 245-253 (2012).

*James Flett,* Separate Opinion: Dispute Settlement System of the World Trade Organization (WTO) (A. Peters/R. Wolfrum eds).

*Hans Flick,* Zur Auslegung von Normen des internationalen Steuerrechts, 151-171 (G. Felix ed., Pöschel 1958).

*Zachary Flowers,* The Role of Precedent and Stare Decisis in the World Trade Organization's Dispute Settlement Body, 47 International Journal of Legal Information 2, pp. 90-104 (2019).

*Karsten Flüchter,* Ein Mindeststandard für Verständigungsverfahren, peer reviews und die Aussicht auf mehr Schiedsklauseln, 24 Internationales Steuerrecht 24, pp. 943-952 (2015).

*Karsten Flüchter,* Das 'EU-Doppelbesteuerungs-Streitbeilegungsgesetz' ist in Kraft, 9 Internationale Steuer-Rundschau 2, pp. 56-64 (2020).

*Karsten Flüchter,* Streitbeilegungs-Richtlinie (H. Schaumburg/J. Englisch eds, Otto Schmidt 2020).

*Jutta Förster,* Das EG-Schiedsübereinkommen, 45 Betriebswirtschaftliche Forschung und Praxis 5, pp. 487-498 (1993).

*Jutta Förster,* Vermehrte Streitschlichtung durch Schiedsverfahren – eine 'Konkurrenz' für die nationale Finanzgerichtsbarkeit?, pp. 143-156 (D. Gosch et al. eds, C.H.Beck 2019).

*Evelyn Frink,* Verständigungs- und Schiedsverfahren im Internationalen Steuerrecht (Peter Lang 2015).

*Malcolm Gammie,* Judicial Precedent in the English Legal System, 73 Bulletin for International Taxation 8, pp. 417-422 (2019).

*Bryan A. Garner,* Black's Law Dictionary (West Academic Publishing 2019).

*Arno E. Gildemeister,* Chapter 12: Germany (M. Lang et al. eds, 2017).

*Christian Gloria,* Das steuerliche Verständigungsverfahren und das Recht auf diplomatischen Schutz: *Zugleich ein Beitrag zur Lehre von der Auslegung der Doppelbesteuerungsabkommen* (Duncker & Humblot 1988).

*Dietmar Gosch,* Über die Auslegung von Doppelbesteuerungsabkommen, 2 Internationale Steuer-Rundschau 3, pp. 87-95 (2013).

*Dietmar Gosch, Heinz-Klaus Kroppen, Siegfried Grotherr & Gerhard Kraft* (eds), DBA-Kommentar: *Doppelbesteuerungsabkommen* (NWB 2019).

*Dietmar Gosch, Arne Schnitger & Wolfgang Schön* (eds), Festschrift für Jürgen Lüdicke (C.H.Beck 2019).

*Sriram Govind,* The New Face of International Tax Dispute Resolution: Comparing the OECD Multilateral Instrument with the EU Dispute Resolution Directive, 27 EC Tax Review 6 (2018).

*Sriram Govind,* Chapter 10: *Personal Scope of the Mutual Agreement Procedure and Arbitration Provisions, and the Mutual Assistance Provisions* (M. Lang et al. eds, IBFD 2019).

*Sriram Govind & Shreya Rao,* Designing an Inclusive and Equitable Framework for Tax Treaty Dispute Resolution, 46 Intertax 4, pp. 313-338 (2018).

*Sriram Govind & Laura Turcan,* Cross-Border Tax Dispute Resolution in the 21st Century: A Comparative Study of Existing Bilateral and Multilateral Remedies, 19 Derivatives & Financial Instruments 5 (2017).

*Sriram Govind & Laura Turcan,* The Changing Contours of Dispute Resolution in the International Tax World: Comparing the OECD Multilateral Instrument and the Proposed EU Arbitration Directive, 71 Bulletin for International Taxation 3/4 (2017).

*Stefan Greil & Stephan Rasch,* Germany, pp. 263-290 (International Fiscal Association ed. 2016).

*Florian Grisel,* The Sources of Foreign Investment Law, pp. 213-233 (Z. Douglas et al. eds, Oxford University Press 2014).

*Ivo Grlica,* Chapter 14 – Baseball Arbitration: *Comparison of the Rules under the U.S.-Canada Tax Treaty with the Rules under the Multilateral Instrument,* pp. 317-336 (A. Majdanska/L. Turcan eds, Linde 2018).

*Gerrit Groen,* Arbitration in Bilateral Tax Treaties, 30 Intertax 1, pp. 3-27 (2002).

*Juliane Gröper,* The Mutual Agreement Procedure in International Taxation: *The Need for Procedural and Administrative Rules* (utzverlag 2020).

*Juliane Gröper,* Chapter 9: Can Mediation Improve (the Efficiency of) the MAP? (P. Pistone/J.J. de Goede eds, IBFD 2021).

*Gilbert Guillaume,* The Use of Precedent by International Judges and Arbitrators, 2 Journal of International Dispute Settlement 1, pp. 5-23 (2011).

*Florian Haase* (ed.), Außensteuergesetz Doppelbesteuerungsabkommen (C.F. Müller 2016).

*Florian Haase*, Internationales und Europäisches Steuerrecht (C.F. Müller 2020).

*Katharina Hafner & Marion Stiastny*, Die EU-Streitbeilegungsrichtlinie – eine Vorstellung, Steuer und Wirtschaft International, pp. 12-20 (2018).

*Berthold Hannes*, Qualifikationskonflikte im Internationalen Steuerrecht (S + W Steuer- und Wirtschaftsverlag 1992).

*Werner Haslehner*, Tax Treaty Disputes in Germany, pp. 290-358 (E. Baistrocchi ed., Cambridge University Press 2017).

*Lucas de Heer & Paul Kraan*, Legal Protection in International Tax Disputes – How Investment Protection Agreements Address Arbitration, 52 European Taxation 1, pp. 3-10 (2012).

*Walter Hellerstein*, Dispute Resolution and Dispute Prevention under the EU VAT: A Global Perspective, pp. 69-84 (M. Lang ed., Linde 2017).

*Michael Hendricks*, Instrumente zur Beseitigung und Vermeidung von Verrechnungspreiskonflikten, pp. 1209-1256 (F. Wassermeyer/H. Baumhoff eds, Verlag Dr. Otto Schmidt 2014).

*Michael Hendricks*, Joint Audits und Abkommensrecht, pp. 565-572 (W. Wassermeyer ed., C.H. Beck 2015).

*Michael Hendricks*, Internationale Verfahren, pp. 513-552 (H. Schaumburg/M. Hendricks eds, Verlag Dr. Otto Schmidt 2018).

*Sonja Heppner*, Procedural Transparency in Investor-State Arbitration (Dissertation, Trinity College Dublin, 2019).

*Matthias Herdegen*, Interpretation in International Law (A. Peters/R. Wolfrum eds).

*Andreas Herlinghaus*, Gedanken zum abkommensrechtlichen Schiedsverfahren nach Art. 25 Abs. 5 OECD-MA, 19 Internationales Steuerrecht 4, pp. 125-130 (2010).

*Edgar Herzfeld*, Probleme des internationalen Steuerrechts unter besonderer Berücksichtigung des Territorialitätsprinzips und des Qualifikationsproblems, 6 Vierteljahresschrift für Steuer- und Finanzrecht, 422-496 (1932).

*F. Sebastian M. Heselhaus & Carsten Nowak* (eds), Handbuch der Europäischen Grundrechte (C.H. Beck 2020), https://beck-online.beck.de/Bcid/Y-400-W-HeselhausNowakHdbEUGR.

*Johanna Hey*, Steuerplanungssicherheit als Rechtsproblem (Dr. Otto Schmidt KG 2002).

*Luc Hinnekens*, The European Tax Arbitration Convention and Its Legal Framework: *Part 2*, British Tax Review 3, pp. 272-311 (1996).

*Lothar Hintzen & Sigrid Hintzen*, Die Systematik des völkerrechtlichen Verständigungsverfahrens der Doppelbesteuerungsabkommen (I): *Der Weg zu einer internationalen Steuergerichtsbarkeit – Zugleich eine praktische Anleitung zur Durchführung*, 32 Der Betrieb 40, pp. 1907-1911 (1979).

*Lothar Hintzen & Sigrid Hintzen*, Die Systematik des völkerrechtlichen Verständigungsverfahrens der Doppelbesteuerungsabkommen (II): *Der Weg zu einer internationalen Steuergerichtsbarkeit – Zugleich eine praktische Anleitung zur Durchführung*, 32 Der Betrieb 41, pp. 1953-1957 (1979).

*Kaj Hober*, Investment Treaty Arbitration: A Brief Overview, 42 Intertax 3, pp. 189-193 (2014).

*Rainer Hofmann,* Separate Opinion: International Court of Justice (ICJ) (A. Peters/R. Wolfrum eds).

*Norbert Horn,* Current Use of the UNCITRAL Arbitration Rules in the Context of Investment Arbitration, 24 Arbitration International 4, pp. 587-602 (2008).

IBFD Observatory on the Protection of Taxpayers' Rights, 2018 General Report on the Protection of Taxpayers' Rights.

International Fiscal Association (ed.), Interprétation judiciaire des convention des doubles impositions et nécessité ou opportunité d'une jurisdiction fiscale internationale (Imprimerie Berichthaus 1951).

International Fiscal Association (ed.), Dispute resolution procedures in international tax matters: *Subject 1* (2016).

*Roland Ismer,* Compulsory Waiver of Domestic Remedies Before Arbitration under a Tax Treaty - A German Perspective, 57 Bulletin for International Taxation 1, pp. 18-23 (2003).

*Roland Ismer,* Rechtswidrige Gewährung von Rechtsschutz? - Zugleich eine Besprechung des Urteils FG Hamburg vom 13. 7. 2000 V 2/97 -, 12 Internationales Steuerrecht 11, pp. 394-396 (2003).

*Roland Ismer* (ed.), Doppelbesteuerungsabkommen: *der Bundesrepublik Deutschland auf dem Gebiet der Steuern vom Einkommen und Vermögen. Kommentar auf der Grundlage der Musterabkommen* (C.H. Beck 2021).

*Roland Ismer & Stefanie Baur,* Verfassungsmäßigkeit von Treaty Overrides, 23 Internationales Steuerrecht 12, pp. 421-427 (2014).

*Roland Ismer & Sophia Piotrowski,* A BIT Too Much: Or How Best to Resolve Tax Treaty Disputes?, 44 Intertax 5, pp. 348-359 (2016).

*Roland Ismer & Sophia Piotrowski,* Internationale Streitbeilegung in Steuersachen und innerstaatliches Verfassungsrecht: Auf zu gerichtsförmigen Verfahren!, 28 Internationales Steuerrecht 21, pp. 845-849 (2019).

*Thomas Jansen & Andreas Mammen,* Kritische Analyse des EU-Doppelbesteuerungsabkommen-Streitbeilegungsgesetzes, 58 Deutsches Steuerrecht 10, pp. 465-475 (2020).

*Hans D. Jarass* (ed.), Charta der Grundrechte der Europäischen Union: *Unter Einbeziehung der vom EuGH entwickelten Grundrechte, der Grundrechtsregelungen der Verträge und der EMRK: Kommentar* (C.H. Beck 2016).

*Alexander Jehlin & Sebastian Löcherbach,* Tagungsbericht zum 18. Münchner Unternehmenssteuerforum: *Verständigungsverfahren im Steuerrecht,* DStR-Beihefter, pp. 1-8 (2016).

*Michelle Johnson, Justin Radziewicz & Jay Hudson,* Chapter 1: *Overview/Best Practices,* pp. 3-68 (Duff & Phelphs ed., Kluwer Law International 2017).

*Ghislain T.J. Joseph,* Transfer Pricing: The EC Arbitration Convention as a Dispute Resolution Mechanism, 28 International Tax Journal 37 (2002).

*Benja Anglès Juanpere,* The Resolution of Tax Disputes and International Tax Arbitration, 5 European Journal of Business and Management Research 1 (2020).

*Heiner Kahlert,* Vertraulichkeit im Schiedsverfahren (Mohr Siebeck 2015).

*Pawel Kamocki & Jim O'Regan,* Privacy Issues in Online Machine Translation Services – European Perspective, pp. 4458-4462 (N. Calzolari et al. eds, European Language Resources Association (ELRA) 2016).

*Sven Kaufmann,* P. II. Vorabentscheidungsverfahren (M.A. Dauses/M. Ludwigs eds, C.H. Beck).

*Gabrielle Kaufmann-Kohler,* Arbitral Precedent: Dream, Necessity or Excuse? *The 2006 Freshfields Lecture,* 23 Arbitration International 3, pp. 357-378 (2007).

*Markus Keerl,* Internationale Verrechnungspreise in der globalisierten Wirtschaft (Universitätsverlag Göttingen 2008).

*Pierre Kerlan,* International Disputes With Respect to Tax Conventions – The French View, pp. 219-262 (V. Di Francesco/N. Liakas eds, Matthew Bender 1978).

*Markus Keuthen,* Die Vermeidung der juristischen Doppelbesteuerung im EG-Binnenmarkt: *Die Vereinbarkeit der Anrechnungs- und der Freistellungsmethode mit den EG-Grundfreiheiten* (Duncker & Humblot 2009).

*Paul Kirchhof & Hans Nieskens* (eds), Festschrift für Wolfram Reiß zum 65. Geburtstag (Verlag Dr. Otto Schmidt 2008).

*David Kleist,* A Multilateral Instrument for Implementing Changes to Double Tax Treaties: Problems and Prospects, 44 Intertax 11, pp. 823-830 (2016).

*Fritz E. Koch,* The Double Taxation Conventions (Stevens 1947).

*Georg Kofler,* Doppelbesteuerungsabkommen und Europäisches Gemeinschaftsrecht (Linde 2007).

*Georg Kofler & Pasquale Pistone,* Seminar J: Ist die positive Integration im EU-Steuerrecht wieder auf Schiene? *Gedanken in Vorbereitung auf den 71. IFA Kongress in Rio de Janeiro,* 26 Internationales Steuerrecht 16, pp. 705-711 (2017).

*Juliane Kokott,* Das Steuerrecht der Europäischen Union (C.H. Beck 2018).

*Juliane Kokott,* Taxpayer's Rights, 60 European Taxation 1, pp. 3-7 (2020).

*Juliane Kokott, Pasquale Pistone & Robin Miller,* Völkerrecht und Steuerrecht – Die Rechte der Steuerpflichtigen: *Phase 1 des Projekts der International Law Association zum Internationalen Steuerrecht,* Steuer und Wirtschaft 3, pp. 200-218 (2020).

*Jasmin Kollmann, Petra Koch, Alicja Majdanska & Laura Turcan,* Arbitration in International Tax Matters, 77 Tax Notes International 13, pp. 1189-1195 (2015).

*Jasmin Kollmann & Laura Turcan,* Chapter 2: Overview of the Existing Mechanisms to Resolve Disputes and Their Challenges, pp. 15-77 (M. Lang et al. eds, IBFD 2015).

*Franz A.M. Koppensteiner,* Das 'Welthandelsgericht' als Forum zur Beilegung von Streitigkeiten im Bereich der direkten Besteuerung im Vergleich zu anderen Direktsteuerverfahren (Wirtschaftsuniversität Wien, 9.10.2009).

*Wolfgang W. Kraft & Andreas Striegel* (eds), WCLF Tax und IP Gesprächsband 2017: *Immaterielle Werte als zentrale Komponente internationaler Steuerstrategien* (Springer Gabler 2019), https://doi.org/10.1007/978-3-658-24953-3.

*Katharina Kubik & Laura Turcan,* Chapter 3: Austria (M. Lang et al. eds, IBFD 2020).

*Nina Kuntschik & Axel Bödefeld,* Schiedsverfahren nach den DBA mit Großbritannien, der Schweiz und Liechtenstein, 21 Internationales Steuerrecht 4, pp. 137-140 (2012).

*Gagan Kumar Kwatra*, Arbitration in International Tax Disputes: A New Approach, 5 Journal of International Arbitration 4, pp. 151-164 (1988).

*Michael Lang*, Die Bedeutung des originär innerstaatlichen Rechts für die Auslegung von Doppelbesteuerungsabkommen (Art. 3 Abs. 2 OECD-MA), pp. 298-304 (G. Burmester/D. Endres eds, C.H. Beck 1997).

*Michael Lang*, Der EuGH als Interpret von Doppelbesteuerungsabkommen, pp. 365-381 (J. Lüdicke et al. eds, Haufe-Gruppe 2013).

*Michael Lang*, Introduction to the Law of Double Taxation Conventions (IBFD 2013).

*Michael Lang* (ed.), CJEU - Recent Developments in Value Added Tax 2016 (Linde 2017).

*Michael Lang*, DBA-Interpretation durch den EuGH, 27 Steuer und Wirtschaft International 10, pp. 507-517 (2017).

*Michael Lang, Jeffrey Owens, Jasmin Kollmann & Laura Turcan* (eds), International Arbitration in Tax Matters (IBFD 2015).

*Michael Lang, Jeffrey Owens, Pasquale Pistone, Alexander Rust, Josef Schuch & Claus Staringer* (eds), The Impact of Bilateral Investment Treaties on Taxation (2017).

*Michael Lang, Jeffrey Owens, Pasquale Pistone, Alexander Rust, Josef Schuch, Claus Staringer & Alfred Storck* (eds), Tax Treaty Arbitration (IBFD 2020).

*Michael Lang, Pasquale Pistone, Alexander Rust, Josef Schuch & Claus Staringer* (eds), The UN Model Convention and its Relevance for the Global Tax Treaty Network (2017).

*Michael Lang, Pasquale Pistone, Alexander Rust, Josef Schuch & Claus Staringer* (eds), Tax Treaty Entitlement (IBFD 2019).

*Michael Lang, Pasquale Pistone, Josef Schuch & Claus Staringer* (eds), Introduction to European Tax Law on Direct Taxation (Linde 2018).

*Michael Lang, Pasquale Pistone, Josef Schuch, Claus Staringer & Alfred Storck* (eds), Beneficial Ownership: *Recent Trends* (IBFD 2013).

*Michael Lang & Mario Züger* (eds), Settlement of Disputes in Tax Treaty Law (Kluwer Law International 2003).

*Moris Lehner*, Möglichkeiten zur Verbesserung des Verständigungsverfahrens auf der Grundlage des EWG-Vertrages: *Dargestellt anhand eines Richtlinienvorschlages der EG-Kommission zur Vermeidung der Doppelbesteuerung im Fall der Gewinnberichtigung zwischen verbundenen Unternehmen* (C.H. Beck 1982).

*Moris Lehner*, Beseitigt die neue Verfassung für Europa die Verpflichtung der Mitgliedstaaten zur Vermeidung der Doppelbesteuerung?, 14 Internationales Steuerrecht 12, pp. 397-398 (2005).

*Moris Lehner*, Streitbeilegung im Internationalen Steuerrecht, pp. 665-678 (P. Kirchhof/H. Nieskens eds, Verlag Dr. Otto Schmidt 2008).

*Moris Lehner*, Die autonome Auslegung von Doppelbesteuerungsabkommen im Kontext des Art. 3 Abs. 2 OECD-MA, pp. 383-401 (J. Lüdicke et al. eds, Haufe-Gruppe 2013).

*Moris Lehner*, Neue Regelungsebenen und Kompetenzen im Internationalen Steuerrecht, 28 Internationales Steuerrecht 8, 277-286 (2019).

*Michael Lennard,* Transfer Pricing Arbitration as an Option for Developing Countries, 42 Intertax 3, pp. 179-188 (2014).

*Michael Lennard,* Some Aspects of the Architecture of International Tax Reform (and Their Human Rights-Related Consequences), pp. 209-233 (P. Alston/N. Reisch eds, Oxford University Press 2019).

*Gustaf Lindencrona & Nils Mattsson,* Arbitration in Taxation (Norstedt 1982).

*Gustav Lippert,* Handbuch des internationalen Finanzrechts (Österreichische Staatsdruckerei 1928).

*Sven-Olof Lodin,* The Arbitration Convention in Practice - Experiences, 42 Intertax 3, pp. 173-175 (2014).

*Marina Lombardo,* The Mutual Agreement Procedure (Art. 25 OECD MC) - A tool to overcome interpretation problems?, pp. 457-480 (M. Schilcher/P. Weninger eds, Linde 2008).

*Marina Lombardo & Carlo Garbarino,* Arbitration of Unresolved Issues in Mutual Agreement Cases: The New Paragraph 5, Art. 25 OECD Model Convention, a Multi-Tiered Dispute Resolution Clause, Bocconi Legal Studies Research Paper.

*Gracia M. Luchena Mozo,* A Collaborative Relationship in the Resolution of International Tax Disputes and Alternative Measures for Dispute Resolution in a Post-BEPS Era, 58 European Taxation 1 (2018).

*Gracia M. Luchena Mozo,* Pros and Cons of the New European Tax Dispute Resolution System and the Spanish Attempt at Transposition, 60 European Taxation 4, pp. 141-151 (2020).

*Jürgen Lüdicke, Jörg Manfred Mössner & Lars Hummel* (eds), Das Steuerrecht der Unternehmen: *Festschrift für Gerrit Frotscher zum 70. Geburtstag* (Haufe-Gruppe 2013).

*Joris Luts & Caroline Kempeneers,* Case C-648/15 Austria v. Germany: Jurisdiction and Powers of the CJ to Settle Tax Treaty Disputes Under Article 273 TFEU, 27 EC Tax Review 1, pp. 5-18 (2018).

*Ruth Mackenzie & Philippe Sands,* Judicial Selection for International Courts: Towards Common Principles and Practices (K. Malleson/P.H. Russell eds, University of Toronto Press 2006).

*Guglielmo Maisto* (ed.), Residence of Individuals under Tax Treaties and EC Law (IBFD 2010).

*Guglielmo Maisto, Stéphane Austry, John F. Avery Jones, Philip Baker, Peter Blessing, Robert Danon, Shefali Goradia, Johann Hattingh, Koichi Inoue, Jürgen Lüdicke, Toshio Miyatake, Angelo Nikolakakis, Frank Pötgens, Kees van Raad, Richard Vann & Bertil Wiman,* Dual Residence of Companies under Tax Treaties, 1 International Tax Studies 1, pp. 1-84 (2018).

*Alicja Majdanska & Laura Turcan* (eds), OECD Arbitration in Tax Treaty Law (Linde 2018).

*Kate Malleson & Peter H. Russell* (eds), Appointing Judges in an Age of Judicial Power: *Critical Perspectives from around the World* (University of Toronto Press 2006).

*Andreas Mammen, Thomas Jansen & Sarah-Sophie Rasche,* Instrumente der Verständigung im internationalen Steuerrecht: *Bestandsaufnahme, Anwendungsfragen,*

*Konfliktpotentiale und Reformbedarf,* 28 Internationales Steuerrecht 10, pp. 372-380 (2019).

*Michelle Markham,* Litigation, Arbitration and Mediation in International Tax Disputes: *An Assessment of Whether This Results in Competitive or Collaborative Relations,* 11 Contemporary Asia Arbitration Journal 2, pp. 277-304 (2018).

*Michelle Markham,* Mandatory Binding Tax Arbitration – Is This a Pathway to a More Efficient Mutual Agreement Procedure?, 35 Arbitration International 2, pp. 149-170 (2019).

*Michelle Markham,* The Comparative Dimension Regarding Approaches to Decision-Making in International Tax Arbitration, pp. 115-135 (J.H. Farrar et al. eds, Springer 2019).

*Michelle Andrea Markham,* Arbitration and Tax Treaty Disputes, 35 Arbitration International 4, pp. 473-504 (2019).

*L. Paige Marvel,* Tax Litigation in the Federal Courts of the United States: The Role of Precedent in a Changing Legal Environment, 73 Bulletin for International Taxation 8, pp. 432-437 (2019).

*Yoshihiro Masui,* Treaty Arbitration from a Japanese Perspective, 58 Bulletin for International Taxation 1, pp. 14-16 (2004).

*Michael J. McIntyre,* Comments on the OECD Proposal for Secret and Mandatory Arbitration of International Tax Disputes, Wayne State University Law School Research Paper.

*Luc Meeus,* Settlement of Disputes in Belgian Tax Treaty Law, pp. 87-122 (M. Lang/M. Züger eds, Kluwer Law International 2003).

*Till Valentin Meickmann,* Die Aufklärung und Bewertung grenzüberschreitender Sachverhalte im Steuerrecht: *Eine Untersuchung unter besonderer Berücksichtigung der rechtlichen und tatsächlichen Rahmenbedingungen gemeinsamer Betriebsprüfungen* (Duncker & Humblot 2019).

*Angelika Meindl-Ringler,* Beneficial Ownership in International Tax Law (Kluwer Law International 2016).

*Siegfried Merz & Dirk Sajogo,* Aktuelle Entwicklungen bei internationalen Verständigungs- und Schiedsverfahren, 11 PIStB (Praxis internationale Steuerberatung) 2, pp. 44-50 (2010).

*Jürgen Meyer, Sven Hölscheidt & Norbert Bernsdorff* (eds), Charta der Grundrechte der Europäischen Union (2019).

*Bob Michel,* Austria v. Germany (Case C-648/15): The ECJ and Its New Tax Treaty Arbitration Hat, 58 European Taxation 1, pp. 2-13 (2018).

*Jeff Monhait,* Baseball Arbitration: An ADR Success, 4 Harvard Journal of Sports & Entertainment Law 1, pp. 105-143 (2013).

*Jérôme Monsenego,* Designing Arbitration Provisions in Tax Treaties: Reflections Based on the US Experience, 42 Intertax 3, pp. 163-168 (2014).

*Jérôme Monsenego,* Introduction to Transfer Pricing (Kluwer Law International 2015).

*Jérôme Monsenego,* Does the Achmea Case Prevent the Resolution of Tax Treaty Disputes Through Arbitration?, 47 Intertax 8/9, pp. 725-736 (2019).

*Hans Mooij,* Arbitration Institutes: *An Issue Overlooked,* 47 Intertax 8/9, pp. 737-744 (2019).

*Hans Mooij,* Chapter 14: MAP Arbitration in Tax Treaty Disputes (P. Pistone/J.J. de Goede eds, IBFD 2021).

*Jörg Manfred Mössner,* Internationale Streitbeilegung und internationales Steuerrecht, 29 Recht der internationalen Wirtschaft 5, pp. 360-364 (1983).

*Jörg Manfred Mössner,* Zur Auslegung von Doppelbesteuerungsabkommen, pp. 403-426 (K.-H. Böckstiegel et al. eds, Carl Heymanns Verlag KG 1988).

*Dieter Mülhausen,* Das Verständigungsverfahren im deutschen internationalen Steuerrecht (Duncker & Humblot 1976).

*Aitor Navarro,* Transactional Adjustments in Transfer Pricing (IBFD 2016).

*Florian Navisotschnigg,* Chapter 4: The Beneficial Ownership Test (M. Lang et al. eds, IBFD 2019).

*Thore Neumann & Bruno Simma,* Transparency in International Adjudication, pp. 436-476 (A. Bianchi/A. Peters eds, Cambridge University Press 2013).

*Luciana Nobrega e Silva Loureiro,* Mutual Agreement Procedure: Preventing the Compulsory Jurisdiction of the International Court of Justice?, 37 Intertax 10, pp. 529-544 (2009).

*Carsten Nowak,* § 55 Recht auf effektiven gerichtlichen Rechtsschutz, pp. 1217-1263 (F.S.M. Heselhaus/C. Nowak eds, C.H. Beck 2020).

*Carsten Nowak,* § 57 Recht auf ein faires Verfahren (F.S.M. Heselhaus/C. Nowak eds, C.H. Beck 2020).

*Sarah Nowland,* Three's (Not) a Crowd in International Tax Arbitration: International Tax Arbitration as a Development of International Commercial Arbitration Rather than a MAP Fix, 37 Hastings International and Comparative Law Review 1, p. 183 (2014).

*Philip Nürnberg,* Das Schiedsverfahren nach dem Multilateralen Instrument, Internationale Wirtschaftsbriefe 18, pp. 688-697 (2018).

OECD, Manual on Effective Mutual Agreement Procedures, https://web-archive.oecd.org/2012-06-14/75147-manualoneffectivemutualagreementprocedures-index.htm (accessed 15 January 2024).

OECD, OECD Transfer Pricing Guidelines for Multinational Enterprises and Tax Administrations: *July 2017* (2017).

OECD, Joint Audit 2019: *Enhancing Tax Co-operation and Improving Tax Certainty* (OECD Publishing 2019), https://doi.org/10.1787/17bfa30d-en (accessed 15 January 2024).

OECD, Model Tax Convention on Income and on Capital 2017: *Full Version* (OECD Publishing 2019), https://doi.org/10.1787/g2g972ee-en.

OECD/G20 Base Erosion and Profit Shifting Project, Addressing the Tax Challenges of the Digital Economy, Action 1 – 2015 Final Report (OECD Publishing 2015).

OECD/G20 Base Erosion and Profit Shifting Project, Making Dispute Resolution Mechanisms More Effective, Action 14-2015 Final Report, OECD/G20 base erosion and profit shifting project, http://dx.doi.org/10.1787/9789264241633-en.

OECD/G20 Base Erosion and Profit Shifting Project, Preventing the Granting of Treaty Benefits in Inappropriate Circumstances: *Action 6: 2015 Final Report* (OECD 2015).

OECD/G20 Base Erosion and Profit Shifting Project, Tax Challenges Arising from Digitalisation - Report on Pillar One Blueprint: *Inclusive Framework on BEPS* (OECD Publishing 2020).

OECD/G20 Base Erosion and Profit Shifting Project, Tax Challenges Arising from Digitalisation - Report on Pillar Two Blueprint: *Inclusive Framework on BEPS* (OECD Publishing 2020).

OECD/IMF, 2019 Progress Report on Tax Certainty, https://www.oecd.org/tax/g20-report-on-tax-certainty.htm (accessed 15 January 2024).

*Ingo Oellerich,* DBA-Recht (H. Schaumburg/J. Englisch eds, Otto Schmidt 2020).

*Karin Oellers-Frahm,* International Courts and Tribunals, Judges and Arbitrators (A. Peters/R. Wolfrum eds).

*Harm J. Oortwijn,* Dispute Resolution in Cross-Border Tax Matters, 56 European Taxation 4, pp. 163-168 (2016).

*Hisashi Owada,* Pactum de contrahendo, pactum de negotiando (A. Peters/R. Wolfrum eds).

*Jeffrey Owens, Arno E. Gildemeister & Laura Turcan,* Proposal for a New Institutional Framework for Mandatory Dispute Resolution, 82 Tax Notes International 10, pp. 1001-1013 (2016).

*William W. Park,* Income Tax Treaty Arbitration, 10 George Mason Law Review 4, pp. 803-847 (2002).

*William W. Park & David R. Tillinghast,* Income Tax Treaty Arbitration (Sdu Fiscale & Financiele Uitgevers 2004).

*Anne Paschke,* Digitale Gerichtsöffentlichkeit (Duncker & Humblot 2018).

*Joost Pauwelyn,* Baseball Arbitration to Resolve International Law Disputes: Hit or Miss?, 22 Florida Tax Review 1, pp. 40-76 (2018).

*Steve Peers, Tamara K. Hervey, Jeff Kenner & Angela Ward* (eds), The EU Charter of Fundamental Rights (Nomos; C.H.Beck; Hart 2014).

*Katerina Perrou,* Taxpayer Participation in Tax Treaty Dispute Resolution (IBFD 2014).

*Katerina Perrou,* Tax Law Disputes Before Investment Arbitration Panels: Practical Experience, European Taxation 10, pp. 451-457 (2016).

*Katerina Perrou,* Taxpayer Rights and Taxpayer Participation in Procedures Under the Dispute Resolution Directive, 47 Intertax 8/9, pp. 715-724 (2019).

*Katerina Perrou,* Chapter 11: Using Mediation for the Resolution of Cross-Border Tax Disputes (P. Pistone/J.J. de Goede eds, IBFD 2021).

*Anne Peters & Rüdiger Wolfrum* (eds), Max Planck Encyclopedia of Public International Law, http://opil.ouplaw.com/home/EPIL.

*Holger M. Peters & Lars H. Haverkamp,* Verbesserte Möglichkeiten zur Beseitigung von Doppelbesteuerungen: *Vergleich des Schiedsverfahrens nach Art. 25 Abs. 5 OECD-MA und des EU-Schiedsverfahrens,* Betriebsberater, pp. 1303-1312 (2011).

*Carla de Pietro,* Tax Treaty Override and the Need for Coordination between Legal Systems: Safeguarding the Effectiveness of International Law, 7 World Tax Journal 1, pp. 73-97 (2015).

*Sophia Piotrowski,* Schiedsverfahren in deutschen DBA nach dem MLI, 27 Internationales Steuerrecht 7, pp. 257-265 (2018).

*Sophia Piotrowski, Roland Ismer, Philip Baker, Jérôme Monsenego, Katerina Perrou, Raffaele Petruzzi, Ekkehart Reimer, Fernando Serrano Antón, Lukasz Stankiewicz, Edoardo Traversa & Jasna Voje,* Towards a Standing Committee Pursuant to Article 10 of the EU Tax Dispute Resolution Directive: A Proposal for Implementation, 47 Intertax 8/9, pp. 678-692 (2019).

*Pasquale Pistone,* Chapter 1: General Report (M. Lang et al. eds, 2017).

*Pasquale Pistone,* Chapter 8: *EU Cross-Border Tax Disputes Settlement* (P.J. Wattel et al. eds, Wolters Kluwer 2018).

*Pasquale Pistone,* Chapter 1: General Report (M. Lang et al. eds, IBFD 2020).

*Pasquale Pistone & Jan J.P. de Goede,* Chapter 19: The Flexible Multi-Tier Dispute Resolution Framework and Our Final Conclusions and Recommendations (P. Pistone/J.J. de Goede eds, IBFD 2021).

*Pasquale Pistone & Jan J.P.* de *Goede* (eds), Flexible Multi-tier Dispute Resolution in International Tax Disputes (IBFD 2021).

*Harm Mark Pit,* Arbitration under the OECD Multilateral Instrument: Reservations, Options and Choices, 71 Bulletin for International Taxation 10, pp. 568-591 (2017).

*Harm Mark Pit,* Dispute Resolution in the EU (2018).

*Christoph Pleil & Stefan Schwibinger,* Confronting Conflicts of Qualification in Tax Treaty Law: The Principle of Common Interpretation and the New Approach Revisited, 10 World Tax Journal 3, pp. 427-470 (2018).

*Arwed von Poser und Groß-Naedlitz,* Der Qualifikationskonflikt bei Doppelbesteuerungsabkommen (1972).

*Lisa Ramharter & Rita Szudoczky,* Chapter 3: Limitation on Benefits Clauses: Limiting the Entitlement to Treaty Benefits (M. Lang et al. eds, IBFD 2019).

*Adalberto Ramos Huerta,* Conflicts of Qualification and the Interpretation of Tax Treaty Law, pp. 19-38 (E. Burgstaller/K. Haslinger eds, Linde 2007).

*Stephan Rasch & Katharina Mank,* Verständigungs- und Schiedsverfahren als Instrumente zur Vermeidung der Doppelbesteuerung, 8 Internationale Steuer-Rundschau 2, pp. 68-74 (2019).

*Markus Reich,* Das Verständigungsverfahren nach den internationalen Doppelbesteuerungsabkommen der Schweiz (Schulthess Polygraphischer Verlag 1976).

*Selina Reif,* Die Profit-Split Methode zur Bestimmung von Verrechnungspreisen (Dissertation, Ludwig-Maximilians-Universität München, 2019).

*Ekkehart Reimer,* Interpretation of Tax Treaties, 39 European Taxation 12, pp. 458-474 (1999).

*Ekkehart Reimer,* Meilenstein des BEPS-Programms: Das Multilaterale Übereinkommen zur Umsetzung der DBA-relevanten Maßnahmen, 26 Internationales Steuerrecht 1, pp. 1-9 (2017).

*Ekkehart Reimer & Alexander Rust* (eds), Klaus Vogel on Double Taxation Conventions (Wolters Kluwer Law & Business 2015).

Report of the International Law Commission, General Assembly - Official Records, http://legal.un.org/ilc/documentation/english/reports/a_61_10.pdf (accessed 15 January 2024).

*Richard Xenophon Resch,* Home Sweet Home: Tax Treaty Interpretation and the Problem with Language Under Consideration of the Permanent Home Tie-Breaker, British Tax Review 2, pp. 205-231 (2019).

*Aurora Ribes Ribes,* Compulsory Arbitration as a Last Resort in Resolving Tax Treaty Interpretation Problems, 42 European Taxation 9, pp. 400-404 (2002).

*Limor Riza,* Taxpayers' Lack of Standing in International Tax Dispute Resolutions: An Analysis Based on The Hybrid Norms of International Taxation, 34 Pace Law Review 3, 1064-1092 (2014).

*Stefano M. Ronco,* Chapter 17: The EU Directive on Tax Dispute Resolution Mechanisms in the European Union: A Flexible but still Perfectible Tool for Resolving International Tax Disputes (P. Pistone/J.J. de Goede eds, IBFD 2021).

*Oliver Rosenberg,* Verständigungs- und Schiedsverfahren nach dem Multilateralen Instrument und der EU-Streitbeilegungsrichtlinie, pp. 165-176 (W.W. Kraft/A. Striegel eds, Springer Gabler 2019).

*H. David Rosenbloom,* Chapter 7 - Mandatory Arbitration of Disputes Pursuant to Tax Treaties: The Experience of the United States, pp. 159-186 (M. Lang et al. eds, IBFD 2015).

*Marlies de Ruiter,* Supplementary Dispute Resolution, 48 European Taxation 9, pp. 493-499 (2008).

*David Rüll,* Die Streitbeilegungsrichtlinie und ihre Umsetzung in Deutschland, 28 Internationales Steuerrecht 18, pp. 728-738 (2019).

*David Rüll,* Chapter 14: Germany, pp. 339-366 (M. Lang et al. eds, IBFD 2020).

*Berndt R. Runge,* The German View of the Prevention and Settlement of International Disputes on Tax Law, 25 Intertax 1, pp. 3-6 (1997).

*Sachin Sachdeva,* Overriding Tax Treaty Overrides: Proposing a Solution, 53 European Taxation 9, pp. 468-474 (2013).

*Spyridon Samonas & David Coss,* The CIA Strikes Back: Redefining Confidentiality, Integrity and Availability in Security, 10 Journal of Information System Security 3, pp. 21-45 (2014).

*Philippe J. Sands & Ruth Mackenzie,* International Courts and Tribunals, Amicus Curiae (A. Peters/R. Wolfrum eds).

*Jacques Sasseville,* History and Interpretation of the Tiebreaker Rule in Art. 4(2) of the OECD Model Tax Convention: *Chapter 7* (G. Maisto ed., IBFD 2010).

*Harald Schaumburg,* Schiedsverfahrenskonvention zu Verrechnungspreiskorrekturen (H. Schaumburg/J. Englisch eds, Otto Schmidt 2020).

*Harald Schaumburg & Joachim Englisch* (eds), Europäisches Steuerrecht (Otto Schmidt 2020).

*Heide Schaumburg & Michael Hendricks* (eds), Steuerrechtsschutz (Verlag Dr. Otto Schmidt 2018).

*Michael Schilcher & Patrick Weninger* (eds), Fundamental Issues and Practical Problems in Tax Treaty Interpretation (Linde 2008).

*Stephan W. Schill*, The Multilateralization of International Investment Law (Cambridge University Press 2009).

*Wolfgang Schön*, International Tax Coordination for a Second-Best World (Part I), 1 World Tax Journal 1, pp. 67-114 (2009).

*Wolfgang Schön*, Persons and Territories: *On the International Allocation of Taxing Rights*, British Tax Review 6, pp. 554-562 (2010).

*Wolfgang Schön*, Seminar E (IFA/OECD): Das Multilaterale Instrument, 26 Internationales Steuerrecht 16, pp. 681-688 (2017).

*Wolfgang Schön*, Internationalisierung des Internationalen Steuerrechts, pp. 923-947 (K.-D. Drüen et al. eds, Verlag Dr. Otto Schmidt 2018).

*Jens Schönfeld & Xaver Ditz* (eds), Doppelbesteuerungsabkommen (Verlag Dr. Otto Schmidt 2013).

*Jens Schönfeld & Xaver Ditz* (eds), Doppelbesteuerungsabkommen: *Kommentar* (Verlag Dr. Otto Schmidt 2019).

*Luís Eduardo Schoueri*, Chapter 8: Arbitration and Constitutional Issues, pp. 187-208 (M. Lang et al. eds, IBFD 2015).

*Luís Eduardo Schoueri & Mateus Calicchio Barbosa*, Transparency: From Tax Secrecy to the Simplicity and Reliability of the Tax System, British Tax Review 5, pp. 666-681 (2013).

*Jonathan Schwarz*, Schwarz on Tax Treaties (Croner-i; Kluwer Law International 2018).

*Magdalena Schwarz*, Report on Pillar Two Blueprint: *Endlich mehr Klarheit zur Income Inclusion Rule und zur Switch-Over-Klausel*, 30 Internationales Steuerrecht 5, pp. 158-165 (2021).

*Magdalena Schwarz*, Report on Pillar Two Blueprint: *Neue Details zur Undertaxed Payments Rule und zur Subject-to-tax-Klausel*, 31 Internationales Steuerrecht 6, pp. 198-203 (2021).

*Anne Scully-Hill & Hans Mahncke*, The Emergence of the Doctrine of Stare Decisis in the World Trade Organization Dispute Settlement System, 36 Legal Issues of Economic Integration 2 (2009).

*Roman Seer*, Thematic Report – Purpose and Problems of Tax Transparency: The Legal Perspective, pp. 17-38 (F. Başaran Yavaşlar/J. Hey eds, IBFD 2019).

*Roman Seer*, Internationales Steuerverfahrensrecht: *Kommentierung der Art. 26, 27 OECD-MA* (NWB 2020).

*Sam Sim & Mei-June Soo* (eds), Asian Voices: *BEPS and Beyond* (IBFD 2017).

*Elizabeth Snodgrass*, Tax Controversies and Dispute Resolution under Tax Treaties: Insights from the Arbitration Sphere, 19 Derivatives & Financial Instruments 5 (2017).

*Pia Spanböchl & Laura Turcan*, Das neue EU-Besteuerungsstreitbeilegungsgesetz (EU-BStbG), Steuer und Wirtschaft International, pp. 187-197 (2019).

*Armin Spitaler*, Empfiehlt sich die Errichtung eines Internationalen Steuergerichtshofes zur Entscheidung zwischenstaatlicher Steuerkonflikte?, Steuer und Wirtschaft, 803-812 (1950).

*Carl M. Stevens*, Is Compulsory Arbitration Compatible with Bargaining?, 5 Industrial Relations 2, pp. 38-52 (1966).

*Isidor F. Stone*, The Trial of Socrates (Anchor Books 1989).

*Rudolf Streinz* (ed.), EUV/AEUV: *Vertrag über die Europäische Union, Vertrag über die Arbeitsweise der Europäischen Union, Charta der Grundrechte der Europäischen Union* (C.H. Beck 2018).

*Jakob Strobl*, Mutual Agreement Procedure and Practice: *National Report Germany*, 66a Cahiers de Droit Fiscal International, pp. 171-187 (1981).

*Noemi Strotkemper*, Das Spannungsverhältnis zwischen Schiedsverfahren in Steuersachen und einem Internationalen Steuergerichtshof: *Möglichkeiten zur Verbesserung der Streitbeilegung im Internationalen Steuerrecht* (Nomos 2017).

*Noemi Strotkemper*, Reformiertes Streitbeilegungsverfahren für Doppelbesteuerungskonflikte in der EU: *Überblick zum Richtlinienvorschlag vom 25.10.2016*, Internationale Wirtschaftsbriefe 2, pp. 55-64 (2017).

*Noemi Strotkemper*, Schiedsgerichtsurteil des EuGH v. 12.9.2017 in Sachen Republik Österreich/Bundesrepublik Deutschland: Kritische Analyse und Folgen für die Praxis, 28 Internationales Steuerrecht 7, pp. 235-242 (2019).

*David R. Tillinghast*, Issues in the Implementation of the Arbitration of Disputes Arising under Income Tax Treaties, 56 Bulletin for International Taxation 3, pp. 90-99 (2002).

*Laura Turcan*, Chapter 10: Dispute Resolution (M. Lang et al. eds 2017).

United Nations, Model Double Taxation Convention: *Between Developed and Developing Countries – 2017 Update* (United Nations 2018).

United Nations, E-Government Survey 2020 *With addendum on COVID-19 Response*, https://publicadministration.un.org/egovkb/en-us/Reports/UN-E-Government-Survey-2020 (accessed 15 January 2024).

*Edwin van der Bruggen*, Unless the Vienna Convention Otherwise Requires: *Notes on the Relationship between Article 3(2) of the OECD Model Tax Convention and Articles 31 and 3 32 of the Vienna Convention on the Law of Treaties*, 43 European Taxation 5, pp. 142-156 (2003).

*Monique van Herksen*, 2003 IRS Report on APAs: A Case for Increased Arbitration Procedures, 10 International Transfer Pricing Journal 5, pp. 173-177 (2003).

*Monique van Herksen*, Chapter 3: International Developments (A. Bakker/M.M. Levey eds, IBFD 2011).

*Monique van Herksen & David Fraser*, Comparative Analysis: Arbitration Procedures for Handling Tax Controversy, 16 International Transfer Pricing Journal 3, pp. 143-160 (2009).

*Diana van Hout*, Is Mediation the Panacea to the Profusion of Tax Disputes?, 10 World Tax Journal 1, pp. 43-97 (2018).

*Diana van Hout*, Introduction, pp. xxv–xlix (P. Pistone/J.J. de Goede eds, IBFD 2021).

*Kees van Raad* (ed.), International and Comparative Taxation: *Essays in Honour of Klaus Vogel* (Kluwer Law International 2002).

*Kees van Raad,* International Coordination of Tax Treaty Interpretation and Application, pp. 217-230 (K. van Raad ed., Kluwer Law International 2002).

*Jean-Philippe van West & Christine Zöhrer,* The EU Arbitration Convention and Directive: *Chapter 10,* pp. 311-331 (M. Lang et al. eds, Linde 2018).

*Frans Vanistendael,* Democracy, Revolution and Taxation, 71 Bulletin for International Taxation 8, pp. 444-451 (2017).

*Richard Vann, Pasquale Pistone & Betty Andrade* (eds), Global Tax Treaty Commentaries (IBFD 2014).

*Emer de Vattel,* The Law of Nations: *Or, Principles of the Law of Nature, Applied to the Conduct and Affairs of Nations and Sovereigns, with Three Early Essays on the Origin and Nature of Law and on Luxury* (Liberty Fund 2008), https://oll.libertyfund.org/titles/vattel-the-law-of-nations-lf-ed (accessed 15 January 2024).

*Martin Vock & Pia Spanböchl,* Das EU-Besteuerungsstreitbeilegungsgesetz im Überblick, Österreichisches Recht der Wirtschaft 3, pp. 192-196 (2019).

*Klaus Vogel,* Doppelbesteuerungsabkommen und ihre Auslegung: *Teil I,* Steuer und Wirtschaft 2, pp. 111-124 (1982).

*Klaus Vogel,* Doppelbesteuerungsabkommen und ihre Auslegung: *Teil II,* Steuer und Wirtschaft 3, 286-301 (1982).

*Klaus Vogel* (ed.), Grundfragen des Internationalen Steuerrechts (Dr. Otto Schmidt KG 1985).

*Klaus Vogel,* Transnationale Auslegung von Doppelbesteuerungsabkommen, 12 Internationales Steuerrecht 15, pp. 523-529 (2003).

*Klaus Vogel & Moris Lehner* (eds), Doppelbesteuerungsabkommen der Bundesrepublik Deutschland auf dem Gebiet der Steuern vom Einkommen und Vermögen: *Kommentar auf der Grundlage der Musterabkommen* (C.H. Beck 2015).

*Klaus Vogel & Rainer G. Prokisch,* General Report: *Interpretation of Double Taxation Conventions,* 78a Cahiers de Droit Fiscal International, pp. 55-85 (1993).

*Jasna Voje,* EU Tax Dispute Resolution Directive (2017/1852): Paving the Path Toward a European Tax Court?, 58 European Taxation 7 (2018).

*Jasna Voje,* The Limits to the Participation of the Taxpayer in Tax Dispute Resolution Procedure Under the Dispute Resolution Directive, 48 Intertax 2, pp. 157-176 (2020).

*Robert Walz,* Final-Offer-Arbitration – oder: Drittentscheidung anhand verbindlicher Angebote, 1 Zeitschrift für Schiedsverfahren 3, pp. 119-123 (2003).

*Franz Wassermeyer & Hubertus Baumhoff* (eds), Verrechnungspreise international verbundener Unternehmen (Verlag Dr. Otto Schmidt 2014).

*Franz Wassermeyer, Christian Kaeser & Michael Schwenke,* Art. 3 OECD-MA (F. Wassermeyer et al. eds, C.H. Beck).

*Franz Wassermeyer, Christian Kaeser, Michael Schwenke & Klaus-Dieter Drüen* (eds), Wassermeyer: *Doppelbesteuerung. Kommentar zu allen deutschen Doppelbesteuerungsabkommen* (C.H. Beck).

*Franz Wassermeyer, Christian Kaeser, Michael Schwenke & Klaus-Dieter Drüen* (eds), Wassermeyer: *Doppelbesteuerung: DBA* (C.H. Beck 2019).

*Wolf Wassermeyer* (ed.), Doppelbesteuerung: *Festgabe zum 75. Geburtstag von Prof. Dr. Dr. h.c. Franz Wassermeyer. 75 Beiträge zum Recht der DBA* (C.H. Beck 2015).

*Peter J. Wattel, Otto Marres & Hein Vermeulen* (eds), European Tax Law (Wolters Kluwer 2018).

*Rainer Wernsmann,* Internationale Doppelbesteuerung als unionsrechtliches Problem – am Beispiel grenzüberschreitender Erbschaften und Schenkungen, pp. 371-381 (J. Damrau/K. Muscheler eds, Verlag C.H. Beck 2012).

*Siegfried Widmann,* Zurechnungsänderungen und Umqualifikationen durch das nationale Recht in ihrem Verhältnis zum DBA-Recht, pp. 235-257 (K. Vogel ed., Dr. Otto Schmidt KG 1985).

*Astrid Wiik,* Amicus Curiae before International Courts and Tribunals (Nomos Verlagsgesellschaft mbH & Co. KG 2016).

World Justice Project, Rule of Law Index 2020, https://worldjusticeproject.org/sites/default/files/documents/WJP-ROLI-2020-Online_0.pdf (accessed 15 January 2024).

*Isabella Zimmerl,* Joint Tax Audits als Ausgangspunkt zur Effektuierung des Verständigungsverfahrens (C.H.Beck 2022).

*Tim Zinowsky & Jens Schönfeld,* Verfahren zur Beilegung von Streitigkeiten in Doppelbesteuerungssituationen – Überblick über die neue EU-Richtlinie, 6 Internationale Steuer-Rundschau 3, pp. 7-15 (2017).

*Mario Züger,* The ECJ as Arbitration Court for the New Austria–Germany Tax Treaty, 40 European Taxation 3, pp. 101-105 (2000).

*Mario Züger,* Schiedsverfahren für Doppelbesteuerungsabkommen: *Möglichkeiten zur Verbesserung des Rechtsschutzes im internationalen Steuerrecht* (Linde 2001).

*Mario Züger,* Arbitration under Tax Treaties: *Improving Legal Protection in International Tax Law* (IBFD 2002).

# Index

**T**



**U**



**V**

## SERIES ON INTERNATIONAL TAXATION

1. Alberto Xavier, *The Taxation of Foreign Investment in Brazil,* 1980 (ISBN 90-200-0582-0).
2. Hugh J. Ault & Albert J. Rädler, *The German Corporation Tax Law with 1980 Amendments,* 1981 (ISBN 90-200-0642-8).
3. Paul R. McDaniel & Hugh J. Ault, *Introduction to United States International Taxation,* 1981 (ISBN 90-6544-004-6).
4. Albert J. Rädler, *German Transfer Pricing/Prix de Transfer en Allemagne,* 1984 (ISBN 90-6544-143-3).
5. Paul R. McDaniel & Stanley S. Surrey, *International Aspects of Tax Expenditures:* A *Comparative Study,* 1985 (ISBN 90-654-4163-8).
6. Kees van Raad, *Nondiscrimination in International Tax Law,* 1986 (ISBN 90-6544-266-9).
7. Sijbren Cnossen (ed.), *Tax Coordination in the European Community,* 1987 (ISBN 90-6544-272-3).
8. Ben Terra, *Sales Taxation. The Case of Value Added Tax in the European Community,* 1989 (ISBN 90-6544-381-9).
9. Rutsel S.J. Martha, *The Jurisdiction to Tax in International Law: Theory and Practice of Legislative Fiscal Jurisdiction,* 1989 (ISBN 90-654-4416-5).
10. Paul R. McDaniel & Hugh J. Ault, *Introduction to United States International Taxation* (3rd revised edition), 1989 (ISBN 90-6544-423-8).
11. Manuel Pires, *International Juridicial Double Taxation of Income,* 1989 (ISBN 90-6544-426-2).
12. A.H.M. Daniels, *Issues in International Partnership Taxation,* 1991 (ISBN 90-654-4577-3).
13. Arvid A. Skaar, *Permanent Establishment: Erosion of a Tax Treaty Principle,* 1992 (ISBN 90-6544-594-3).
14. Cyrille David & Geerten M.M. Michielse (eds), *Tax Treatment of Financial Instruments,* 1996 (ISBN 90-654-4666-4).
15. Herbert H. Alpert & Kees van Raad (eds), *Essays on International Taxation,* 1993 (ISBN 90-654-4781-4).
16. Wolfgang Gassner, Michael Lang & Eduard Lechner (eds), *Tax Treaties and EC Law,* 1997 (ISBN 90-411-0680-4).
17. Glória Teixeira, *Taxing Corporate Profits in the EU,* 1997 (ISBN 90-411-0703-7).
18. Michael Lang et al. (eds), *Multilateral Tax Treaties,* 1998 (ISBN 90-411-0704-5).
19. Stef van Weeghel, *The Improper Use of Tax Treaties,* 1998 (ISBN 90-411-0737-1).

20. Klaus Vogel (ed.), *Interpretation of Tax Law and Treaties and Transfer Pricing in Japan and Germany,* 1998 (ISBN 90-411-9655-2).
21. Bertil Wiman (ed.), *International Studies in Taxation: Law and Economics; Liber Amicorum Leif Mutén,* 1999 (ISBN 90-411-9692-7).
22. Alfonso J. Martín Jiménez, *Towards Corporate Tax Harmonization in the European Community,* 1999 (ISBN 90-411-9690-0).
23. Ramon J. Jeffery, *The Impact of State Sovereignty on Global Trade and International Taxation,* 1999 (ISBN 90-411-9703-6).
24. A.J. Easson, *Taxation of Foreign Direct Investment,* 1999 (ISBN 90-411-9741-9).
25. Marjaana Helminen, *The Dividend Concept in International Tax Law: Dividend Payments Between Corporate Entities,* 1999 (ISBN 90-411-9765-6).
26. Paul Kirchhof, Moris Lehner, Kees van Raad, Arndt Raupach & Michael-Rodi (eds), *International and Comparative Taxation: Essays in Honour of Klaus Vogel,* 2002 (ISBN 90-411-9841-5).
27. Krister Andersson, Peter Melz & Christer Silfverberg (eds), *Liber Amicorum Sven-Olof Lodin,* 2001 (ISBN 90-411-9850-4).
28. Juan Martín Jovanovich, *Customs Valuation and Transfer Pricing: Is It Possible to Harmonize Customs and Tax Rules?,* Second Edition, 2018 (ISBN 978-90-411-6134-5).
29. Stefano Simontacchi, *Taxation of Capital Gains under the OECD Model Convention: With Special Regard to Immovable Property,* 2007 (ISBN 978-90-411-2549-1).
30. Michael Lang, Josef Schuch, & Claus Staringer (eds), *Tax Treaty Law and EC Law,* 2007 (ISBN 978-90-411-2629-0).
31. Duncan Bentley, *Taxpayers' Rights: Theory Origin and Implementation,* 2007 (ISBN 978-90-411-2650-4).
32. Sergio André Rocha, *Interpretation of Double Taxation Conventions: General Theory and Brazilian Perspective,* 2008 (ISBN 978-90-411-2822-5).
33. Robert F. van Brederode, *Systems of General Sales Taxation: Theory, Policy and Practice,* 2009 (ISBN 978-90-411-2832-4).
34. John G. Head & Richard Krever (eds), *Tax Reform in the 21st Century: A Volume in Memory of Richard Musgrave,* 2009 (ISBN 978-90-411-2829-4).
35. Jens Wittendorff, *Transfer Pricing and the Arm's Length Principle in International Tax Law,* 2010 (ISBN 978-90-411-3270-3).
36. Marjaana Helminen, *The International Tax Law Concept of Dividend,* Second Edition, 2017 (ISBN 978-90-411-8394-1).
37. Robert F. van Brederode (ed.), *Immovable Property under VAT: A Comparative Global Analysis,* 2011 (ISBN 978-90-411-3126-3).
38. Dennis Weber & Stef van Weeghel, *The 2010 OECD Updates: Model Tax Convention & Transfer Pricing Guidelines - A Critical Review,* 2011 (ISBN 978-90-411-3812-5).
39. Yariv Brauner & Martin James McMahon, Jr. (eds), *The Proper Tax Base: Structural Fairness from an International and Comparative Perspective— Essays in Honour of Paul McDaniel,* 2012 (ISBN 978-90-411-3286-4).
40. Robert F. van Brederode (ed.), *Science, Technology and Taxation,* 2012 (ISBN 978-90-411-3125-6).

41. Oskar Henkow, *The VAT/GST Treatment of Public Bodies*, 2013 (ISBN 978-90-411-4663-2).
42. Jean Schaffner, *How Fixed Is a Permanent Establishment?*, 2013 (ISBN 978-90-411-4662-5).
43. Miguel Correia, *Taxation of Corporate Groups*, 2013 (ISBN 978-90-411-4841-4).
44. Veronika Daurer, *Tax Treaties and Developing Countries*, 2014 (ISBN 978-90-411-4982-4).
45. Claire Micheau, *State Aid, Subsidy and Tax Incentives under EU and WTO Law*, 2014 (ISBN 978-90-411-4555-0).
46. Robert F. van Brederode & Richard Krever (eds), *Legal Interpretation of Tax Law*, 2014 (ISBN 978-90-411-4945-9).
47. Radhakishan Rawal, *Taxation of Cross-border Services*, 2014 (ISBN 978-90-411-4947-3).
48. João Dácio Rolim, *Proportionality and Fair Taxation*, 2014 (ISBN 978-90-411-5838-3).
49. Paulo Rosenblatt, *General Anti-avoidance Rules for Major Developing Countries*, 2015 (ISBN 978-90-411-5839-0).
50. Gaspar Lopes Dias V.S., *Tax Arbitrage through Cross-Border Financial Engineering*, 2015 (ISBN 978-90-411-5875-8).
51. Geerten M.M. Michielse & Victor Thuronyi (eds), *Tax Design Issues Worldwide*, 2015 (ISBN 978-90-411-5610-5).
52. Oktavia Weidmann, *Taxation of Derivatives and Cryptoassets*, Second Edition, 2024 (ISBN 978-94-035-2383-5).
53. Chris Evans, Richard Krever & Peter Mellor (eds), *Tax Simplification*, 2015 (ISBN 978-90-411-5976-2).
54. Reuven Avi-Yonah & Joel Slemrod (eds), *Taxation and Migration*, 2015 (ISBN 978-90-411-6136-9).
55. Alexander Bosman, *Other Income under Tax Treaties: An Analysis of Article 21 of the OECD Model Convention*, 2015 (ISBN 978-90-411-6610-4).
56. John Abrahamson, *International Taxation of Manufacturing and Distribution*, 2016 (ISBN 978-90-411-6664-7).
57. Frederik Boulogne, *Shortcomings in the EU Merger Directive*, 2016 (ISBN 978-90-411-6713-2).
58. Angelika Meindl-Ringler, *Beneficial Ownership in International Tax Law*, 2016 (ISBN 978-90-411-6833-7).
59. Andreas Waltrich, *Cross-Border Taxation of Permanent Establishments: An International Comparison*, 2016 (ISBN 978-90-411-6832-0).
60. Sergio André Rocha & Allison Christians (eds), *Tax Sovereignty in the BEPS Era*, 2017 (ISBN 978-90-411-6707-1).
61. Peter Antony Wilson, *BRICS and International Tax Law*, 2018 (ISBN 978-90-411-9435-0).
62. Louise Otis, Brigitte Alepin & Blanca Moreno-Dodson (eds), *Winning the Tax Wars: Tax Competition and Cooperation*, 2018 (ISBN 978-90-411-9460-2).

63. Marta Castelon, *International Taxation of Income from Services under Double Taxation Conventions: Development, Practice and Policy*, 2018 (ISBN 978-90-411-9594-4).
64. D.M. Broekhuijsen, *A Multilateral Tax Treaty: Designing an Instrument to Modernise International Tax Law*, 2018 (ISBN 978-90-411-9872-3).
65. John Abrahamson, *International Taxation of Energy Production and Distribution*, 2018 (ISBN 978-90-411-9101-4).
66. Leopoldo Parada, *Double Non-taxation and the Use of Hybrid Entities*, Second Edition, 2024 (ISBN 978-94-035-4666-7).
67. Richard Snoeij, *International Tax Aspects of Sovereign Wealth Investors: A Source State Perspective*, 2018 (ISBN 978-90-411-9431-2).
68. Aleksandra Bal, *Taxation, Virtual Currency and Blockchain*, 2019 (ISBN 978-94-035-0103-1).
69. Werner Haslehner, Georg Kofler, Katerina Pantazatou & Alexander Rust (eds), *Tax and the Digital Economy: Challenges and Proposals for Reform*, 2019 (ISBN 978-94-035-0361-5).
70. Eva Escribano, *Jurisdiction to Tax Corporate Income Pursuant to the Presumptive Benefit Principle: A Critical Analysis of Structural Paradigms Underlying Corporate Income Taxation and Proposals for Reform*, 2019 (ISBN 978-94-035-0640-1).
71. Jérôme Monsenego & Jan Bjuvberg (eds), *International Taxation in a Changing Landscape: Liber Amicorum in Honour of Bertil Wiman*, 2019 (ISBN 978-90-411-9234-9).
72. Kasper Dziurdź, *Non-discrimination in Tax Treaty Law and World Trade Law: The Impact of Formal, Substantive and Subjective Approaches*, 2019 (ISBN 978-94-035-0904-4).
73. Félix Daniel Martínez Laguna, *Hybrid Financial Instruments, Double Nontaxation and Linking Rules*, 2019 (ISBN 978-94-035-1074-3).
74. Jan Gooijer, *Tax Treaty Residence of Entities*, 2019 (ISBN 978-94-035-1301-0).
75. John Abrahamson, *International Taxation of Banking*, 2020 (ISBN 978-94-035-1094-1).
76. Richard Krever & François Vaillancourt (eds), *The Allocation of Multinational Business Income: Reassessing the Formulary Apportionment Option*, 2020 (ISBN 978-94-035-0614-2).
77. Ajit Kumar Singh, *Exploring the Nexus Doctrine in International Tax Law*, 2021 (ISBN 978-94-035-3363-6).
78. Galya Savir, *Regulation and Tax in Space*, 2021 (ISBN 978-94-035-3393-3).
79. Rita Julien, *Credit Method Compatibility and Constraints under EU Law: An Analysis of the Case Law of the CJEU*, 2022 (ISBN 978-94-035-2363-7).
80. Sergio André Rocha & Allison Christians (eds), *A Multilateral Convention for Tax: From Theory to Implementation*, 2022 (ISBN 978-90-411-9428-2).
81. Brigitte Alepin, Lyne Latulippe & Louise Otis (eds), *Coordination and Cooperation: Tax Policy in the 21st Century*, 2022 (ISBN 978-94-035-3740-5).
82. Chunyang Zhang, *The Role of Tax Law in Mergers and Acquisitions: A Chinese Perspective*, 2022 (ISBN 978-94-035-3741-2).

83. Florian Navisotschnigg, *Substance in International Tax Law: DEMPE Approach, Substantial Activity Requirement and Beneficial Ownership*, 2022 (ISBN 978-94-035-4895-1).
84. Mees Vergouwen, *The Effect of Directives Within the Area of Direct Taxation on the Interpretation and Application of Tax Treaties*, 2023 (ISBN 978-94-035-0907-5).
85. Rachna Matabudul, *Tax Treaty Dispute Resolution: Lessons from the Law of the Sea*, 2023 (ISBN 978-94-035-3407-7).
86. David Orzechowski-Zölzer, *The Taxation of Fees for Technical Services on the Basis of Article 12A UN Model Convention*, 2024 (ISBN 978-94-035-4297-3).
87. David Rüll, *The Resolution of International Tax Disputes: From the Established Mechanisms Towards an Institutionalised International Instrument*, 2024 (ISBN 978-94-035-2088-9).